You are lov[...] [...]

Thx for your co-ministry

& faithfulness to our Lord

& His call to Your Ministry

Straight Ahead!

The Pyramid and the Box

The Pyramid and the Box

The Decision-Making process in
A Local New Testament Church

JOEL TETREAU

MARTHA BAUDER, General Editor

RESOURCE *Publications* · Eugene, Oregon

THE PYRAMID AND THE BOX
The Decision-Making process in A Local New Testament Church

Resource Publications
An Imprint of Wipf and Stock Publishers
199 W. 8th Ave., Suite 3
Eugene, OR 97401

www.wipfandstock.com

ISBN 13: 978-1-62032-636-7

Manufactured in the U.S.A.

This book is dedicated to four families that have impacted me at the deepest levels. Their practice of unconditional love has been life-changing. The first family is the Tetreau-Carmack Family. The second family is the one at Southeast Valley Baptist Church in Gilbert, Arizona. The third family would be the family of the Institute of Biblical Leadership. The final family would be the one comprised of my mentors and friends. Thanks for your continued friendship and support throughout the years.

"opinionum varietas et opinantium unitas non sunt hasusta"
("variety of opinion and unity of opinion are not incompatible")

—Jeremiah Burroughs, 1600–1646

Contents

Foreword

You may be asking, *"Why should I invest my time and energy in reading this book?"* Allow me to provide a perspective that may assist you in answering that question. The act of making decisions permeates every dimension in our lives; i.e., in personal decisions, in family decisions, in business decisions, and in the decisions affecting the church. It is upon this latter category, decisions affecting the Bride of Christ, that this book is focused. As such, we should be motivated all the more to gain God's insight to so lead our churches that we further the cause of Christ in this lost and dying world as we await His triumphant return.

From his twenty years in ministry Pastor Tetreau has come to realize that church leadership involves numerous responsibilities but, among the most important, is making decisions. Moreover, when those decisions are "right" decisions the ministry thrives and trust in the leadership grows. As well, a church can be profoundly harmed when its leaders are indecisive.

Pastor Tetreau also understands that church leaders cannot avoid making decisions, some of which carry such critical importance that they will impact every member of the church and will have an enduring effect for years to come. He has learned that effective leaders rise to prominence because they make right decisions consistently and repeatedly. Timely and competent decision-making is the mark of a true leader.

So, given the compelling nature of the above, you and I should be hungry for insight into what God has said to us about this important subject. What insights has He given to equip us to so manage His Bride that the Holy Spirit is unleashed to harvest a great crop?

Dr. Tetreau helps us to first understand what God's Word teaches about the "notion" or the "concept" of decision-making. From that foundation, Dr. Tetreau then turns his attention to those individuals in the local church to whom the Bible gives authority to make decisions, and the topical areas in which that authority is given. Then, a methodology for making decisions in the local church is recommended. As a measure of the time he has spent in the trenches as a pastor, and as an added touch of reality, Dr. Tetreau includes insight into how to recover from a bad decision. It's a refreshing addition.

Perhaps the contribution this book makes to the literature on this subject is best summarized by Dr. Tetreau's closing comment and appeal for *". . .a strong and spiritually vibrant servant leadership coupled with an involved and spiritually adept congregation gives the best balance of harmony and peace. . ."* for decision-making. How true! This balance is essential for biblical decision-making to take place and to become woven into the fabric of a church culture. If either is lacking then God-honoring decision-making is at best elusive.

Russel F. Lloyd, Ph.D.
Founder & President, *Institute of Biblical Leadership*
Lake Lure, NC

Preface

Effective decision-making is an indispensable part of life. It is also one of the most important dynamics in a congregation. The premise of this book is that bad decision-making affects churches more than almost any other challenge that a typical fellowship of believers will face. Church conflict results more often from a deficient approach to decision-making than from almost any other cause. This book will present principles that, when applied to the decision-making process of a church, will enable unity and health to flow through the congregation.

This work is the result of fourteen years of study, writing, thinking, talking, experimenting, re-writing and rethinking the principles of decision-making. God's grace has allowed these thoughts to crystallize into a coherent work that hopefully he can use in the lives of believers and his church. This book is purposefully shorter rather than longer. I have worked hard to be concise—not easy for those of us who like to talk.

The topic of decision-making has been of special interest for much of my twenty years of ministry. In fact, my thesis project for my Doctorate of Ministry degree was "The Deacons' Role in the Decision-Making Process at Southeast Valley Baptist Church (Gilbert, AZ)." This book is an expansion of that thesis, intended to reach outside the world of academics and into the world of congregations. The burden here is for the average church attendee, congregation and leadership.

My initial motivation in writing this book was to shed light on the destructive power of poor decision-making. Three extremes exist in the world of decision-making in Christian ministry. The first is the classic one-man dictatorship, which may or may not be benevolent. This man can easily fall prey to the adage, "power corrupts; absolute power corrupts absolutely." In this model, one man believes that he alone has the right, the responsibility and the insight to make all, or certainly most, of the decisions for the ministry. This classic extreme is captured by the title of this book (The Pyramid and the Box). The leader looks at himself as sitting on the tip of the pyramid, guarding the physical fortress—his box!

The second common extreme is often a reaction against the first, namely, the "oligarchy." In the first extreme, one man makes the decisions for the entire group. In the second extreme, a (typically) small group of leaders controls everything. This small group will tell the pastor what he can and cannot do. The idea behind this is, "Pastor, you preach and teach, but we will make the decisions," or, "You take care of the sheep, we'll take care of the church."

The third extreme in decision-making is the "pure democracy" extreme. The leaders in this model are not given the authority to lead. Independent churches that utilize this model bring the body together to make decisions on a monthly or quarterly basis. The leadership waits until the body has spoken on the decisions. In more extreme cases, these assemblies are characterized by infighting, caucusing and politics.

This book will look at Scripture to determine who, what and how decision-making should be done in the local assembly, in the hope that congregations of all types can receive help and become healthier in their decision-making, no matter what their polity is.

Acknowledgments

This project has been a long journey, and through it I have been dependent on kind acts of advice, help and editing from a number of people. What is true of leaders in general is especially true of pastors. We're a needy lot. We ask for God's people to give of their time, talents and money; we ask for help all the time.

Now it's my turn to thank all of those who have selflessly given of whatever talents they have to help make this book a reality. First and foremost, I am grateful to Jesus of Nazareth for his mercy. God has a plan; I am humbled that he would redeem me and use me in spite of all my failures and shortcomings.

My family has been an enduring encouragement and source of support. Toni, my precious partner in life, marriage and ministry gives me a constant mixture of love, strength and sacrifice. My sons, Jonathan, Jeremy and Joshua have grown into young men of honor with tender faith and commitment to Jesus. Thank you for your sweet spirit and patience. My parents, Dr. Jerry and Kit Tetreau have supported me and shown me what living a Christian life of integrity and discipleship means. Mom and dad, thanks for your steady hand of love and direction. My prayer is that I could be half the parent to my children that you both were to Heather and me. To my sister, Heather and her husband, Dr. David Smith, thanks for your humor and encouragement.

The professors in every place that I've studied (International Baptist College & Seminary, Detroit Baptist Theological Seminary, Calvary Baptist Theological Seminary and Central Baptist Theological Seminary), as well as the two bearded guys at the Jerusalem Center of Biblical Studies, had to endure my musings about ecclesiastical leadership. Thanks to all of them for their patience.

Acknowledgments

To my dear friends at Tri-City Baptist Church, where I grew up in the Lord, was called to minister, attended the Christian high school and graduated from its Bible College with two degrees and one wife, and was ordained into the gospel ministry, praise God for how he has used you over the decades.

Thank you to the congregation and leadership of Tri-Lakes Baptist Church in Brighton, MI, where I served during my seminary days. I needed you more than you needed me! Thank you, Pastor Art Larson, for your patience and kindness in mentoring me and helping me develop into a principled leader. You, more than any other mentor, demonstrated what "decisive decision-making" looks like.

To the congregation of Mildred Bible Chapel in Backus, MN, thank you for your gracious relationships for the three years that we served together. It's a shame that God doesn't usually put the wisdom of a sixty year old into the body of a twenty-seven year old!

To my present church family, Southeast Valley Baptist Church in Gilbert, AZ, I have no words to communicate how much I have grown to love you. Other than my wife, Toni, you have had to bear the most sacrifice during this project. Without your willingness to allow the organizational structure of our church to be formed, tested, analyzed and reformed, this project would have died. Thank you for your love and acceptance, your constant encouragement and faithfulness. Thank you to the elders and deacons of SVBC for the combined leadership. Your friendship is worth more than platinum. The love you have for the Lord and his ministry makes it a privilege to serve with you.

Special thanks for their feedback on the material in this book go to Gary Davis, Roger Geiger, Garland Miller, Chris Melvin, Paul Warf and Dan Warf. Thanks, my dear brothers, for your "iron-sharpening" as fellow elders here at SVBC. Thanks also to the Expanded Leadership Team (ELT) of SVBC and those who have served as deacons or have led ministries in the church.

Thanks to Dr. Russell Lloyd, founder and president of Institute of Biblical Leadership in Lake Lure, NC, as well as to my friends on the board of IBL; Dr. Kevin Bauder, former president and chair of postgraduate studies at Central Baptist Theological Seminary in Plymouth, MN; Dr. W. Edward Glenny, Bible department of Northwestern Christian College near Minneapolis, MN; Dr. David Doran, president of Detroit Baptist Theological Seminary in Allen Park, MI; Dr. David Burggraff, former president of

Calvary Baptist Theological Seminary in Lansdale, PA; Dr. Jerry Tetreau, Chancellor of International Baptist College in Chandler, AZ.

A precious group of leaders, a group of brothers who serve in similar ministries, deserves thanks. The group includes Pastor Steven Hair, lead pastor of Calvary Baptist Church in Show Low, AZ. Pastor Tony Bartolucci, senior pastor of Clarkson Community Church in Clarkson, NY; Pastor Bob Bixby, senior pastor of Morning Star Church and founder of Global Grace Missions in Rockford, IL; Pastor Jeremy Scott, former co-pastor of Morning Star Church, presently lead pastor at Memorial Baptist Church in Verona, WI; Chris Metras, former music pastor of Morning Star Church and presently serving on the teaching faculty of Northland International University in Dunbar, WI; Pastor Mike Durning, former senior pastor of Mount Pleasant Bible Church in Goodles, MI; Dr. Gheorghe Motoc, senior pastor of Foothill Baptist Church in Castro Valley, CA; Dr. Bob Snyder, former senior pastor of Open Door Bible Church in Hudson, MI; Pastor John Kane, senior pastor of Sun Oak Baptist Church in Citrus Heights, CA; Thomas Pryde, former pastor of Berean Baptist Church in Fremont, CA and founder of "Sermons in Songs;" Pastor Roger Willis, senior pastor of Lighthouse Bible Church, Simi Valley, CA; Brian McCrorie, senior pastor of Heather Hills Baptist Church in Indianapolis, IN, Pastor Rob Krause, lead pastor of Serenissima Bible Church in Fontanafredda, Italy; Dr. David Parker, senior pastor of Amazing Grace Fellowship in Prescott, AZ; and Pastor Jason Janz, senior pastor of Providence Bible Church in Denver, CO and founder of sharperiron.org. Jason, thanks for letting me use *sharperiron* in its early days (www.sharperiron.org) as a place to think out loud on ecclesiastical decision-making and Type B fundamentalism.

To my editors and proofreaders, you will receive crowns in heaven for everything that you've had to endure. Thanks to Larry Oats, John Pinkerton, Jack Watters, Robert Fall, John Robinette, Kevin Bauder and Martha Bauder. Special thanks to Martha for serving as the chief editor of this book project. Your friendship and interaction on the project has been herculean. Thanks to my good friends, Randy and Matt Wilson at Grand View Camp in Alpine, AZ for letting me compose half of my book at your camp. The pine trees and fresh air were inspirational. Thanks to my friends at Central Seminary and Fourth Baptist Church in Plymouth, MN for the use of your library in the final stages of writing. Thanks to Dan and Tina Gibbs for your hospitality during my seasons of research and writing in the Twin Cities.

Thanks to my new friends at Resource Publications and Wipf & Stock Publishers in Eugene, Oregon.

To my mentors: First, my parents, Dr. Jerry and Kit Tetreau—Mom and Dad, thanks for giving me my philosophy of life (oh, yeah, thanks for giving me life!). Second, to the late Dr. James Singleton—Mary, next to my father, your husband was my closest mentor. Words cannot communicate the love I have for him and for you. Praise God for his faithfulness to Jesus and his church. Third, to Dr. Russ Lloyd, director of Institute of Biblical Leadership in Lake Lure, NC—you are my mentor in the area of church leadership. Thanks for allowing me the thrill of co-ministry both here and abroad. I'm grateful for the Institute of Biblical Leadership (www.iblministry.com) and how God is using it in the lives of leaders and ministries worldwide. Fourth, to Dr. Rolland McCune, former chair of Systematic Theology at Detroit Baptist Theological Seminary in Allen Park, MI—thanks for showing me who my God is. The theological grid that is stuck in my heart and brain was introduced to me by your faithful depositing of its wealth and beauty. Fifth, to Dr. Douglas McLachlan, former senior pastor of Fourth Baptist Church in Plymouth, MN and former president of Central Baptist Theological Seminary—thanks for demonstrating what authentic ministry looks like today. Thanks for a balanced and Biblical model of historic fundamentalism. Thanks for making it easier for my generation to appreciate the term.

To those who will buy this book and encourage others to do the same, may your tribe increase! Feel free to interact with me any time on this subject. You can reach me at jtetreau@cox.net. Shalom and straight ahead! Philippians 3:12–14 and Romans 8:28.

SECTION I

What Is Decision-Making?

1

Introduction

KEY CHAPTER PRINCIPLE:

Because decision-making in the church is an important aspect of body-life, and because body-life is a part of corporate worship and corporate edification, we must strive to honor God and each other with a healthy and Biblical approach to decision-making.

IMPORTANT QUESTIONS ABOUT THE DECISION-MAKING PROCESS FOR THE LOCAL CHURCH:

What is decision-making for the church? Who are the legitimate decision-makers for each decision? How are decisions made in the church?

Decision-making in a local church is in many ways very different from decision-making in business, military or governmental organizations. The bottom line is not the bottom line. An implication from Matthew 6:24 for local church ministry is that we do not use the ministry to make money, but we do use money to accomplish the ministry.

A biblically-oriented local church does not see the profit-or-loss column as the ultimate evidence of whether a ministry is successful. That doesn't mean that congregations should not be careful stewards of physical resources, but that the church must first of all be biblically motivated in regard to its doxological standing. Does it glorify God? Glorifying God is motivation to utilize resources effectively for worship, instruction, fellowship and evangelism. This is the foundation upon which ecclesiastical decision-making must rest. Churches that mirror the world's values by making profit and loss the main ruler for decision-making have already set themselves up for failure. Churches and leaders that give in to this kind of worldly "porridge" will ultimately jettison the authority of Scripture and demands of Jesus in favor of the consumerism of modern-day evangelicalism, which is both fickle and narcissistic. Even in a church where God's glory is pursued, decision-making can be difficult.

"We've never done it that way before!" is an all-too-common complaint. The objection in one instance was to a change in the way the division of leadership in that church was organized. The issue was whether the change was biblical, not whether it was what had always been done.

"But it's not what our kind of church has done before!"

Again, is the issue whether it's been done before (in this instance, it had, and with great success), or is the issue whether it violates the Bible's view of ecclesiology?

"But I just don't like this."

Does that mean God doesn't like it? If it doesn't violate his principles, then the answer is "no."

So who should be making the decisions in a local church? How should those decisions be made?

Ministry can be both exhilarating and challenging. Our ability to navigate the decision-making process will determine in large part whether our ministry will be smooth or rough. After more than twenty years of pastoral ministry, serving in a variety of ministry leadership positions, I have witnessed firsthand the carnage that can result from unclear and irresponsible decision-making in the context of gospel ministry. While our work could be applied to a variety of ministries, we concern ourselves here with the decision-making process of a local New Testament church.

Decision-making is especially important in the facilitation of biblical leadership, which can be defined as "a Holy Spirit-led process whereby a Christ-like individual with a heart to glorify God influences others to embrace God's objectives" (courtesy of Institute of Biblical Leadership). Ineffective decision-making reveals ineffective leadership.

This book is presented, not as the ultimate authority on the topic, but as an attempt to generate discussion amongst those who cherish the local church as Christ does. After we look at what decision-making is in the local body and who should be making those decisions, we will end by examining the important issue of how decisions should be made. By applying the principles presented in this book, leaders may be able to increase their effectiveness.

The issue of local church decision-making is of vital importance. Most church leaders have had the experience of proposing or making a decision, only to have that decision second-guessed by a co-leader or church member. Many have had their motives questioned because others disagree with what they say or do. An unnecessarily adversarial relationship develops. Does it have to be "my way" or "your way?" Why can we not come together prayerfully to work through the scenario? If we are united in finding the will of God on the matter, the body of Christ will be strengthened.

The principles presented in this book have evolved over many years of observation, both of local ecclesiastical communities and of churches in many other countries around the globe. Universally, there appears to be a startling amount of apathy or ignorance concerning what the Scriptures state about church organization.

> "A study of Scripture provides a number of snapshots of the early church. A number of ecclesiastical patterns emerge, and specific commands appear periodically as well. . .While there is no precise manual on church government and polity, a survey and analysis of the Biblical material reveals definite patterns and discernible guidelines on how the churches of the New Testament functioned."[1]

This book targets three major groups:

1. Future Christian leaders who are preparing themselves by way of study and mentorship for the gospel ministry.

2. Colleagues, both in the parish and in the academic world, who are in gospel ministry.

3. The average church member who is interested in the topic of congregational decision-making and church health, especially as it applies to his own assembly.

This book is aimed at those who actually make the decisions and live with the results—the pastors and youth leaders, the missionaries, deacons and Sunday school teachers, the choir members, janitors, nursery workers and ushers, the prayer warriors who faithfully attend prayer meetings.

---

1. Brand and Norman, *Perspectives on Church Government,* 25–26.

Section I: What Is Decision-Making?

It's not enough to talk about making decisions. We must have people who actually make the decisions.

The principles presented here can be applied to churches of any size, and may be of special help to the medium and small congregations dealing with the special perplexities of decision-making with limited resources. John Hiemela, Chafer Theological Seminary, says that "a congregation of one hundred people in the New Testament times would have been exceptionally large."[2] He further states that the majority of early assemblies were in essence "house churches."[3]

Smaller congregations today probably look more like the typical local assembly of the early New Testament church than do larger North American assemblies. Often, in larger congregations, when a leader makes a decision, he is protected by layers of leaders, associate leaders, secretaries and more. The effect is that many times a leader does not really experience the hurting effects of an unpopular decision. On the other hand, the pastor of a small congregation—not to mention his spouse—feels the jolt over every decision.

The leader of a large congregation can be shielded from those that might not agree with a decision. He has other leaders, and a number of other congregants who will agree with the decision. However, the shepherd of a small congregation, because he may have a closer shepherding relationship with those in his congregation, may intimately feel the hurt of a dear brother who doesn't understand why his pastor made an unpopular decision. The pastor of the large congregation won't lose sleep over the decision he made. In contrast, the pastor of the small congregation will be in tearful prayer over the hurt that his decision causes.

Bad decision-making can have a negative effect on all churches, but if public enough, will especially undermine the morale of the medium and smaller congregations. Smaller congregations must understand that most churches in North America and around the world are small. Glenn Daman notes that seventy-five percent of North American churches have a membership of 150 or less.[4] The vast majority of assemblies in the time of the early church would have numbered fewer than 100 souls.

---

2. Hiemela, "*Especially Those Who Labor In the Word: 1 Timothy 5:17 and the Plurality of Elders,*" 10:2

3. Ibid.

4. Daman, *Shepherding the Small Church,* 23.

When a smaller congregation has to work through a difficult decision, this can have a discouraging effect on the members. David Ray says that *"low self-esteem is a cancer that kills small churches. It reduces the amount of available money, results in poor building upkeep, repels new members, discourages leaders, erodes organizational effectiveness, changes communication from positive to negative, causes church fights, undermines planning and limits relationships with those on the outside. In short, it undermines the ministry and mission of the church. Efforts to enhance personal and church self-esteem and build morale need to top a church's priority list."*[5]

One aspect of man being created in the image of God is his ability to make decisions. Basic theology tells us that because sin is bequeathed to us and practiced by us, we will be plagued with impure motives in decision-making. Man is fallible; this is bad news when it comes to making decisions. Making poor decisions is a natural outgrowth of our sin nature. Now add to those foundational challenges our propensity to fear. Most of us have failed in decision-making at times because we were afraid to make the correct decision. We often suffer from a moral paralysis. Napoleon Bonaparte once said, "Nothing is more difficult, and therefore more precious, than to be able to decide."

Former President Ronald Reagan once had an aunt who took him to a cobbler for a new pair of shoes. The cobbler asked young Reagan, "Do you want square toes or round toes?" Unable to decide, Reagan didn't answer, so the cobbler gave him a few more days. Several days later, the cobbler saw Reagan on the street and asked him again what kind of toes he wanted on his shoes. Reagan still couldn't decide, so the shoemaker said, "Well, come by in a couple of days. Your shoes will be ready." When the future President did so, he found one square-toed and one round toed shoe! "This will teach you to never let people make decisions for you," the cobbler told his indecisive customer. "I learned right then and there," Reagan said later, "if you don't make your own decisions, someone else will."[6]

The issue of decision-making as a leader becomes even more difficult in the midst of struggle, which is both a normal and a regular part of organizational life. Frequently, leaders are faced with decisions that at first seem like lose-lose situations. During World War II, Winston Churchill was forced to make a painful choice. The British Secret Service had broken the Nazi code and informed Churchill that the Germans were planning

5. Ray, *The Big Small Church Book*, 141–42.
6. *Today in the Word*, MBI, 16.

to bomb Coventry. He had two alternatives: (1) evacuate the citizens and save hundreds of lives at the expense of alerting the Germans that the code was broken; or (2) take no action, which would kill hundreds but keep the information flowing and possibly save many more lives in the long run. Churchill had to choose and followed the second course.[7]

Former President George W. Bush describes a similar type of decision on September 11, 2001:

> *"We needed to clarify the rules of engagement. I told Dick that our pilots should contact suspicious planes and try to get them to land peacefully. If that failed, they had my authority to shoot them down. Hijacked planes were weapons of war. Despite the agonizing costs, taking one out could save countless lives on the ground. I had just made my first decision as a wartime Commander-in-Chief."*[8]

FAMILY CHURCH VS. INSTITUTIONAL CHURCH

A leader will often face decisions that are complex and emotionally debilitating. That is as true in ministry as anywhere else. A wrong decision will leave not only an immediate wound, but can cause a domino effect that may result in a string of organizational or personal conflicts. Decision-making reveals much about a church; for instance, whether it is an "institutional" church or a "family" church.

An institutional church is a congregation that sees the organizational machinery as more important than the individual families of the church. That means that ministries, buildings and other physical resources take priority over people. Two major concepts have troubled effective ecclesiastical decision-making. The first, represented by a pyramid, is a leader who is power-hungry. He sees himself as not unlike an Egyptian pharaoh, sitting on top of his own pyramid. This is his domain. The second, represented by a box, speaks of the ministry priority. When a local church cares more for its budget, buildings and reputation than for its people, it takes on a "box" mentality. Both the pyramid and the box come straight out of the institutional church.

A family church has the opposite commitment. The family church is willing to 'sell the farm' if necessary for the sake of its members. People are

7. Snodgrass, *Between Two Truths*, 179.
8. Bush, *Decision Points*, 129.

far more important than physical resources in a family church. Evangelical churches that are willing to discard families or use up individuals are acting like cut-throat corporations. Jesus' actions were the opposite—he didn't disregard the individual for the sake of the masses. His concern was with the spiritual and physical needs of the individual.

While some might conclude that larger churches are more likely to be institutional, and smaller churches are more likely to be family-oriented, reality doesn't always work that way. There are a number of larger churches that demonstrate their commitment to families by the way they protect their commitment to individual believers. On the other hand, there are many smaller congregations that are extremely territorial and even blindly loyal to the 'status quo' at the expense of members. In these cases potential new individuals and families are actually viewed as a threat to the equilibrium of the congregation. This is as blindly institutional as the mega-churches that are careless of their members.

In an institutional church, decisions are often codified, if not petrified, as part of the concrete policy of the church. In other words, policy is just a level or two lower than the voice of God himself. Often, no effort will be made to respond to the negative effects of hard decisions. Decision-makers are seen as uncaring. In a family church, the congregation or leaders are painfully aware and care very much for how a decision may negatively affect leaders or families. Efforts will be made to lessen the hurtful effects of a hard decision.

Later in this book, we will examine closely the method of making church decisions. In one sense, it's not much different from an individual believer making a personal decision. God's Word gives direction (Psalm 119:105). Wise counselors give wisdom (Proverbs 12:15). God's providence opens an opportunity (1 Cor. 16:9). God's child prays over that option (James 1:5). God's Spirit gives us peace that passes understanding (Phil. 4:7). Proverbs 3:5-6 gives us a normative expectation from believers to Heaven—"Trust in the Lord. . .acknowledge Him and He shall direct thy path" (KJV).

This method can be applied not only to daily decisions, but to the decision-making dynamic of a congregation. Initially, at the "inception stage," leaders (possibly led by the passion and considerations of a visionary type of individual) are given a new or renewed concept which would result in a change or a new path. Next is the "endorsement stage," where the leadership does all in its power to convince not only the internal leaders but the membership at large to understand and buy in to the decision being proposed. Finally is the "implementation stage" where the decision is actually put into practice.[9]

Lyle E. Schaller, in his work entitled, "The Change Agent," describes a twelve-step process for a decision to go from its embryonic form to its birth into reality. Schaller sees 1) Preliminary agreement on the question; 2) Analysis of the facts; 3) Listing of alternative courses of action; 4) Review in the context of overall policy; 5) A more detailed examination of the facts; 6) Review of probable consequences of each alternative; 7) Elimination of several alternatives; 8) Analysis of all possible consequences of each of the remaining alternatives; 9) Selection and recommendation of one or two alternative courses of action; 10) Formal communication of that recommendation to members of the final decision-making group; 11) A formal decision; 12) Implementation.[10]

In his work on decision-making, Errol Wirasinghe lists a variety of ways that individuals make decisions. Many of the methods that he notes reflect closely the methods employed by Christian leaders in the context of ministry decision-making. Some of the examples he uses are: praying to higher powers; seeking advice from fortune-tellers (the ecclesiastical version of fortune-tellers might be ministry consultants and church growth gurus); dictatorial/monarchical; egotistical; delegate to subordinates; pass-the-buck; rely on gut feelings (this one is sometimes called intuition); postpone; by consensus; follow established rules; pattern recognitions; tradition/superstition; gambling; heuristics; decision analysis; forecasting; and the use of tools. The author gives a number of examples of tools, such as the decision tree and the process of elimination; intelligent databases; the scaling technique; the distribution technique and finally knowledge-based systems.[11] While several of these appear to be healthy, many more are at best comical and at worst, dangerous. In the following chapters we will note that some of these are legitimate and even exegetically defensible when working through ministry decision-making with a group of believers.

---

9. Schaller, *The Decision-Makers*, 43.

10. Schaller, *The Change Agent*, 33–120.

11. Wirasinghe, *The Art of Making Decisions*, 31–42.

POLITY

Polity has been an issue of division for centuries. Steven Cowen referred to the schisms from differences over church government in seventeenth-century England. He noted, *"The Presbyterians and Congregationalists separated from the Church of England and from each other in part over the nature of church government. Baptists parted ways with all of the above over disagreements involving either infant baptism or church government."*[12]

Historians Joel R. Beeke and Randall J. Pederson cite the example of the schism between Henry Ainsworth and fellow Puritan leader Francis Johnson:

> *"The two came to a parting of the ways over a much-mooted point of Congregationalist polity, viz., whether decisions of the church's officers should be subject to review by the congregation. After many efforts at reconciliation, Ainsworth and his supporters withdrew in 1610 to go their own ways as the 'Ainsworthians.'"*[13]

Jeremiah Burroughs is another example of the divide among the Puritans over matters of polity. In 1644, Burroughs and several of his fellow Puritans presented a work to Parliament entitled, "Apologetical Narration," an apologetic for a kind of independency of church polity. Beeke and Pederson comment that this approach was *"an attempt to steer a middle course between Presbyterianism, which they regarded as too authoritative, and Brownism, which they regarded as too democratic. This led to division between the Presbyterians and Independents. . ."*[14]

Burroughs was passionate to bring unity. His motto was *Opinionum varietas et opinantium unitas non sunt hasustata* (literally, "Variety of opinion and unity of opinion are not incompatible."). In perhaps one of the greatest examples of his commitment to peace in Christ's Church is the testimony that he had to his fellow Puritans. Richard Baxter once noted, *"If all Episcopalians had been like Archbishop Ussher, all the Presbyterians like Stephen Marshall, and all the Independents like Jeremiah Burroughs, the breaches of the church would soon have been healed."*[15]

Puritan Thomas Cartwright's (1535–1603) work on the Book of Acts caused controversy when he argued that the Church of England should

---

12. Cowen, *Who Runs the Church*, 8.
13. Beeke and Pederson, *Meet the Puritans*, 16.
14. Ibid., 119.
15. Ibid.

replace the prelatic offices such as archbishop and archdeacon for a system of church government where each congregation would be led by its own elders, and each elder should be chosen by each church instead of the by the state. Furthermore, he felt that an elder should only lead one congregation.[16]

This book seeks to present a set of principles which can have application to any Bible-believing community despite its choice of polity, as long as the congregation is willing to assume that the Bible gives us the best template for when and how decisions are to be made in church life. These principles will apply to a Baptist church, led by a single pastor aided by a group of deacons, as well as to a Presbyterian or Bible church led by a team of elders. They also apply to independent community churches directed by an aggressive form of congregational or committee-run leadership as well as to denominational or convention churches that give up a measure of autonomy to a collective of assemblies.

What is the final court of appeal if a clear decision cannot be made but must be made? The biblical principles of mutual submission, gifted ministry and division of labor are not undermined, regardless of one's position on the final authority of the congregation—pastor, elders or deacons. One's approach to decision-making may be affected to some degree by one's view of polity, but any Bible-believing church can have a biblical and healthy approach to decision-making by applying the principles presented here. One of the goals of this work is to demonstrate with scriptural data the leadership principles which can help delineate certain decision-making guidelines of the deacons, pastors and other leaders. These principles can give concrete help, no matter what form of polity the local church prefers.

SITUATIONAL DECISION-MAKING

Regardless of one's polity, evaluating an approach and response to decision-making may be difficult. Many leaders, even seasoned ones, struggle in this critical area of leadership. Sometimes, after a decision has been made, the leader needs to rescind the decision because of new information that comes to his attention. Sometimes he needs to consult additional counselors before making or implementing a decision. And sometimes a decision must be made immediately, with little time for reflection because of some special challenge in the life of the ministry. Occasionally, a leader must come before his congregation and tell them that he doesn't know which way is right

16. Ibid., 129.

when facing a decision, and ask their prayers and counsel to discern the correct decision.

Any decision can have its share of detractors. When is it right to reconsider? When is it right to pursue the decision that has already been made? An effective leader will be able to respond with situational decision-making, an important dynamic that may take years to hone. It is at this point that a leader may come under fire. Ineffective leaders often criticize strong leaders because they themselves lack the ability to lead with this kind of decisiveness.

The Institute of Biblical Leadership (www.iblministry.org) suggests an approach to situational decision-making that will allow a leader or a team of leaders to determine whether a decision should be by command, consult, majority or consensus. The following two charts illustrate this. Notice that when time and other critical factors (such as the decision being critical to the overall success of the ministry, or the effects of the decision on the group as a whole) are limited, the leader must exert more control. However, when time and other factors are favorable, higher levels of agreement may be used to make the decision.

The first chart will help a leader decide how to make a decision in the context of limited resources, time or support. The second chart couples the number of options with the "willingness factor" to give a point score that can help a leadership team decide when a decision should be a team effort versus when it should be made by a few. These charts will help leaders to think through situational decision-making.[17] A similar matrix can be developed for specific groups, remembering the biblical principles of decision-making. This approach to decision-making in a congregation is important so that a ministry has a "buy-in" or "ownership" that goes beyond the executive leadership.

17. Used by permission from Dr. Russ Lloyd and IBL ministries (www.iblministry. com).

A Practical Model for Organizational Decision-Making

the Institute of Biblical Leadership

FACTORS									High/Open
Available time?	1	2	3	4	5	6	7	8	9
Need for	1	2	3	4	5	6	7	8	9
	1	2	3	4	5	6	7	8	9
	1	2	3	4	5	6	7	8	9
	1	2	3	4	5	6	7	8	9
	1	2	3	4	5	6	7	8	9

HIGH ←——————— LEADER CONTROL ———————→ LOW

Decision Styles:	Command	Consult	Majority	Consensus
Description:	Leader makes the decision alone	Leader gathers input; makes decision self	Majority opinion is the group decision	Decision is what ALL members can support
Critical Factors:	+Limited time +Little support req'd	+More info req'd +Some support req'd	+Time somewhat ltd. +Sig. support req'd	+Time available +Critical to success +Support mandatory

Decision Making — ©2006 the Institute of Biblical Leadership

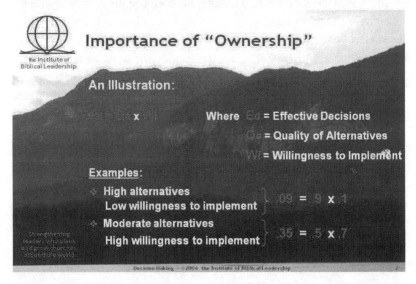

Importance of "Ownership"

the Institute of Biblical Leadership

An Illustration:

$$Ed = Qa \times Wi$$

Where Ed = Effective Decisions
Qa = Quality of Alternatives
Wi = Willingness to Implement

Examples:

- High alternatives
  Low willingness to implement } $.09 = .9 \times .1$
- Moderate alternatives
  High willingness to implement } $.35 = .5 \times .7$

Decision Making — ©2006 the Institute of Biblical Leadership

There are many types of decisions that a congregation—or the parts of a congregation—may encounter. Many times, the decision is not about "right" or "wrong," but about which of several possibilities is the best. In a situation like that, the discussion is not about morality so much as it is about the right criteria for the choice at hand. According to sociologist and Harvard professor Talcott Parsons, there are three types of decisions found in any organization. The first is the policy decision, the second is the allocative decision (what resources an organization is willing to expend to accomplish their goal or objective), and the third is the integrative decision (the type of decision that needs to be made on a regular basis to accomplish the ultimate purpose of the organization's existence).[18]

These different spheres of decision-making face each congregation regularly. For example, a policy decision might be to take the teens on a ministry youth trip only if an adequate number of adults go along to supervise. An allocative decision would state that the youth budget could contribute a certain amount of funding as long as each young person's family contributed the remainder. The integrative decision would be the ministry goals and how the youth leaders would accomplish those goals.

Questions or potential issues might arise with each aspect of the single ministry initiative of a youth trip. Multiply that by the number of ministries a congregation might have throughout the year. That's still just one small slice of ministry decision-making!

Take this illustration one step further: imagine being the youth leader. Who are you trying to please in the execution of this youth ministry trip? Is it an extension of your philosophy of ministry? You must be aware of a number of expectations from the lead pastor, the deacons or elders, the teenagers and their parents, and the youth staff. And don't forget your own goals as youth leader. In reality, all of these goals and expectations could be miles apart. How do you handle that?

There is another matrix or taxonomy that could be placed over the landscape of ecclesiastical decision-making. Decisions can be divided into four groupings. The first group is those decisions that take place under certainty. An example would be the weekly sermon.[19] The minister knows that he will be preaching on Sunday. The only unknown is what he'll preach on.

The second category is the decisions that take place under risk. Say that a parishioner is in the ICU, but the condition that put him there is unlikely to be fatal. You as his leader/minister visit him and find he is improving, so you proceed with the three-day camping trip that you had already planned with your sons. You run the risk of your parishioner's health worsening, in which case your weekend getaway with your sons will be ended prematurely.

The third category of decisions is those that take place under conflict. An ultimatum is issued—get rid of the music director or a prominent

---

18. Parsons, *Structure and the Process in Modern Societies*, 29–35.

19. Schaller, *The Decision-Makers*, 34–36.

family threatens to leave the church. You make the decision that the music leader is doing a great job and that God is honored with the ministry, and that this is a personal angst issue between the prominent family and the music leader.

The fourth and last category is of the decision that takes place under uncertainty.[20] Your congregation wants to reach out to the local community college students. Even though you don't have an identifiable core of Christian students to form a team the same age as the target ministry in your congregation, you launch the program anyway.

Every congregation will feel the effects of decision-making differently, especially during times of transition. A large congregation going through a change of personnel may not be impacted to the same degree as a smaller congregation. Likewise, older congregations may not be disturbed by an unexpected turn of events, whereas a young work or church plant experiences significant upheaval. For a larger congregation, some decisions made mid-crisis might feel like hitting a speed bump at a slow speed, but for a smaller congregation, the same decision could feel like hitting a brick wall at a high speed in a Volkswagen bug!

Critical decisions are often emotionally draining and socially challenging. Examples abound in the local church: appropriate use of leaders in the most appropriate positions; drawing straying members back to the fold; personal issues such as smoking or gluttony among the leadership team; directing members to the areas of service most suited to them without hurting their feelings or asking too much of them. The wrong decision can be ecclesiastical suicide as you tiptoe through the minefield of ministry.

No matter what size your congregation or what type of ministry, at some point conflict will arise. Believers are people, and people are sinners, and sinners sin. The conflict may be simply your approach to decision-making. True biblical leadership is key, because the question is not "if" conflict will arise, but rather, "when."

Godly men who are passionate but cool-headed enough to separate the wheat from the chaff will have learned to avoid the toxic mess.[21] Applying biblical principles will protect the process of working through the disagreement to come to a decision. Many times, when a leader is working through an intense time of conflict, he will find himself on the pointed end of unjust accusations. One of the biblical principles to remember is found in

20. Ibid.

21. Shawchuck, *How to Manage Conflict in the Church*, 21–27.

1 Timothy 5:19. For an accusation to be proven, multiple witnesses must have seen it with their own eyes. This is a reiteration of an Old Testament precept documented in Numbers 35:30 and Deuteronomy 17:6 and 19:15 as part of the Mosaic Law. An individual can only be condemned if there are multiple witnesses who actually saw firsthand the questioned act. This is what is considered a legitimate testimony. This single principle will do more to protect the integrity of God's leaders (and keep the irresponsible accusations of jaded believers out of the life of the church) than any other.

OPEN OR CLOSED?

No matter what the polity of a particular congregation, its approach to church government and decision-making will be either "open" or "closed." Congregations that choose the closed approach have official decision-makers, and anyone not so designated will likely not be privy to how or why decisions are made. This approach is most common in the institutional church. This turns the previously mentioned box mentality into a titanium box!

In an "open" approach to decision-making, the leadership of the church communicates with and encourages church members to share their thoughts about any number of decisions being made by the congregation or its leadership. This leaves the leaders open to a peer review by the congregation. This approach understands that the leaders and congregants are brothers in Christ, although with differing roles in the church. Just as the disciples of Jesus had a sense of equality and unity, so do modern-day brothers and sisters in Jesus.[22] In contrast, the closed system often gives the attitude of "there are no peers to review." One leader has even said (albeit in jest), "I'm not a dictator, I'm the only 'tator!" Some leaders aren't joking when they say that.

Those that take the closed view do so in seeming contradiction to the wisdom of Solomon in the Proverbs. Consider the following: "*Where there is no counsel, the people fall; but in an abundance of counselors there is victory*" (Prov. 11:14). "*He who separates himself seeks his own desire, He quarrels against all sound wisdom. A fool does not delight in understanding, But only in revealing his own mind.*" (Prov. 18:1–2). "*Prepare plans by consultation.*" (Prov. 20:18). One more thought: If the Apostle Peter submitted

---

22. Brown, *Corporate Decision-Making in the Church of the New Testament*, 68–75; 78–82.

his actions to the judgment of the body of believers in Jerusalem (Acts 11:1–17), how much more should leaders today, who are two thousand years removed from apostleship, be open and not closed to the review of ministry decision-making?

OVERVIEW

Constant tension has existed within many local assemblies of Bible believers throughout the history of the church.[23] The core of this tension has been focused on the place of the church leader, his authority and his role in local church decision-making.[24] This tension becomes even more complex in light of scriptural texts which seem to contradict each other in supporting different church leadership models. The believer may be easily confused when comparing the different approaches to decision-making. Do the elders take the lead? What is the role of the deacons? Does the congregation make the final decision?

This is a corollary to the issue of authority in the church. Many leaders have pretended that this issue doesn't need to be addressed. Robert Saucy notes, "*Traditionally this issue has been practically ignored. Church constitutions are often vague as to the place of final authority. Functionally, the issue depends more on the particular personality and effectiveness of the pastor and other leaders than on any formal church law. The search for a Biblically based ecclesiology, however, has called for a more definitive explanation of the place of authority in the local church. All agree that the only valid ultimate authority is Christ, the head of the church. However, the question of authority in the church concerns the functional application of Christ's authority as it is expressed in the local assembly.*"[25]

Understanding what kind of decisions the pastor-teacher, elders, deacons and congregations of the New Testament church made can help congregations today determine which decisions should be given to each group within the flow of the local ministry. Three significant scholastic works have been aimed at the issue of church order and decision-making. These works, while helpful, are limited to the academic world and only cover a portion of what this book will address. The first is by Vernon Doerksen, "*An Inductive Study of the Development of Church Organization in the New Testament*"

23. Schaff, *History of the Christian Church*, 2: 653–60.

24. Hendrix, *Management for Christian Leaders*, 22–24.

25. Saucy, *Walvoord: A Tribute*, 219–20.

(ThD diss., Grace Theological Seminary, 1971). Also see Jeffrey Brown, *"Corporate Decision-Making in the Church of the New Testament"* (Ph.D. diss., Central Baptist Theological Seminary, 2009), and Lyle E. Schaller, *The Decision Makers* (Nashville: Abingdon Press, 1974).

The number and types of questions that church leaders hear regarding decision-making show the level of confusion on the subject. How does a congregation balance the biblical function of the pastor as leader and follow his leadership, while at the same time discouraging him from having an abusive and dictatorial demeanor?[26] How do the deacons aid the pastor in oversight and leadership? What is the relationship between the pastor's/elders' authority and responsibility and the deacons' authority and responsibility? What decisions should be passed on to the individual church member or the entire congregation? Once an understanding of the relationship of these offices is developed, how does that information get translated into a working model of the local church? How does the process of decision-making in a local church differ from the approach found within secular society? How might individual and corporate disciplines such as prayer impact decision-making? What process should a church use when working through decisions?[27]

At the heart of these questions lies the issue of decision-making. At least six different levels of decision-making should exist in the local church. First is the lead pastor. The New Testament evidence will demonstrate that on some occasions, only the lead pastor may properly give the final word.[28] This final authority does not mean that the senior pastor cannot or should not consult or seek advice from other pastors or elders. Ideally, the senior pastor should consult the team of elders within that local church. This demonstrates wisdom. A shepherd would also do well to consult both deacons and godly church members in various settings. Even after receiving advice and wisdom, the senior pastor often must make the final decision.[29]

The second level of decision-making lies with the group of pastors/elders of the local church. Scripture gives examples of occasions when many pastors conferred together.[30] While this level may not exist in smaller churches that have only one pastor, the third level should exist in all

26. Finzel, *The Top Ten Mistakes Leaders Make,* 81–96.

27. Whitehead, *Method in Ministry,* ix.

28. Anderson,*The Effective Pastor,* 99–100.

29. Westing, *Multiple Church Staff Handbook,* 25–39.

30. Ibid., 15–23.

churches, whatever their size. This level consists of those decisions that the pastors and deacons make together. Homer Kent explains that Paul mentioned these two offices together so that order in the assembly would not be bypassed. Additionally, it was a clear endorsement of the authority of both offices. Kent explains the possible connection between the monetary gift sent with Epaphroditus and the joint leadership and mutual involvement of both the deacons and overseers in connection with the financial support of Paul's ministry.[31]

The fourth level includes those decisions that the deacons oversee.[32] They may gain insight or wisdom from the pastor(s) or members of the congregation. Scripture sets aside certain decisions that fall under the leadership and stewardship of the deacons.

The fifth level of decision-making requires the attention and action of the congregation of the local church.[33] The sixth and final sphere of decision-making belongs to individual church members. Whatever their polity, most churches would agree that these six basic levels exist in the process of decision-making.

ASSUMPTIONS

This book assumes that the reader and the Bible-believing congregation recognize the differences and accept the categorical distinctions between the senior pastor, the elders, the deacons, the congregation and the individual congregant. Some who read this work do not practice the division or recognize each of these in the same way that the author does.

Some participate in a congregation where a single pastor is aided by a group of deacons. Sometimes the deacons take on a surrogate "elder" function but are still referred to as "deacons." In other cases, the pastor is viewed as the only pastor and either because of position or because of a certain stage of ministry, the congregation simply does not have a team of elders. Some denominations have a view that each church might have an assistant pastor (or two), but there will only ever be one "bishop."

A second group of potential dissenters are congregants who have a team of elders but who reject the notion of a single senior pastor who would lead as "first among equals." The elders in the team are all equal in their

31. Kent, Jr., "Philippians," 103–4.

32. Lenski, *The Interpretation of the Acts of the Apostles*, 239–47.

33. Marshall, "Acts," 127.

leadership roles. Many Brethren-type churches have this kind of leadership structure. The New Testament allows the presence of a single pastor leading a congregation without the aid of a team of fellow pastors. This is what an evangelist was in the early church. While some see a distinction with the pastor-teacher, it is technically not a separate or third office.

Some congregations have not or will not name official deacons. While perfectly legitimate and logical in a new church, the normative passages of New Testament church life show that congregations will need to add deacons for the role that they serve.

EXTREMES

Within the discussion of elder, pastor, deacon and congregational decision-making, some extremes must be noted:

Extreme #1—The Dictatorship Extreme (the monarchy)

The Problem: A single leader (pastor, elder or deacon) demonstrates an attitude that some have called "The Messiah Syndrome."[34] The assumption of this extreme is that all decisions must have the leader's stamp of approval before they can legitimately be implemented. The underlying conviction is that the leader always knows best. These so-called leaders lead with a harsh and unloving demeanor. While a pastor (especially a senior pastor) can be forceful or show strong emotion in his leadership, he is to have that energy checked by a personal code of conduct and character that is consistent with 1 Timothy 3. There are some men who function as benevolent dictators— dictators with a loving demeanor. Even this brings up problems that will be addressed later in this book.

A. What God thinks about this attitude: "*Therefore, I exhort the elders among you, as your fellow elder and witness of the sufferings of Christ, and a partaker also of the glory that is to be revealed, shepherd the flock of God among you, exercising oversight not under compulsion, but voluntarily, according to the will of God; and not for sordid gain, but with eagerness; nor yet as lording it over those allotted to your charge, but proving to be examples of the flock (1 Peter 5:1–3).*"

34. Hartog II, *Pastors and Deacons*, 19–24.

B. What can we say about this approach? Some dictators have genuine warmth and love for both the Lord and His sheep, but feel that because they have a special degree of responsibility; this gives them the authority for all the decisions of the local assembly.

Extreme #2—The Board-Run Extreme (the oligarchy)

The problem: A small group of individuals—deacons or trustees chosen from the laity—make all or most of the decisions for the church. This problem is s imilar to the dictator, except it involves more than just one person. The attitude from this board is often, "I'll get my way," rather than, "May I serve you?"

In Extreme #1, one man is abusing his authority. In Extreme #2, the pastor is often abused by being stripped of his rightful decision-making role. The congregation may also be stripped of its function in this system. In extreme cases, the pastor and congregation become hostages to the will of a few controlling individuals or families. It these are God-loving and fearing leaders, the problem may not always be visible, which then makes it especially disastrous.

A. What God thinks about this attitude: "*. . .The kings of the Gentiles lord it over them, and those who have authority over them are called 'Benefactors.' But it is not this way with you, but the one who is the greatest among you must become like the youngest, and the leader like the servant.*" (Luke 22:25–26).

B. What can we say about this approach? Some ministries have rightly discovered the New Testament practice of a plurality in leadership. Many of these ministries want to protect against the first extreme. Frequently, the small group of decision-makers in these ministries is made up of God-fearing and congregational-caring men.

Extreme #3—The Congregational/Democracy Extreme (the anarchy)

The Problem: These congregations are under the self-deception that they are to instruct the leadership on what to do, instead of being willing to submit to God-ordained and placed leadership. The assumption in these churches is that the relationship between pastors and deacons is the equivalent of the relationship between the executive and legislative branches of American government. In other words, deacons serve a two-fold purpose: 1) to represent special interests of groups (this generates an ecclesiastical form of lobbying and politics in these types of churches) within the congregation, and 2) they provide a balance of power.

A. What God thinks about this: *"Remember those who led you, who spoke the word of God to you, and considering the result of their conduct."* (Heb. 13:7). The author of Hebrews continues: *"Obey your leaders and submit to them, for they keep watch over your souls as those who will give an account. Let them do this with joy and not with grief, for this would be unprofitable for you."* (Heb. 13:17).

B. What can we say about this approach? These ministries have a deep appreciation for congregational polity. They are concerned about losing not only autonomy of the local church, but their ability to ensure that they have Biblical leadership.

Decision-making is at its core an important part of what we are. Luke Johnson says, *"If we identify the church as a community of faith, the process of decision-making ought to make the structures and implications of this response to reality called 'faith' more explicit. Reaching decisions in the church should be an articulation of faith."*[35] In the following chapters, we will defend the congregation's right to make congregational decisions. We will defend the pastor's right to make pastoral decisions. We will defend the elders' ability to lead the congregation in decision-making. We will defend the deacons in their right to use decision-making as a tool of service. And we will defend the individual church member's right to make decisions about his place as believer-priest, gifted by the Holy Spirit. At the conclusion, we will analyze how decisions should be made in each sphere.

35. Johnson, *Decision Making in the Church*, 11–12.

2

Let The Scriptures Speak
Key Passages and Concepts

KEY CHAPTER PRINCIPLE:

Because we find principles of decision-making unfolded for us in both the Old and New Testaments, a Biblical theology of decision-making can help answer the question of what decision-making is in the church.

Systematic theology, while important, borrows from a wide spectrum of testimony. Biblical theology is constrained by both a chronology as well as an author. When using biblical theology, Bible students and teachers have a reasonable degree of certainty that their pre-conceived biases are not affecting the meaning, interpretation or application of the text that they are studying. This chapter will present a biblical theology of leadership and decision-making with application to the church.

In the previous chapter, we explored the need for a balanced approach to effective decision-making in regards to both a pragmatic efficiency as well as loyalty to the authoritative teaching of Scripture. This chapter will present a suggested method for decision-making in Bible-believing local assemblies. First, we will examine biblical passages and theological implications which demonstrate the roles of the pastors, the deacons, the members and the congregation by using concepts that come from principles of leadership in both the Old Testament and in the life of Jesus. By exegesis of these concepts, we will then extrapolate a philosophy of leadership as well as examine modern-day secular leadership theory. While authority is found only in the Scriptures, secular theory and leadership practice often illustrate the spirit and biblical teaching of both leadership and decision-making.

The Hebrew word meaning "to choose," when speaking of men making a choice or a decision, is the word *bahar*.[1] The term may have a theological meaning, as with God choosing or electing men to salvation. John N. Oswalt notes that when the word is used for man making a choice or decision, "it always involves a careful, well thought out choice."[2] In Scripture, decision-making is often being directed by God himself, directly through a prophet or an apostle. Many today believe that the work of prophets and apostles was finished with the completion of the canon of Scripture. Where does that leave the people of God today in the area of decision-making? Were there times in either the Old Testament community of Israel or the New Testament community of the church where decisions were made outside of the direct instruction of God via his spokesperson?

In 1982, a group of conservative evangelical thinkers, most of whom had been connected with Dallas Theological Seminary, dedicated a well-written theological treatise to Dr. John Walvoord in honor of his thirty years of teaching and writing. Published by Moody Press, the work was entitled, "*Walvoord: a Tribute*," and was edited by Donald K. Campbell. A chapter written by Robert Saucy focused attention on the question of authority in the church. In that chapter, Saucy explains the transmission of Christ's authority, previously apostolic, to today's assemblies. While holding at bay the Roman Catholic view of a perfect transmission of apostolic succession, he notes that although the apostles have passed on,

> ". . . *their authoritative ministry in a unique sense continues in the deposit of Scripture, there is another sense in which it has been passed on to succeeding generations of the church. Those who continue to execute leadership in the local church may be said to be successors of the apostolic authority. Of course, they do not exercise apostolic authority in an absolute sense since their authority is not based on the special commission of the risen Lord. Yet in a functional sense they*

1. Harris, Archer, and Waltke, *Theological Wordbook of the Old Testament*, 1:100–101.
2. Ibid.

*are instructed with communicating the authoritative commands of
the Lord through teaching and modeling His word in the church."*[3]

The challenge, then, is to allow leaders to exercise the right measure of
authority and leadership without "lording it over God's sheep" (1 Peter 5:3).

ELDERS

Churches that wish to protect themselves from the possibility of pastoral
dictatorships will sometimes remove legitimate pastoral authority. Alexander Strauch says that oftentimes churches allow *"deacons to act more like
corporation executives than ministering servants. . .Even more troublesome
is the fact that deacons are often placed into a competitive role with the shepherds of the local church."*[4] Since Scripture nowhere assigns a specific list of
decision-making responsibilities, these must be inferred from passages that
deal with the function and responsibility of church offices.

In Acts 20:17, 28, the Apostle Paul addresses the same office with
three different titles. First, in Acts 20:17, he summons the πρεσβυτέρους.[5]
The meaning of this term is "elder." It has two major uses—one describes
someone who is advanced in life. The other describes someone who has
a specific rank or office (such as a member of the Sanhedrin). The term
became connected with the second meaning in the context of church leadership. Joseph Henry Thayer wrote, *"That they did not differ at all from the
bishops or overseers (as is acknowledged also by Jerome in Tit. 1:5) is evident
from the fact that the two words are used indiscriminately. . .and that the duty
of presbyters is described by the terms* ἐπισκοπεῖν *and* ἐπισκοπὴ[6]

After calling these men "elders," Paul instructs them in verse 28 to
watch carefully over themselves and God's flock, because God has called
them to the task of being overseers (ἐπισκόπους) and that, by being such,
they have the added responsibility to shepherd (ποιμαίνειν) the church.[7]

Obviously, from a comparison of the two verses, Paul assumes that the
elder is also to serve as 'bishop,' in addition to being 'the shepherd.'[8] Paul

---

3. Saucy, *Walvoord: A Tribute,* 224.

4. Strauch, *The NT Deacon,* 9.

5. BDAG, 862.

6. Thayer, *The New Thayer's Greek-English Lexicon of the New Testament,* 535–36.

7. BDAG 379c, 842d.

8. Lenski, *Acts,* 847–48.

stresses the point that the pastor, who feeds the children of God, should also lead and guide them through loving and direct leadership. Paul is laying the responsibility of spiritual oversight on the office of pastor.[9] Paul also commands these elders to care for God's flock, the church. This reminds the pastor that the sheep ultimately do not belong to him, but to God. The pastor is to view his job as that of a steward.[10]

One more point must be made. As the texts of Acts 20:17, 21:18 and Philippians 1:1 demonstrate, each congregation had a plurality of elders. This does not undermine the possibility of a single pastor leading a congregation (as was the pattern of the New Testament evangelist), but it does demonstrate the pattern of a plurality of elders for each fellowship. When one sees the almost universal practice of a plurality of both elders and deacons within the New Testament church, the burden of proof is on those who would suggest that a single-led pastorate is more consistent with Scripture.

One of the passages that implies that the pastor does have biblical authority is 1 Timothy 5:17.[11] In this verse, the spiritual leaders are called upon to rule the church well. The verb προιστη appears four times to describe this duty (see also 1 Timothy 3:4, 5; 1 Thessalonians 5:12).[12] The literal meaning of the verb is "to stand first" or "to rule."[13] While it is true that the congregation must grant τιμης, the responsibility of the pastor/elder/bishop is to both manage and communicate God's word. Guthrie states, "*The word rule (proistemi) means general superintendence, and describes the duties allotted to all presbyters.*"[14] Reicke writes that "*the verb has in the New Testament the primary sense of both 'to lead' and 'to care for'. . .this agrees with the distinctive nature of office in the New Testament, since according to Luke 22:26 the one who is chief. . .is to be as he who serves.*"[15]

A similar term appears in Hebrews 13:7, 17, and 24. The term, ἡγέομαι, suggests the same type of leadership. The most common meaning is simply 'to lead.'[16] It was used specifically of one who was 'to go before.'[17] Addition-

---

9. Marshall, "Acts," 333–34.

10. MacArthur, Jr. *Rediscovering Pastoral Ministry*, 111.

11. Ibid.

12. BDAG 870c.

13. Ibid.

14. Guthrie, "The Pastoral Epistles," 105.

15. Reicke, "προῖστημι" *TDNT,* 6:700.

16. BDAG, 434a.

17. Ibid.

ally, it referred to one whose job it was 'to be a leader, to rule, command; to have authority over,' often in the context of military leaders.[18] Further uses of the term illustrate the application of leading.[19]

A secondary usage of this term is to 'think, consider or have regard for.'[20] Paul uses the same term to instruct the Thessalonian believers to respect their leadership.[21] Lenski, demonstrating the significance of this secondary usage, states:

> To consider them very much in love on account of their work implies appreciation, esteem, and thus willingness to be led and trained. Intelligent Christian love is to be the inward motive for this consideration, and the work these faithful men do is to be the outward motive.[22]

One more significant textual issue must be highlighted in this passage. Note that these elders were deserving of double honor, not only because they were ruling well, but because they were also effective in teaching. Here, the Greek word διδασκαλία shows that in the early New Testament church, the pastor was expected to exercise both pastoral leadership and biblical teaching. This is important, because many people today insist that the pastor does not inherently have the right to exercise oversight or authority. Richards and Heltdke have taken this position:

> The emerging picture of the local church leader (speaking of elder/ bishop/pastor), then is not that of the manager of an enterprise or a decision maker, but of one who with the wisdom gained by personal experience builds an intimate relationship with others whom he cares for. . .The responsibility of leaders is not to manage the church. They are not to be God's voice of authority in the body. The responsibility of leaders is the care and nurture of believers.[23]

The New Testament pastor/elder/bishop has the responsibility to exercise pastoral leadership and at the same time has a responsibility to

18. Ibid.

19. BDAG, 434a. Other usages include a description of Joseph's position in the land of Egypt; God's goodness leading to repentance; the Spirit's leading of Jesus.

20. BDAG, 434a.

21. Ibid.

22. Lenski, *The Interpretation of St. Paul's Epistles to the Colossians, to the Thessalonians, to Timothy, to Titus and to Philemon,* 354.

23. Richards and Hoeldtke, *A Theology of Church Leadership,* 92.

care for the sheep.[24] While some pastors abuse their authority and, in so doing, fail to understand and demonstrate the Christ-like quality of servant leadership, it is important that Christians do not over-react by asserting that the pastor has no significant authority in making decisions for a local congregation.[25]

Seeing then that Scripture, both through the titles and the descriptions of the pastor's work and responsibility, gives the pastor authority for oversight, three questions arise. First, does Scripture limit that authority? Second, if Scripture does limit the authority, how and to what extent is it limited? And third, how should the pastor exercise the rightful authority that is legitimately his responsibility?

While the previous passage indicates that the pastor, functioning as elder, bishop and shepherd, does have a God-given authority, Scripture also sets limits to that authority. Colossians 1:18 shows that ultimate and sovereign authority rests not with a man, but with Jesus Christ. The pastor's relationship to the other elders limits his authority. An exegetical analysis of Acts 6 shows the roles of deacons and the congregation in decision-making, thus limiting the pastor's authority.

In Colossians 1:18, the Apostle Paul argues that Jesus, and he alone, is to have the place of πρωτότοκος[26]. While it is true that the passages examined in Acts, 1 Timothy, and Hebrews 13 all point to the pastor's authority, Scripture ultimately places the κεφαλὴ (literally, 'head') of the church in Jesus of Nazareth. The language found in the Greek in vv. 17–18 stresses strongly that "Christ, and no one else, is the head." The New Testament appears to show that even the early church had pastors who, because of a misunderstanding of their own importance, abused the authority that was delegated to them. Diotrephes (3 John) is one example.[27] In contrast to John's disciple Gaius, who had a consistent testimony of walking in the truth, Diotrephes was publically repudiated because he falsely acquired the position of φιλοπρωτεύων.[28] Connected with Diotrephes' abuse of power

24. Gangel, *Feeding and Leading,* 9–12.

25. McLachlan, *Reclaiming Authentic Fundamentalism,* 22–51.

26. BDAG, 892d.

27. Lenski, *The Interpretation of I and II Epistles of Peter, the Three Epistles of John and the Epistle of Jude,* 584–89.

28. Ibid.

and authority is his action of excommunicating from the fellowship brethren who were not willing to abide by his abusive authority and power.[29]

A similar injunction against this spirit occurs in 1 Peter 5:3, where Peter states that the πρεσβυτέρους are not to abuse those whom they are to feed by κατακθπιεύοντες.[30] The NASB (New American Standard Bible) has correctly translated this as 'not lording it over those allotted to your charge.' In this verse, Peter no doubt remembers the Lord's explanation that this attitude of 'lording it over,' while certainly characteristic of the world's perversion of authority, should never characterize God's ministers and servants (Matthew 20:25–28).[31] Certainly, because Jesus Christ is ultimately the head, the pastor must first be concerned that he is dedicated to pursuing Christ and that which corresponds to His will. Paul is able to ask those who follow him to do so as long as he follows Christ.[32]

While this first limitation to the pastor's authority is his relationship to God, the next three are related to the Christian brethren. A second limitation is introduced in 1 Peter 5:1.

As Peter addresses the 'elders' in this passage, he speaks of himself as a συμπρεσβύτερος, literally as a 'co-elder' or 'fellow elder.'[33] Other or 'fellow' pastors are the second limitation to the pastor's authority. Peter is not basing his appeal on his position as apostle, although clearly he was one, but on the fact that he is a 'fellow elder.'[34] Beginning in the book of Acts and stretching on into the epistles, one can detect the role and importance of the elders of each local church.[35] This was a consistent practice in the early church.

While Scripture does give evidence of a type of senior pastor, or first among equals, the practice of a plurality of elders seems to be consistent with the New Testament.[36] Concerning this point, MacArthur states:

> Nearly every church we know in the New Testament is specifically said to have had elders. For example, Acts 20:17 says, "And from Miletus he sent to Ephesus and called to him the elders of the church."

29. Ibid.
30. BDAG 862a.
31. Hiebert, *1 Peter*, 303–5.
32. BDAG, 651d.
33. Hiebert , *1 Peter*, 300.
34. Blum, "1 Peter," 250.
35. MacArthur, *The Master's Plan for the Church*, 179–99.
36. Ibid.

> *It is significant that the church at Ephesus had elders, because all the churches of Asia Minor. . .such as those listed in Revelation 1:11. . .were extensions of the ministry at Ephesus. We can assume that those churches also identified their leadership by the same terms that were set as a pattern in Ephesus. . .a plurality of elders.*[37]

Unfortunately, many church leaders are under the impression that it is impossible to have a plurality of elders and maintain a commitment to a congregational form of ecclesiastical government.[38] Commenting on the biblical precedent of a plurality of elders, nineteenth century American Baptist pastor and leader W. B. Johnson states the following:

> *It is worthy of particular attention, that each church had a plurality of elders, and that although there was a difference in their respective department of service, there was a perfect equality of rank among them. Let us now endeavor to ascertain the respective departments of service assigned to the members of the bishopric. . .The particular department of service which each shall occupy, will be determined by the talent which he has for one or the other line of duty. For example, one of the bishops may have a particular talent for presiding over the body, for regulating its affairs by advice, admonition, rebuke. Let such an one be the presiding bishop. Another may have a particular capacity for reaching the flock by exposition or scripture and exhortation, and in visits to the members. Let this be his department. A third may be endowed with the talent for superintending a Sabbath school, directing the course of studies, gathering up children for the school, and alluring them to the reading of the Scriptures and religious work. To this service, then, let him be devoted. And a fourth may be endowed with the gift of laboring in the word and doctrine, that is, of preaching the gospel of Christ. This one should give himself wholly to the ministry of the word.*[39]

Some try to suggest that because the plurality of elders simply is seen historically, as opposed to commanded didactically, the modern church is not under compulsion to seriously consider the number of elders in each congregation. However, unlike the practice of head coverings in the Corinthian church, the practice of a plurality of elders is seen regularly in the New Testament, and not relegated simply to one region.[40] A church that

---

37. Ibid.
38. Dever, "*Polity*," 34.
39. Johnson, "*Polity*," 192–93.
40. Strauch, *Biblical Eldership,* 36–38.

does not have more than one pastor isn't necessarily out of order, but the health of the congregation is usually improved when it is served by more than one elder.[41]

The word 'elders,' in the plural (πρεσβύτεποι), is found fifty-nine times in the New Testament, while in its singular form it is found only four times (πρεσβύτερου). As noted, the burden of proof seems to be more on those who assert that the New Testament practice of a plurality of eldership has fallen out of practice rather than with those who believe its practice should continue.[42] That is especially true when one considers passages such as Acts 14:23 and Titus 1:5, which speak of a fairly normative practice of having πρεσβύτεροι in each congregation.[43] Many struggle to understand how a common and seemingly important leadership practice in the early church could be considered to have fallen out of practice without a single verse to explain its end or reveal a transition to a different system. A plurality of elders may not be imperative but may be superior.[44]

J.L. Reynolds, a Baptist contemporary of Johnson, asserted that while a plurality of elders did exist in the New Testament, it functioned more consistently as represented by Baptist polity than by Presbyterian.[45]

> A distinction has sometimes been made between teaching and rul-
> ing elders. This was formerly the custom of Congregational churches,
> and obtains, at the present time, in the Presbyterian Church. For
> the support of this distinction, the passages of Scripture principally
> relied on are 1 Tim. 5:17; 1 Cor. 12:28. The latter passage is too
> indefinite in its phraseology to establish the distinction, and would
> probably never have been supposed to contain it, had not an errone-
> ous interpretation of the former passage previously led to the belief
> that such a distinction really existed.[46]

Other scriptural principles seem to coincide with the idea of a multiple eldership.[47] Concerning the value and wisdom of having more than
one person's insight in the decision-making process, Solomon writes this:
"*Where there is no guidance the people fall, But in abundance of counselors*

41. Ibid.

42. BDAG 862a.

43. Strauch, *Biblical Eldership*, 36–38.

44. Glasscock, "The Biblical Concept of Elders," 66–79.

45. Reynolds, "*Polity*," 350.

46. Ibid.

47. Ibid.

there is victory."(Proverbs 11:14). Of course, this passage assumes the value of multiple counselors when the counselors are 'wise and intelligent.'[48]

Another scriptural factor which impacts the administration of a plurality of elders is the variety of gifts, as seen in a variety of leaders. When one considers the emphasis the New Testament places on team ministry, and that no one believer has all of the gifts, it would seem to follow that the church would benefit from a team of leaders instead of only one man exercising leadership and decision-making. In 1 Corinthians 1, Paul, Cephas and Apollos each appears as a talented man in his own right.[49] An important message in 1 Corinthians 3:4–8 is that ultimately God gives both 'the gifts' as well as 'the increase.' The New Testament says much concerning the giving of spiritual gifts. Clearly, the message is that no one has all the gifts; therefore, every believer needs every other believer (1 Corinthians 12:8, 27–30; Romans 12:3–8). This same principle is true of the leaders of the Church as described in Ephesians 4:11.[50]

Although the scriptural evidence points to a multiple eldership, the authority ascribed to each elder is not necessarily equal, but shows a hierarchy of authority.[51] The first evidence of this hierarchy appears in 1 Timothy 3:1, where Paul lists the qualifications of the ἐπισκοπῆς, (Titus also uses the singular in Titus 1:7). This is in contrast to verse eight, where Paul lists the qualifications of the deacons in the plural (διακόνους). In contrast to the plural number of the deacons is the role demonstrated by James in the Jerusalem church. While James did not lead without the wisdom and leadership of the rest of the elders, he did function as a sort of 'first among equals.' This relationship between James and the other Jerusalem elders is apparent in Acts 15, the occasion of the Jerusalem Council. A similar phenomenon is also seen in Acts 21 showing the position of Peter within Paul's report to the Church.[52]

A third evidence of a hierarchy of elders, with one serving as a 'presiding' elder, is the mentioning of the 'angel' (ἀγγέλω) within the context of each of the seven churches of Asia Minor addressed by John.[53] A fourth evidence appears in the theological discussion of the work and charac-

48. Ross, "Proverbs," 5:962.
49. Westing, *Multiple Church Staff Handbook*, 58–71.
50. Lowery, *The Bible Knowledge Commentary*, 2:511.
51. Doran, "The Foundation of the Pastorate," 1–2.
52. Ibid.
53. Ibid.

ter of God. In the other God-ordained institutions, an order of authority appears (as found within civil government, Israel, and the family). The fifth and perhaps strongest argument for this internal leader among equals is 1 Timothy 5:17. Here Paul speaks of an elder who receives 'double honor' for his excellent leadership in ruling the congregation. The elder is worthy of this type of honor because of his careful attention to Word and doctrine. This speaks of a special recognition by the congregation at large, especially honoring the presiding pastor-teacher.

While the evidence emphasizes the idea of a hierarchical relationship within the eldership of a local church, it does not give the senior pastor the right to refuse to submit to the wisdom and leadership of other elders. This is analogous to the authority of a husband. While the wife is to submit to the husband (Ephesians 5:22), the husband and wife are also to submit to each other (Ephesians 5:21).[54] In this relationship, the husband is to be the leader of the home, but within the domestic sphere, he needs to submit to the wisdom of his wife. However, after listening closely and honestly to his wife's suggestions, the husband does have the right to make a different choice as long as he does so in a loving manner.

In a similar fashion, the senior pastor needs to learn to submit to the wisdom of other elders as well as to the wisdom of godly laymen within the context of his biblical relationship to the deacon(s) and to the collective discernment of the congregation. This leads to the third and fourth limiting elements to the pastor's authority—the leadership of the deacons and the collective discernment of the congregation as seen in Acts 6:1–6.[55]

DEACONS

After describing the great growth and blessings of the early church in Jerusalem, Luke directs the reader's attention to Stephen. In doing so, he sets up the story by explaining the situation that existed in the early Jerusalem church, which resulted in the formation of the office of διάκονος.[56] The growth of the Jerusalem church was remarkable;[57] however, this quick growth of believers created a problem.[58] The Hellenists' widows, who were

54. Stott, *The Message of Ephesians*, 206–9.

55. Longenecker, *Acts*, 9:331.

56. Ibid.

57 R.C.H. Lenski, *The Interpretation of The Acts of the Apostles*, 239.

58. Marshall, *Acts*, 124–28.

in need of financial and physical support, were apparently being over-looked because of the workload that the Jerusalem assembly placed on the apostles.[59] In response to the problem, the apostles gathered the assembly of believers and explained that their priority as apostles was the ministry of Word and prayer (v. 4). The apostles told the assembly to choose seven men characterized by integrity, spirituality, and wisdom who would have oversight of the benevolent and physical aspects of the ministry.[60] This group of seven would enable the spiritual leaders (then apostles, today pastors) to focus on the Word and prayer.[61] Verse five states that the multitude nominated and then elected these Godly men to the office of deacon. Following the discernment of these believers, the spiritual leaders submitted to the collective discernment of the congregation and laid hands on the new deacons to bless them and pray for them.

In the early church, the deacons had the authority to oversee the financial and benevolent affairs of the church's ministry. One of the most important principles of this text is that administrative responsibility was given to the deacons for the completion of these temporal ministries. This transfer of responsibility allowed the spiritual leadership to keep their primary focus on ministry of the Word and prayer. The importance of the office of deacon is underlined by the fact that the deacons' qualifications are nearly identical to those for the bishop. Furthermore, the congregation decided who was eligible to become a deacon and who was not. The text shows no involvement of the spiritual leadership in this process other than praying over the selected deacons and the apostles' hands being laid upon them.

What do the Scriptures say about the role and authority of the deacon? How should the contemporary church appropriate these passages that describe the pastor, his role and his authority? Furthermore, how do these passages limit the pastor's decision-making authority?

Christians need to understand the part that deacons play in a local church's decision-making. An examination of the description and genesis of the office can explain how deacons contribute to the decision-making process. While the believer benefits from a number of passages that foster an understanding of the role of the pastor, the New Testament reader will

59. Ibid.

60. Lenski, *The Interpretation of I and II Epistle of Peter, and Three Epistles of John, and the Epistle of Jude,* 215–17.

61. Ibid.

find far fewer passages that outline the function and role of the deacon. An understanding of the term 'deacon' can be discerned through the linguistics and etymology of the word.

An Etymological Analysis of διακονέω, διακονία, and διάκονος

While a study of the etymology of a word will help with its understanding, the ultimate meaning and significance of the office and function of the διάκονος is determined by the context of each scriptural passage.[62] Context is paramount to its understanding, but the intended meaning of a word—the literal meaning—is relevant too. This can be illustrated by examining the meanings of the words διακονέω, διακονία, and διακονος.

διάκονος

This noun form, found twenty-nine times in the New Testament, primarily denotes a person who is a 'servant,' as in Matthew 20:26. This word also refers to someone who serves as a 'helper of people who render service as Christians.' In this sense, the word is used as a description of how all believers should serve both the Lord and others (2 Corinthians 6:4, 11:23; Ephesians 6:21). At some time after the establishment of the church, the term became an official title for the office of 'deacon' (Romans 16:1; Philippians 1:1; 1 Timothy 3:8, 12).[63]

διακονία

This form, found thirty-two times in the New Testament, is used in reference to 'service' (Acts 6:4; 2 Corinthians 11:8; Ephesians 4:12). It also refers to those people who 'aid, support, or distribute.' (See Acts 6:1; 11:29).[64] Beyer notices the connection between this word and the office of deacon because its wider meaning is 'the discharge of a loving service.'[65] Beyer makes the point that διακονία of Stephanas is an example.[66] He also states

---

62. Carson, *Exegetical Fallacies*, 26–32.

63. BDAG, p. 230a.

64. BDAG, p. 230a.

65. Ibid.

66. Ibid.

that the term, '. . .is linked with works, faith, love, and patience in Rev. 2:19.'[67] However, this type of activity is not limited to the deacon. One will see that διαχονία refers to 'the discharge of certain obligations' as it relates to apostles (Rom. 11:13; 2 Cor. 4:1), evangelists (2 Tim. 4:5), or assistants, such as Mark (2 Tim. 4:11).[68] This reference should not be surprising when one considers the occasional universal usage of διάκονος in reference to all believers, as opposed to the official function of deacon.[69]

διακονέω

This verb, found thirty-four times in the New Testament, speaks primarily of those who are 'serving.' In Luke 12:37 and John 12:2, the usage is that of one who is 'waiting on tables.' In 2 Corinthians 3:3, the term speaks of those who would take care of the needs of others.[70] Beyer makes the point that for the Greeks, this type of service was considered 'undignified.'[71] By contrast, Jews believed this concept of service was noble.[72] Beyer also notes that this concept of serving in Judaism came to be viewed as 'sacrificially meritorious.'[73]

An Analysis of Key Passages

Because there are no specific or detailed listings of the job description for New Testament deacons, it is up to the student to examine the Scriptures to identify principles that outline the deacon's responsibilities and authority. While Scripture may not be as clear on this issue as on some others, it gives sufficient guidance to define a consistent working arrangement for the deacon in his decision-making role.

67. Ibid.
68. Ibid.
69. Ibid.
70. Ibid.
71. Ibid.
72. Ibid.
73. Ibid., 153.

Acts 6

In order to understand the deacons' role in the decision-making process, one must examine the origins of this important office.[74] The spiritual leadership (then 'apostle,' today 'elder') was initially overwhelmed with the load of temporal ministry in the early church.[75] The Hellenistic Christian widows were being neglected and so a new group of ministers was needed in order to relieve the spiritual leadership from such duties.[76] The intended benefit was to allow the spiritual leaders the time they needed to focus upon ministry of the Word and prayer. The temporal ministry was specifically given to these 'proto-deacons' in order to allow a stewardship of Word and prayer.[77]

From the beginning of the church at Pentecost until Acts 6, the church's shepherds and overseers were the apostles themselves ('the twelve,' as Luke calls them).[78] They were not only responsible for the spiritual care of the early church, but also for the collection, oversight and distribution of finances for the benevolent needs of the church.[79] These material tasks began to accumulate to the point that spiritual aspects of the ministry were choked.[80] Greek-speaking Jews (called 'Hellenist Jews') began to be converted at an aggressive rate.[81] Hellenistic Jews, unlike the Aramaic-speaking Palestinian Jews, often carried a more 'foreign' identity (more Greek or Roman than Jewish). Quickly, a division began to unfold.[82] With the majority of the Jerusalem church having a more Palestinian identity, the material needs of many Hellenist widows were being neglected.[83]

With the arrival of this potential conflict, the apostles recognized the need for a God-honoring solution. The apostles cut to the core of the issue by stating, "It is not desirable for us to neglect the Word of God in order to serve tables."[84] They were accounting for, serving and overseeing the fi-

---

74. Irenaeus, *Against Heresies*, 3:12:10.

75. Strauch, *Biblical Eldership*, 144.

76. Nichols, *The Work of the Deacon and Deaconess*, 9–10.

77. Strauch, *The NT Deacon*, 47–49.

78. Decker, "Polity and the Elder Issue," 257–79.

79. Marshall, *Acts*, 125–26.

80. Ibid., 126.

81. Ibid.

82. Toussaint, "Acts," 2:367.

83. Longenecker, *Acts*, 9:330–331.

84. Strauch, *The NT Deacon*, 15–24.

nances of early church ministry; as a result, their involvement with these tasks undermined the spiritual ministry of God's Word.[85]

1 Timothy 3:11—Romans 16:1

In considering the issues related to deacons, one must decide whether deaconesses existed in the New Testament.[86] At the heart of this question is the identity of the γυναῖκας in 1 Timothy 3:11. The difficulty of the passage is that γυναῖκας can mean simply 'wives,'[87] but it can also refer to 'widows' 'brides,' or 'adult women.'[88] Those who believe that the context demands that the γυναῖκας are deacons' wives often point out that the verses preceding and following this verse refer to the deacon.[89] Those people who interpret this word as a reference to a third office, often point to Phoebe (Romans 16:1), who is called διάκονον τῆς ἐκκλησίας.[90]

A third interpretation is that γυναῖκας refers to some unmarried women in the church who dedicated themselves to aiding the ministry of the local church deacons.[91] These problems also raise the issue of how one views the role of women within the local church.[92] The three most common views are the non-evangelical egalitarian, the evangelical egalitarian, and the hierarchical.[93]

Most likely γυναῖκας in 1 Timothy 3:11 refers to the wives of the deacons (and/or perhaps that of the elders). Phoebe, however, most likely did serve as a deacon.[94] Phoebe would have ministered as a deaconess in such a way as not to violate the prohibition of women exercising authority over men (1 Timothy 2:12).[95] Therefore, churches that appoint deaconesses do

---

85. Ibid.

86. Piper and Grudem, *Recovering Biblical Manhood & Womanhood*, 213–14.

87. BDAG, p. 208d.

88. Ibid.

89. Lewis, "The Women of 1 Timothy 3:11," 168–69.

90. Ibid., 170–172.

91. Ibid., 172–76.

92. Hoch, "The Role of Women in the Church: A Survey of Current Approaches," 242–51.

93. Ibid.

94. Hiebert, *First Timothy,* 70–71.

95. Ibid., 60–61.

have some Biblical basis. Furthermore, the wives of the deacons could also function as deaconesses just as Phoebe did. C.A. Trentham says,

> *"It seems very plausible to interpret this passage in the light of the fact that deacons' wives who made pastoral visits with their husbands would easily fall prey to the temptations to gossip and over-indulgence in drink and would, therefore, need to be warned against these. Where the deacons handled church monies, their wives would also share in the responsibility of guarding the money given through them to the church, and must refrain from laying greedy hands upon it."*[96]

The local church faces practical needs that suit the nature of women.[97] On some occasions women make better ministers than men.[98] The New Testament seems to leave room for women to help as deaconesses by assisting the deacons in some ways.[99] Most churches have a group of women who already function in this capacity even if they are not designated as deaconesses. They are typically found cleaning the floors and kitchen and vacuuming the nursery. These are also the ones who minister to the personal needs of other women in the church. As long as these women understand the nature of their tasks and continue to heed both the spirit and the letter of 1 Timothy 2:12, the local church may be enriched by their ministry.

This is not to say that churches should appoint women to exercise authority in the office of deacon.[100] If a church does employ the use of deaconesses, the nature and authority of the office of deacon must be distinguished from the function of the deaconess.[101] Many churches who do not have officially designated deaconesses expect that some women (especially the wives of the pastors and deacons) will function in the spirit of Phoebe. With the agreement and blessing of the elders and deacons, these women oversee much of the serving, planning, ministry to women, aid in the general hospitality, and help to organize and meet the physical and practical needs of church functions (such as dinners, fellowships and activities).

---

96. Trentham, *Studies in Timothy*, 46.
97. Guthrie, "The Pastoral Epistles," 85.
98. Ibid.
99. Ibid.
100 Hoch, "The Role of Women in the Church," 244–46.
101. Ibid., 247–50.

Philippians 1:1

Deacons are here named along with bishops in Paul's greeting to the church at Philippi. While most of the time διάκονος is used to mean a 'servant,' here the Apostle Paul uses the term in a more technical way.[102] Here and in 1 Timothy 3:8, 12, Paul uses the term to designate an office.[103] While this text says little about the nature of these deacons, one can nevertheless draw several conclusions from it.

First, the office of deacon was apparently part of the established order of local church government by the time of the writing of Philippians (A.D. 61).[104] This means that from the time of Acts 6, the office of deacon had progressed past its introductory stage. Second, Paul recognized deacons as an identifiable group.[105] Third, Paul's recognition of both deacons and elders implies an endorsement of their leadership and service.[106] Perhaps Paul pointed out the deacons because of their role in the collection and subsequent sending of the church's gift to Paul by the hand of Epaphroditus (2:15; 4:18).[107] Building on this observation, Strauch argues that the work and qualifications of deacons indicate that the 'diakonate' was indeed a recognizable office.[108]

The last point here is that these deacons were identified in the plural, not the singular. This provides evidence of a team approach to ministry. James Boice effectively notes:

> "...there is no reference anywhere in the New Testament to the appointment of only one elder or one deacon to a work. We would tend to appoint one leader, but God's wisdom is greater than our own at this point. In appointing several persons to work together, the church at God's direction provided the mutual encouragement among those who shared in the work..."[109]

---

102. Strauch, *The NT Deacon*, 71.
103. Ibid.
104. Ibid., 69.
105. Kent, Jr., "Philippians," 103.
106. Ibid.
107. Martin, "The Epistle of Paul to the Philippians," 57–58.
108. Strauch, *The NT Deacon*, 71.
109. Boice, *Foundations of the Christian Faith*, 632.

Section I: What Is Decision-Making?

I Timothy 3:8–13

One of the most compelling reasons to see the deacon as a significant leadership role in the local church is found in the comparison between the qualifications for the overseer and the qualifications for the deacon.[110] These similar qualifications imply an important slate of tasks for deacons as one of the primary purposes for their existence.[111] The establishment of deacons in Acts 6 was intended to allow the spiritual leadership to give themselves to the ministry of the Word and prayer.[112]

This passage focuses attention on the qualifications for the office of deacon.[113] First, Paul mentions four personal qualifications (v. 8). These deal with the deacon's character. He is to be a man of dignity, one who controls his tongue, one who is not a drunkard, and one who demonstrates financial integrity.[114] Second, Paul names two spiritual qualifications (v. 9). The deacon is to know and obey the Word of God.[115] Third, Paul lists three domestic qualifications (vv. 11–12). These include having a wife of Godly character, consistently being a 'one-woman man,' and being in control of his family.[116]

Paul concludes this passage by noting that the deacon who serves faithfully will enjoy a special standing. This standing is based on the extended observation of the deacon's character. It includes an external testimony that demonstrates the quality of the inner man. This special standing or rank is probably alluding to the opinion in which God and perhaps others in the church would hold the deacon.[117] The deacon himself would enjoy a greater amount of faith and assurance.[118]

---

110. Hiebert, *First Timothy,* 68–72.

111. Earle, *1 Timothy,* 367.

112. Ibid.

113. Strauch, *The NT Deacon,* 83–143.

114. Litfin, "*1 Timothy,*" 2:737–38.

115. Ibid., 738.

116. Ibid.

117. Earle, *1 Timothy,* 11:368–69.

118. Ibid., 369.

GENERAL LEADERSHIP LESSON FROM THE OLD TESTAMENT

One of the more intense hermeneutical discussions today concerns the application of Old Testament teaching to the New Testament church.[119] The target audience for the Old Testament writings was Israel. The New Testament, however, teaches that all Scripture is God-breathed and is profitable (2 Timothy 3:16). Therefore, New Testament believers must be able to extrapolate Old Testament truths for application to contemporary life and ministry. The New Testament offices of elder and deacon do not function like the Old Testament offices of prophet, priest or king. General lessons of leadership found in the Old Testament, however, may be applied to the elder and deacon and to the decision-making process of the local New Testament church.[120]

Dispensationalists see significant discontinuity between the Testaments.[121] Even dispensationalists, however, are able to discover principles and examples that can be applied trans-dispensationally. A tough challenge exists for the consistent and honest dispensationalist to reconcile these points. There must be a way of doing just that.[122]

In 1 Corinthians 10, Paul suggests that Old Testament principles should serve as an example for obedient Christian living.[123] It would be a mistake for the New Testament believer to ignore helpful leadership principles from the Old Testament. Grant Osborne demonstrates how that is especially true when dealing with the use of Old Testament allusions applied to New Testament Church settings. In looking for a biblical approach to New Testament leadership, such trans-dispensational principles can help the modern deacon learn to function effectively in local church decision-making.[124]

Moses provides a ready pattern for trans-dispensational principles of leadership.[125] Moses was protected by the Lord. Bringing the right kind of leadership into a local church is consistent with God's character. God

---

119. Hays, "Applying the Old Testament Law Today," 21–35.

120. Steinbron, *The Lay Driven Church*, 88–99.

121. Ryrie, *Dispensationalism Today*, 43–47.

122. Zuck, *Basic Bible Interpretation*, 284–89.

123. Waltke, *Continuity and Discontinuity*, 276–77.

124. Osborne, *The Hermeneutical Spiral*, 134–35.

125. Baron, *Moses on Management*,

throughout redemptive history has provided his people with leaders. Throughout the Old Testament, God ordained and guided those whom he would use as leaders.[126] Moses demonstrates several key leadership principles that can help the church leader.[127]

Moses, being a potential heir to the throne of the Egyptian empire, would have been given the best education Egyptian gold could buy.[128] Some believe that Moses would have been trained not only in mathematics and the sciences, but also as a military tactician.[129] This must have been part of God's plan to develop Moses' leadership skills. After forty years in Midian, Moses was not convinced of his leadership ability. After God dramatically communicated his will to Moses, Moses became a more effective leader.[130] That effectiveness can be seen in several ways. Myron Rush writes that Moses' leadership is shown by his delegation.[131] Delegation is especially applicable to local church decision-making. Many deacons and pastors, though, have an attitude of reluctance toward sharing of authority. Lloyd M. Perry and Norman Shawchuck express the damage this attitude causes:

> "*The whole idea of creating a powerful, active laity is met with mixed emotions on the part of clergy, many of whom are not fully willing to accept the laity as genuine co-workers in the church. Many clergy fear that if the power of the laity increases, their own power will decrease. They wish to control and direct the extent of lay involvement by giving assignments to the laity rather than fully involving them in all phases of planning and decision-making about the church's ministry, what should be done and who should do it. Pastors who fail to train and equip the laity and then turn them loose to plan and carry out the church's ministry need never to expect to build their congregations into truly vital forces for God. They will instead be 'people shrinkers,' reducing the laity to a point of passive dependence upon them. . .*"[132]

Moses certainly could have made most of the decisions that others would eventually make. Prior to his exhortation by Jethro, Moses was

126. Woolfe, *The Bible on Leadership*, 24–48.

127. Strauch, *The NT Deacon*, 75.

128. Marshall, *Acts*, 139.

129. Josephus, *Flavius Josephus*, 2.10.7.

130. Baron, *Moses on Management*, 1–8.

131. Rush, *Management: A Biblical Approach*, 142.

132. Perry and Shawchuck, *Revitalizing the 20th Century Church*, 59.

making the overwhelming majority of the decisions.[133] After receiving Jethro's warning, however, Moses consistently turned to God's people for their help in accomplishing what had to be done. Melvin Steinbron calls this 'The Moses Principle.'[134]

The Moses Principle, if applied to New Testament churches, can aid the overall health of a congregation. Moses identified those leaders who were trustworthy men of ability.[135] Then, instead of hoarding authority and responsibility, he spread the load so that only the most important issues came to him. Hans Finzel cites the following quote from Theodore Roosevelt: "*The best executive is the one who has sense enough to pick good men to do what he wants done, and self-restraint enough to keep from meddling with them while they do it.*"[136] Moses didn't pass all issues off to others, but issues that were less important or pressing were delegated to the other leaders to handle. This is impressive and instructional for several reasons.

Moses provides an example of exercising discernment to recognize good leaders.[137] Moses carefully identified which leaders should serve in each capacity. Moses also illustrates the willingness to release important tasks to other leaders.[138] Insecure leaders do not do this because they are always threatened by giving away authority.[139] The implication for church leaders should be obvious: biblically qualified believers should be trusted with authority and responsibility.[140] They should also be willing to give away authority and to trust other gifted and committed individuals.[141] As he learns to delegate effectively, the leader will see more of his responsibility being fulfilled as more people participate in the ministry.

David provides a second example of effective Old Testament leadership. If Moses models delegation, David illustrates the ability to balance the tasks of leading compassionately while following respectfully. David had to develop this ability because of the insecurity of King Saul. The New Testament believer should take special notice. He must at times be willing

133. Rush, *Management: A Biblical Approach*, 142.

134. Steinbron, *The Lay Driven Church*, 88–89.

135. Ibid., 88.

136. Finzel, *The Top Ten Mistakes Leaders Make*, 101.

137. Hannah, "Exodus," 2:136–37.

138. Ibid., 136.

139. Finzel, *The Top Ten Mistakes Leaders Make*, 100.

140. Strauch, *The NT Deacon*, 77–79.

141. Steinbron, *The Lay Driven Church*, 94.

to defer in matters of personal preference. Other times, however, he must lead from conviction, and not simply bow out of a discussion because his position is not popular.[142] The ability to disagree while maintaining a spirit of respect is absolutely necessary for all leaders.

Saul could fly into a rage when he heard people praising David (1 Samuel 18:7). Today, many deacons must serve pastors whose attitude is like Saul's.[143] How disastrous when one of these deacons is praised in the presence of one of these pastors.[144] The New Testament provides a parallel example in the contrast between Gaius and Diotrephes (3 John). Gaius is commended because his spirit was consistent with truth and love. Diotrephes, however, 'loves to have the preeminence.' Sometimes, some pastors manifest this same Diotrephes syndrome.[145] Through all of Saul's anger, David honored God. On an occasion when David could have taken the life of Saul, his response was, "how can I touch God's anointed?"[146]

Proverbs 11:14 states, "*In the multitude of counselors there is safety*" (KJV). This verse assumes that these counselors are wise and correct. Bob Beasley, commenting on the application of this passage, makes the following observation:

> *In seeking advice the temptation is strong to seek only the advice we will like. However, the purpose of advice is not to confirm our thinking, but to establish our thinking. We seek advice from several perspectives. In doing so, we are able to uncover the blind spots in our own thoughts. In forming a board of directors for a corporation, different disciplines are sought in board members because they will all approach decision-making from different angles. From a team of diverse counselors, a business can establish a foundation that will chart profitable and safe course through today's competitive environment.*[147]

The problem with Rehoboam was not that he was unwilling to listen to counsel; the problem was his unwillingness to listen to the right counsel.[148] Rehoboam chose the same route that many pastors and deacons

---

142. Strauch, *The NT Deacon*, 94–97.

143. Finzel, *Top Ten Mistakes Leaders Make*, 23.

144. Barker, "3 John," 12:369–77.

145. Ibid.

146. Youngblood, "1, 2 Samuel," 3:769.

147. Beasley, *The Wisdom of Proverbs*, 101.

148. Ibid.

choose when making a decision in the church. Rehoboam surrounded himself with counselors who were just like himself. He chose to listen to the young men whose thoughts and philosophies reinforced his own. The results were tragic.[149] This is not to say that young leaders always take the wrong side. Often older men become set, stubborn and foolish in regards to new aspects of change. However, usually when mature godly leaders are uneasy about decisions or directions, there are good reasons fueling those fears. This is the same type of disaster that occurs when pastors or deacons attempt to add men to a leadership team on the sole condition of loyalty. While this may create easy leadership meetings, it will result in damage to that ministry.

LEADERSHIP LESSONS FROM JESUS OF NAZARETH

In His divinity, Jesus is unlike humans. In matters pertaining to his deity, he does not necessarily provide an example.[150] Jesus was also human, however, and therefore he does serve as an example in important ways. One of the best works outlining the pattern of Christ in the development of leadership is A. B. Bruce's "The Training of the Twelve."[151] In emphasizing the priority that the Lord placed on developing the disciples' leadership, Kenneth Gangel makes the following observation based on Bruce's work:

> He [Bruce] suggests that the total report of the gospels covers only thirty-three or thirty-four days of our Lord's three-and-one-half-year ministry, and John records only eighteen days. What did Christ do the rest of the time? The clear implication of the Scriptures is that He was training leaders.[152]

The apostles had to learn effective leadership because they would lead believers into a new dispensation. As the transition from the apostles to the church unfolded, the position of leadership passed from apostles to elders. Elders were given the primary leadership role of the local church. One of the elders' responsibilities (shared by the congregation) was to make sure that the deacons were equipped for their role in decision-making and

---

149. Ibid.
150. Erickson, *Christian Theology*, 721.
151. Bruce, *The Training of the Twelve*, 29–40.
152. Gangel, *Competent to Lead*, 13.

leadership. In a secondary sense, the deacons themselves are responsible for their ability and effectiveness.[153]

2 Timothy 2:2 gives the reason why this process of equipping must take place: "*And the things which you have heard from me in the presence of many witnesses, entrust these to faithful men who will be able to teach others also.*" Bruce makes the following observation:

> "'. . .Follow me,' said Jesus to the fishermen of Bethsaida, 'and I will make you fishers of men.' These words. . .show that the great Founder of the faith desired not only to have disciples, but to have about Him men whom He might train to make disciples of others. . .Both from His words and from His actions we can see that He attached supreme importance to that part of His work which consisted in training the twelve. In the intercessory prayer, e.g., He speaks of the training He had given these men as if it had been the principal part of His own earthly ministry. . .[154]

These dynamics have to be 'caught' as much as 'taught.' Bruce brings out a similar point from John 21: "*[Christ] will have all His followers, and especially the heads of His people, to be heroes, 'Ironsides,' prompt to do bidding, fearless of danger, patient of fatigue, without a trace of selfish softness. He will give no quarter even to natural weaknesses, disregards present pain, cares not how we smart under rebuke, provided only He gain His end, the production of character temptation-proof.*"[155]

Every local church has the right and authority to take the Scriptures and draw its own conclusions.[156] If a pastor or a deacon tries to undermine the authority and agreement of the congregation, he is ultimately undermining an important biblical distinctive in regards to the local church.[157] A church's decision-making process should not be dictated to it by an outside authority. This does not mean that an autonomous church cannot cooperate with other churches through a fellowship or an association. Even in those cases, however, the local assembly should have the ultimate determination as to how decisions should be made within the church.[158] God has gifted the

---

153. Nichols, *The Work of the Deacon and Deaconess*, 92–95.

154. Bruce, *The Training of the Twelve*, 12–13.

155. Ibid., 526.

156. Lumpkin, *Baptist Confessions of Faith*, 285–89.

157. Ibid.

158. Hiscox, *Principles and Practices for Baptist Churches*, 311–43.

local assembly with believers who are equipped to handle ministry through the exercise of spiritual gifts.

Deacons' function in ministry and service depends upon their spiritual gifts. In his journal article titled, "Called to Serve: Toward a Philosophy of Ministry," J. Gary Inrig makes the connection between the concept of service and spiritual gifts. This is true not only of elders and deacons, but of all believers brought into the Church.[159] Inrig states:

> *"The New Testament does not depict ministry as a specialized position, occupied by a select few. Gifts are God's provision for serving each other (1 Peter 4:10). In fact Peter divided gifts into major categories of speaking and serving gifts (1 Peter 4:11), and Paul spoke of a particular gift of service (Romans 12:7). Service takes place by means of spiritual gifts, which shape and define one's ministry.*[160]

Inrig continues by applying this truth to those men who are called to positions of leadership, when he quotes Paul's admonition to Archippus, "Take heed to the ministry which you have received in the Lord, that you may fulfill it." (Colossians 4:16)[161]

The ideal role of the New Testament deacon can be constructed from the biblical evidence. The key distinction between the elder's function and that of the deacon is his sphere of ministry. By attending to the Word and prayer, the elders are to oversee the spiritual sphere of ministry. Deacons are to assist the elders by overseeing the material sphere of ministry. According to Acts 6, deacons were to free up the spiritual leadership to spend the necessary time and attention on the ministry of the Word and prayer.[162]

In the early church, the deacons were responsible to oversee the church's finances.[163] The term 'tables' in Acts 6 most likely refers to tables used to count money and manage finances.[164] One interpretation of Acts 6:2 could read, "It is not right for us to neglect the preaching of God's Word in order to handle finances." This interpretation seems consistent with the context of Acts 4:34–35. These first deacons demonstrate oversight of the finances by collecting money and goods contributed to the needy (Acts 4:34,

159. Inrig, "Called to Serve," 336–50.

160. Ibid.

161. Ibid.

162. Cianca, "The Nature of Biblical Leadership: From Theocracy to Community," 147–49.

163. Strauch, *The NT Deacon*, 32–33.

164. Ibid., 33.

35, 37; 5:2). Following the collection, the resources were distributed to the needy (Acts 4:35). These men were given the responsibility to ensure that funds were distributed justly and fairly (Acts 6). Finally, they coordinated the church's overall financial affairs and oversaw the various ministries of benevolence.[165]

There are at least three foundational areas of decision-making that existed in the early New Testament church that carry on today. First, those issues that involve spiritual concerns and biblical ministry must be overseen by the elders.[166] The preaching, teaching and discipling ministries of the church fall under the authority of the elders. In one sense, the elders do have a responsibility for the oversight of the overall life of the congregation. In certain areas, however, elders must submit themselves to the wisdom of godly deacons.[167] Therefore, this second category of decisions, those that are of a physical, financial, benevolent or practical nature, should be led by the deacons. Often, however, a decision in a church body affects the spiritual realm as well as the physical realm. On those occasions, these two groups of leaders should work through mutual submission toward unanimity and consensus.[168]

RELATIONSHIP BETWEEN ELDERS AND THE CONGREGATION

Before examining the decision-making relationship between the deacon and the congregation, one must understand the relationship between the pastor/elder/bishop and the congregation. In many churches the relationship that exists between the deacons and the congregation is actually one that the elders should fulfill. Baptists typically believe that the ultimate human authority of a church resides within the congregation. Each individual within the assembly must choose to submit himself to the office of pastor or deacon.[169] John Gill explains the necessity of this delegation of authority and the decision of the church member to submit to leadership when he states,

---

165. Ibid., 33.

166. Mayhue, *Rediscovering Pastoral Ministry*, 336–50.

167. Cianca, *The Nature of Biblical Leadership*, 149–51.

168. Foshee, *Now That You're a Deacon*, 22–40.

169. Hiscox, *Principles and Practices of Baptist Churches*, 99–100.

> *. . .unless persons voluntarily give up themselves to a church and its pastor, they can exercise no power over them, in a church-way; they have nothing to do with them that are without, they have no concern with the watch and care of them; nor are they entitled thereunto, unless they submit themselves to one another in the fear of God; they have no power to reprove, admonish, and censure them in a church-way; nor can the pastor exercise any pastoral authority over them, except by agreement they consent to yield to it; nor can they expect he should watch over their souls as he that must give an account, having no charge of them by any act of theirs. . .*[170]

Once that occurs, the congregation should lovingly submit to the guidance and wisdom of these duly appointed leaders.[171] In answer to those who ask, '*why?*' Gill again explains that,

> *These pastors, teachers, bishops and elders are called rulers, guides and governors. A pastor, or shepherd is the governor and guide of his flock; a teacher, and a ruling elder are the same, 1 Tim. V. 17. . .1 Tim. III. 1, 4, 5. These, indeed are not to lord it over God's heritage, or rule according to their own wills, in an arbitrary manner; but according to the laws of Christ, as King of saints; and then they are to be respected and obeyed. . .*[172]

God has given the elders of each congregation the responsibility to oversee decision-making within the spiritual sphere. Each local assembly must apply these principles to its own process for decision-making. For instance, the elders may oversee the church calendar, the maintenance of ministry staff, special speakers, ministry policy (with the help of the deacons where those policies affect their sphere). They may make final decisions on standards of conduct for worship, Christian education curriculum and expectations for leadership. Areas that pertain directly to the communication of biblical truth, corporate living, and fidelity and doctrine are areas that the elders must lead. The congregation is responsible for God-honoring conduct in these areas, but the elders lead the congregation in such matters.

Those who disagree have to answer the question of why an elder is also called a bishop or overseer. Stretching back into Classical Greek, the term ἐπίσκοπος was often used in the context of a decision-making officer.[173]

170. Gill, *A Body of Practical Divinity,* 2:858.

171. Hiscox, *Principles and Practices of Baptist Churches,* 99–100.

172. Gill, *A Body of Practical Divinity,* 2:864.

173. Lidell and Scott, *A Greek-English Lexicon,* 657.

H.W.Beyer says, *"Athens uses episkopoi for state officials, e.g., supervisors sent by Athens to other cities of the Attic League. . .We also read of similar officials in other states, whether as secret police or as officials with judicial functions (this would perhaps include judicial "authority?"). . .An interesting use occurs in Syria in relation to the erection of a public building in which it is clear that those who have the episcope are supervisors of the work in the interests of the builders and perhaps with control of the funds. . .there is no clearly defined office of episcopos in the LXX but the term is used for 'overseer' in various senses, e.g., officers in Judges 9:28, Is. 60:17, supervisors of funds in 2 Chr. 34:12, 17. . ."*[174] Duane Litfin says that these leaders were to "direct the affairs of the church. Elders have the oversight of the affairs of the congregation. . ."[175]

If the elders do not have decision-making authority within the spiritual sphere of ministry, how is it that they are expected to "rule well" the flock of God? Why is it that the assembly has given the obligation to submit to those who "rule over you, who have spoken the word of God to you. . ." (Hebrews 13:7)? If elders (who are called bishops) cannot make decisions in the spiritual sphere of ministry, they simply cannot rule.[176] If they cannot rule, they cannot administrate (Acts 20:17, 28). If they cannot administrate, they cannot carry out their tasks as bishops. If they cannot accomplish the tasks of bishop, they cannot fulfill their tasks as elders or pastors (1 Peter 5:1–2). Furthermore, if elders do not have the right to exercise decision-making in the spiritual sphere, how can they lead or feed the flock?

For example, if the congregation is to be the primary decision-maker in the spiritual sphere, the pastor should take a poll each Sunday to see what he should preach (i.e., "feed"). The words of Christ seem to indicate that the shepherd is to exercise his discernment in the details of feeding (John 21:15–17; Acts 20:17, 28). How is that devoid of decision-making? If the congregation holds decision-making authority in the spiritual sphere, then the elders should poll the congregation as to where the church is headed and what will be fed. This is contradictory to 1 Peter 5:1–2.

In 1 Peter 5:1–2, elders are commanded to "shepherd," which deals with the task of nurturing and feeding. That means they will need to determine what is fed. This demands decision-making. As elders, they are leaders. Therefore, they will need to determine the direction they will lead

174. Beyer, *TDNT*, 2:608–20.

175. Litfin, *"1 Timothy,"* 2:744.

176. Earle, *1 Timothy*, 11: 380.

the congregation. This also demands decision-making. Then they are commanded to oversee or manage the church of God. Benjamin Griffith, a leading Baptist in the eighteenth century, writing on behalf of the Philadelphia Baptist Association in 1743, said, *"Ruling elders also are to be respected, seeing they are fitted of God, and called by the church to go before the church, or to preside in acts of government and rule, 1 Tim. 5:17."*[177] Again, this demands decision-making. The very fact that 1 Peter 5:1–3 warns about abuse of decision-making indicates that elders do exercise a legitimate form of decision-making.[178]

The congregation does share in the burden of responsibility for their own spiritual health. Passages such as 2 Corinthians 5 demonstrate that the congregation is responsible to make sure that the elders are making decisions in a way that is consistent with Scriptural demands.[179] This balance is difficult but important. Elder rule without congregational accountability is foreign to the New Testament. Congregational polity without elder leadership is equally unscriptural. Consider the observations of Phil Newton, *"There is no evidence that the early church voted on every issue. Rather the plural eldership competently and efficiently handled day-to-day matters."*[180] In many cases, congregations give the elders' rightful duties to the deacons. Then, because no one is left to accomplish the deacon's work, they invent the office of trustee.

RELATIONSHIP BETWEEN DEACONS AND THE CONGREGATION

What is the decision-making relationship between the deacon and the congregation? Deacons are responsible for the areas that concern the physical, financial, benevolent, or service ministries. Qualified deacons must rule their families well, just as the bishop must (1 Timothy 3:12). This ruling involves some form of responsible decision-making. Again we see the Scriptures teaching that if a man cannot manage well at home, he cannot manage well at church. If elders have already been given the responsibility of managing the spiritual sphere of ministry, what is left for the deacons to manage? John Gill describes the type of oversight the deacons are to

177. Griffith, *Polity,* 103.

178. Raymer, "1 Peter," 2:856.

179. Hiscox, *Principles and Practices for Baptist Churches,* 160–191.

180. Newton, *"Elders in Congregational Life,"* 58.

exercise: "...the office of a deacon lies chiefly in the management of temporal things."[181] The deacon has been given to the local assembly to serve the benevolence of the congregation and to exercise oversight over the material sphere of ministry.

RELATIONSHIP BETWEEN ELDERS AND DEACONS

Some decisions affect both the spiritual and material spheres of ministry. These decisions are best made by the two leadership groups working together. This does not mean that the congregation has no role. Passages such as 2 Corinthians 5 imply that the congregation does bear a responsibility for church life. The individual members as well as the congregation at large have specific obligations toward the deacons. Benjamin Griffith comments,

> The officers of the church, whom Christ hath appointed, are to be respected. (l.) the deacons of the church, though they officiate but in the outward concerns of the church, as in the section about deacons is noted, if they are faithful, do purchase unto themselves a good degree, 1 Tim. 3:13, are therefore to be respected."[182]

The corporate body has the right to veto any decision made by the leadership. Indeed, the congregation decides who the leaders will be. In Acts 6, the congregation was involved in both the nomination and election of their deacons, though the apostles ratified the decision through the laying on of hands.[183] The apostles did not ultimately choose the first deacons.[184] Therefore, congregations must have direct involvement in major decisions.[185]

In order to help with the decision-making process, a church needs to establish procedures for its leaders. As a student of Scripture examines God's Word, he can identify at least fourteen principles to guide the process of making decisions. These include:

1. The five laws of direction (Word, Prayer, Open Doors, Wisdom, Peace)

2. The commitment to the vision and mission of the church

181. Gill, *A Body of Practical Divinity,* 2:885.

182. Griffith, *Polity,* 103.

183. Toussaint, *Acts,* 367.

184. Ibid.

185. Hiscox, *Principles and Practices for Baptist Churches,* 153–59.

3. The commitment to the idea that Jesus is preeminent

4. The commitment to consensus

5. The commitment to a process of approval and implementation

6. The commitment to assume the best

7. The commitment to mutual submission

8. The commitment to humility

9. The commitment to division of labor

10. The commitment to communication

11. The commitment to speaking the truth in love

12. The commitment to trust

13. The commitment to being a God-pleaser, not a man-pleaser

14. The commitment to join responsibility with authority

GENERAL LEADERSHIP LESSONS ILLUSTRATED BY SECULAR MODEL'S

While Christians should not appropriate secular models of management while disregarding scriptural principles, some secular models help apply truths that are both practical and biblical. The field of leadership and management theory offers a wealth of practical insight that on few occasions can be surprisingly consistent with biblical thought. These models of leadership demonstrate that biblical principles of leadership are effective even when applied in a secular context.

Douglas McGregor

Warren Bennis notes that Douglas McGregor

> . . .created a new taste across the entire field of management and the newer fields of organizational behavior and organization development. . .since this book (The Human Side of Enterprise), more than any other book on management, changed an entire concept of organizational man and replaced it with a new paradigm that

stressed human potentials, emphasized human growth, and elevated the human role in industrial society.[186]

In *The Human Side of Enterprise,* McGregor contrasts two theories of how workers are motivated. The theory which was most popular at the time was Theory X. The new theory proposed by McGregor was Theory Y.[187] McGregor's work is an important one. In Theory X, one sees the common distrust of pastors and congregations toward deacons. While Theory Y may not be the best solution, it presents a different option with which to view qualified deacons. Instead of assuming the worst of the deacon (Theory X), it would be most consistent with the deacon's character (assuming he is Biblically qualified), to expect a better set of foundational desires toward his work as a Christian and as a leader in the congregation (Theory Y). It may be that pastors who view deacons with the attitude that McGregor labels as Theory X do so as a result of arrogance on the part of the pastor.

Theory X

This theory is based on three major tenets, according to McGregor.[188]

The average human being has an inherent dislike of work and will avoid it if he can.

1. *Because of this human characteristic of dislike of work, most people must be coerced, controlled, directed, threatened with punishment to get them to put forth adequate effort toward the achievement of organized objectives.*

2. *The average human being prefers to be directed, wishes to avoid responsibility, has relatively little ambition, wants security above all.*[189]

Some of Theory X corresponds to a Christian view of depravity, but this seems inadequate as a foundation for leading a regenerate congregation. It provides an even weaker foundation for leading a team of pastors or deacons. The theory fosters a deep distrust of coworkers and subordinates. This distrust becomes devastating when this theory is transported into a

---

186. McGregor, *The Human Side of Enterprise,* iv.

187. Ibid., 33–57.

188. Ibid., 33–35.

189. Ibid.

church setting. In many churches, however, the pastor does view his assistant pastors, deacons and congregation according to Theory X.[190]

Of course, people do need leadership, discipline and direction. The problem is not in these elements of Theory X. The problem is assuming that most believers and even lay leaders will avoid work, need to be constantly threatened, and cannot be trusted.

Theory Y

Here McGregor paints an entirely different view of the average worker in the average organization. The fundamental assumptions of this view are as follows:

1. *The expenditure of physical and mental effort in work is as natural as play or rest.*

2. *External control and the threat of punishment are not the only means for bringing about effort toward organizational objectives. Man will exercise self-direction and self-control in the service of objectives to which he is committed.*

3. *Commitment to objectives is a function of the rewards associated with their achievement.*

4. *The average human being learns, under proper conditions, not only to accept but to seek responsibility.*

5. *The capacity to exercise a relatively high degree of imagination, ingenuity, and creativity in the solution of organizational problems is widely, not narrowly, distributed in the population.*

6. *Under the condition of modern industrial life, the intellectual potentialities of the average human being are only partially utilized.*[191]

While McGregor's Theory Y fails as a description of the natural man, it does describe at least the more mature Christian. Theory Y provides a better foundation for Christian leadership than does Theory X. The distribution and use of spiritual gifts is more compatible with Theory Y than with Theory X.

190. McGregor, *Leadership and Motivation,* 13–14.

191. McGregor, *The Human Side of Enterprise,* 45–57.

Principle-Centered Leadership

Stephen R. Covey's 1989 bestseller, *The Seven Habits of Highly Effective People*, was widely read by both Christians and non-Christians.[192] Nearly a year later, Covey published a book called *Principle Centered Leadership*, in which he mentions many characteristics of effective leadership that are also found in Scripture.

In chapters 16 and 17 of *Principle Centered Leadership*, Covey contrasts four paradigms of management.[193] The first three represent paradigms that are less than ideal, or even destructive. The first, the scientific paradigm, essentially sees others in the organization as stomachs to be motivated by the carrot-and-stick approach. Even if fairly employed, this approach is still very authoritarian.[194] The second, the human relations paradigm, differs only in that it is more benevolent than the first model. In the words of Covey,

> *We see that people have feelings. Hence we treat people not only with fairness, but with kindness, courtesy, civility, and decency. But it may only mean a shift from being authoritarian to being a benevolent authoritarian because we still are the elite few who know what's best.*[195]

The third model, the human resource paradigm, is concerned with fairness (as in the first) and kindness (as in the second); but it is also concerned with efficiency. It appreciates other people in the organization and develops them socially, economically, and psychologically. This paradigm, while much better, still falls short because the leaders still view the followers primarily as resources instead of as souls to be nurtured and valued.[196]

Covey's fourth paradigm and the one that most closely parallels what the deacons and the pastors of the local church should do, is to view all participants in the church as spiritual beings. This is significantly different than viewing them as expendable resources. In this approach, everyone understands the purpose, the objectives, the values, and rationale of the organization.[197] Leaders encourage participation in decision-making as well as other important matters. The more important the decision, or

---

192. Covey, *The 7 Habits of Highly Effective People*.

193. Covey, *Principle-Centered Leadership*, 173–89.

194. Ibid., 176–77.

195. Ibid., 177–78.

196. Ibid., 178.

197. Covey, *Principle-Centered Leadership*, 178–81.

more challenging the problem, the more leaders attempt to tap the talents of their human resources. This results in a group that has clear purpose that is larger than individual fulfillment. Covey concludes,

> *The scientific management (stomach) paradigm says, "Pay me well." The human relations (heart) paradigm says, "Treat me well." The human resource (mind) paradigm suggests, "Use me well." The principle-centered leadership (whole person) paradigm says: "Let's talk about vision and mission, roles and goals. I want to make a meaningful contribution.*[198]

Covey's observations concerning the importance of trusting and sharing the ownership of vision and direction of a team leads to the next major application.[199] The result of creating an atmosphere described by Covey can be seen in the use of Self-Directed Work Teams.

Self-Directed Work Teams

The Self-Directed Work Team (SDWT) was introduced during the late 1980's. The SDWT spreads the workload horizontally among a number of leaders.[200] The theory behind SDWT is that more work can be accomplished when teams are empowered and freed from aggressively authoritarian forms of management. The SDWT approach does not discard accountability. However, these authority-based relationships are viewed differently from other more traditional approaches to management.[201] Here are a few of the distinctions between the SDWT vs. the traditional approach to management and decision-making:

SDWT	Traditional
Multi-skilled work force	Workforce of isolated specialists
Information shared widely	Information limited
Few levels of management	Many levels of management
Whole-business focus	Function/department focus
Shared goals	Segregated goals

---

198. Ibid., 180–181.
199. Ibid.
200. Fisher, *Leading Self-Directed Work Teams,* xxxi.
201. Rees, *How to Lead Work Teams,* 15.

Section I: What Is Decision-Making?

Seemingly chaotic	Seemingly organized
Purpose achievement emphasis	Problem-solving emphasis
High worker commitment	High management commitment
Continuous improvements	Incremental improvements
Self-controlled	Management-controlled
Values/principles-based	Policy/procedure-based[236]

The two premier leaders in this movement are Kimball and Maureen Fisher, co-founders of The Fisher Group, a consulting firm that helps "organizations transform into 'high performance organizations.'" This group mainly focuses on "team-based organizations" or "socio-technical systems."[203]

The SDWT requires some adjustment for use in the church. It should not simply be a "Self-Directed Work Team," but rather a "Spirit-Directed Work Team." A church is a spiritual body. It would be a sad replacement to have leaders of a local church depend more on technical approaches to decision-making than on the leadership and empowering of the Holy Spirit and directed by scriptural-based wisdom. As already noted, decisions on all levels must be bathed in prayer before they are made.[204]

Applying this SDWT approach to the relationship between elders and deacons could in fact bring a measure of health man church leadership teams are missing. First, the deacons are not totally independent from the elders. They are still responsible to communicate with one another, with the elders, and with the body as a whole. Second, the deacons are not free to do whatever they feel like doing. The tasks of each deacon are given in the job description for each Area of Responsibility (AOR). Third, the deacon is granted the freedom to use the financial, intellectual, and personal resources of the church in the way that makes the best sense to him and to others with each AOR. Fourth, each deacon is accountable not only to other deacons, but also to elders. Throughout the function of the various tasks, each deacon is responsible to communicate not only with each other, but also with the elders.

---

202. Fisher, *Leading Self-Directed Work Teams,* 18.

203. Fisher, *Leading Self-Directed Work Teams,* xxxvi.

204. Tetreau, *The Deacons' Role in the Decision-Making Process,* Appendix A.

While the New Testament leaves some room for churches to adopt various patterns of decision-making, those that grant all authority to the pastor and not the deacons will undermine the health of the congregation. The New Testament churches held their leaders accountable even when those leaders were apostles.[205] Modern churches do not have apostles, but if the Scriptures permit accountability in the face of apostolic authority, then local churches should also hold their leaders accountable.

Those churches that allow one man (senior pastor or deacon chairman) to exercise unilateral decision-making authority are creating an office that is not found in Scripture. The only mention of a leader who functioned this way was Diotrephes, and Scripture's commentary on him was not a positive one. 3 John 9 describes this leader as one who liked to have preeminence.

DEFECTIVE APPROACHES TO ECCLESIASTICAL DECISION-MAKING

According to James Cianca, a wrong approach to authority within the congregation naturally leads to an abuse of power. A biblical model of decision-making is in contrast with at least four modes or models of church leadership.[206] A few of the more common alternatives are examined here for the purpose of marking and delineating a healthy approach.

The Dictator

Some churches allow the pastor or the board chairman so much power that the rest of the leadership is essentially silenced.[207] This model is found all over the evangelical spectrum. In some churches, the congregation is gripped by the fear of crossing the one elder or pastor who has a tight grip on the reigns of the church. No one dares to question a point of theology or decision led by the elder. This type of leader leads by way of threats and intimidation. Believers often end up discouraged, frustrated, and eventually leave the congregation. This frustration is especially acute in the presence of a self-centered or insecure leader. What makes these churches even less

---

205. Longenecker, *Acts,* 9:470–472.

206. Cianca, *Biblical Leadership,* 73–79.

207. Finzel, *The Top Ten Mistakes Leaders Make,* 32–33.

healthy is the type of insecure Christians that they typically attract. The churches may also develop an ascetic atmosphere, in which the pastor is expected to chastise the congregation for its failures rather than to praise and encourage them for their successes. This results in an unhealthy church driven by a performance-based acceptance.[208]

These churches do not have a sense of real community because every decision must come down from the top. In some cases, the church will tolerate an abusive and obnoxious leader because of the friendships and traditions he has established. The church will allow the pastor to select the deacons personally, and the deacons are often chosen because of their loyalty to (or friendship with) the pastor. The business meetings may be characterized more by political maneuvering than by consensus.

Benevolent Dictator

Not all churches that have the "dictator" leadership model have an evil or self-centered senior pastor or deacon chairman. Some churches honestly believe that this is the biblical model. One can find examples of men who hold this complete authority, and yet who demonstrate a genuine love for God's people. While the benevolent dictator is to be commended for his avoiding the heavy-handedness of the harsh dictator, his 'modus operandi' is still in error and as such still exhibits danger. A church that has a benevolent yet authoritarian dictator for a leader lacks two important guarantees. First, they are not guaranteed that this leader will remain godly in his ministry. Second, they are not guaranteed that the next pastor will be as benevolent as the first. When discussing the danger of unquestioned authority, many quote the English historian, Lord Acton, who said, "History has proven that. . .power tends to corrupt; absolute power corrupts absolutely." If God had intended for the senior pastor to make every major decision alone, then why wasn't Pastor James doing that for the Jerusalem Church in Acts 15?

The Board

In this model of church decision-making, one typically finds a small group of individuals (usually deacons or trustees chosen from the membership)

---

208. McLachlan, *Reclaiming Authentic Fundamentalism,* 51–52.

making most or all of the decisions for a church.[209] The problem is that the board may behave selfishly. In a dictatorship, the pastor or deacon chairman abuses his authority. A board-dominated oligarchy strips the pastor of his rightful authority and role. Typically the board also strips the congregation of its authority. An all-powerful board may not create a visible problem as long as its members are godly. This model, however, becomes disastrous when they are not. A board-controlled system may evolve when a congregation overreacts against a dictator.

Scripture contains no evidence for a board-like entity to run the congregation and/or rule the pastors/deacons. While there is evidence of an elder or bishop team serving along with a deacon team (Phil. 1), to think that the church of Jesus should be run like a Madison Avenue corporation is naïve. Ministries that place keen businessmen on the leadership team who do not have the character established in the New Testament for church leadership (1 Timothy 3) only complicate this misunderstanding. Churches, while by necessity careful of their financial practices, should not be run primarily as corporations, but as spiritual organisms.

The Democracy

While larger churches seldom operate as a pure democracy, small churches often do.[210] In one such congregation, the newly-elected pastor was surprised to find that the first twenty minutes of his first congregational business meeting was occupied by a spirited discussion on the appropriateness of a thirty dollar phone bill. The problem should be obvious. Some Christians mistakenly try to force the biblical structures of one God-ordained institution upon another, different one.[211] It would be a mistake to try to force the ideas of the division of human government, such as in a democratic republic, upon the New Testament church without clear textual evidence.

God has given the elders of the church the responsibility to function as bishops (1 Peter 5:1–2). Bishops have been given the responsibility to exercise executive leadership and direction (Acts 20:17, 28; 1 Timothy 5:17). The congregation has been given the responsibility to follow that executive leadership (Hebrews 13:7, 17). This of course does not mean that if the elders lead in the wrong direction the congregation must follow. At that

209. Strauch, *Biblical Eldership,* 42.

210. Ibid.

211. Rushdoony, "Biblical Law and Western Civilization," 5–13.

Section I: What Is Decision-Making?

point it would be their responsibility to correct the leadership or find new leadership that is indeed blameless (1 Timothy 3).

SECTION II

Who Are The Decision-Makers?

3

The Decision-Making Role of The Senior Pastor

KEY CHAPTER PRINCIPLE:

"Because the principle role of the Senior Pastor (or Pastor-Teacher) is to lead and shepherd other leaders as well as the body at large, his decision-making authority in the area of shepherding must be protected at all costs."

IMPORTANT DECISIONS A SENIOR PASTOR WILL MAKE:

"His approach to the preaching and teaching ministry; the theology and philosophy of ministry toward which he believes he should lead the congregation; how he will protect his personal Christian disciplines and his personal relationships; who should serve with him in the office of elder; who should potentially serve as deacons; who he will mentor and disciple; how to handle criticism; how to protect the congregation from 'tares' within and 'wolves' without."

There is no analogy to compare with what it's like to serve as the lead pastor in a congregation. No other calling propels a man to such heights and plummets him to such emotional depths on a daily basis as that of the senior or lead pastor. His task is daunting, made worse by the common unfair expectations of too many congregations. R.C Sproul notes,

Section II: Who Are The Decision-Makers?

> *"In churches today, particularly in America, enormous expectations are imposed upon the office of minister. Because of that, sixteen thousand pastors leave the ministry every year. . .Today a pastor is expected to be psychologist, theologian, biblical scholar, administrator, preacher, teacher, and community leader. The minister spends so much time on secondary matters that he has little time to do his principal work, which is to feed the sheep through preaching and teaching."*[1]

In spite of the challenges, pastoral ministry is exhilarating to we who have been called to this wing of the ministry. The victories a pastor experiences in his own life along with the victories experienced by the corporate body and in the lives of others are astounding. A lead shepherd sees God's supernatural fingerprint in the marriages, families and changed lives of his people. Coupled with that, though, is the sting and hurt of failure, betrayal, immaturity and sin in his own life and the lives of others, along with the regular spiritual warfare that the average congregation faces regularly.

To aid the faithful steward in meeting these challenges, a senior pastor has a variety of weapons at his disposal. The congregation must support the pastor, especially if he is pastor-teacher or senior pastor. The pastor that does the bulk of the leading or teaching is worthy of double honor, according to the New Testament. This is possibly because his sacrifice, pain and endurance may be twice that found in the lives of other servants of God.

The bar is high. Because a senior pastor must be faithful in teaching and leading, the level of commitment must also be high. This is similar to what Dr. Rolland McCune says about being the right kind of theologian:

> *". . .(he) need not be a genius, but he must bring to the study the following personal qualities: (1) He must have a love of learning and an insatiable thirst for the doctrine of Scripture; (2) He must be able to organize the material he studies and correlate it with what he already knows; (3) He must be disciplined to go no further than that which is written and be content simply to think God's thoughts after Him. This final quality requires not only mental discipline but intellectual humility as well."*[2]

Timothy and Titus lay out the characteristics of such a call. Coinciding with the responsibility is a set of tools that the senior pastor must have at his disposal. These tools include the prayers, love, respect and encouragement

---

1. Sproul, *1–2 Peter*, 184.
2. McCune, *A Systematic Theology of Biblical Christianity*, 1:31.

of those to whom he ministers. Additionally, a senior pastor needs the resources of study Bibles, commentaries, language helps, and of course the time to prepare accurate and rich sermons and lessons. Last, the senior pastor must have his hands free to make the decisions that are connected to his responsibility to shepherd.

Categories of decisions that the senior pastor should be free to make will be noted in this chapter. These categories flow directly or indirectly from the pages of the Scriptures to the hands of the lead under-shepherd. Occasionally some of these decisions may be delegated to other leaders. Some of the categories may actually overlap with the decision-making sphere of other decision-makers.

This tool of decision-making is connected to his responsibility of leading the leaders. Undoubtedly there will at times be tension, not unlike that of a tightrope walker. Lean too far one way and the pastor will fall from the rope of ministry into the hazards of a dictatorial CEO mentality. Lean too far the other way and he'll end up abdicating his decision-making leadership. It is all too easy, when the pastor or a loved one has been hurt by one extreme, to overcompensate by going to the other extreme. Gene Getz reflects:

> One of the great principles that grabbed my attention during this process was "plurality in leadership." I'd always enjoyed working with a "team," but as I ventured into church planting, I became even more committed to this concept. I saw no other "plan" in the New Testament story—and still don't. . .Let me be perfectly honest. I was initially so committed to the principle of plurality in leadership that I, at times, downplayed and, in some respects, denied how important it is to have a strong primary leader. When I was asked, "Who leads the church?" I would always say, "The elders." In essence, that was a very true statement. And when I was then asked, "Who leads the elders?" I'd answer, "We lead the church, together." Again, this was a true response, but I didn't answer the questions adequately. The facts are that "I led the elders" and together "we led the church." I was then, and always have been, the primary leader in the Fellowship churches where I've served as senior pastor. Unfortunately, in those early years, I communicated a "model of leadership" I was not in actuality practicing.[3]

Because the lead pastor must be a leader of leaders, he must treat with the utmost respect the work and sacrifice the other leaders of the church are

3. Getz, *Elders and Leader,* 18.

giving. He must not allow his co-ministers to be targeted unfairly. Leaders are foolish when they sacrifice co-leaders in an attempt to keep malcontented church members happy.

AUTHORITY OVER THE CONGREGATION

In his essay defending the congregational-led church, James Leo Garrett shows how a congregational government should co-exist with a pastor's legitimate use of authority and leadership.

> *"Mistaken indeed is the notion that the practice of Congregational polity jeopardizes or cripples the legitimate roles of the ordained ministers in the congregation. There is no either/or choice between such polity and such ordained ministry. The earliest Baptist and Congregational documents affirmed the essential roles of ordained ministers as well as congregational polity. The Great Awakening bequeathed to Baptists in the United States a strong conviction as to the indispensability of a divinely called and gifted pastoral ministry. Baptist congregations have every reason to expect of their pastors that they not only engage in preaching, pastor care and nurture, and church administration but also lead by both precept and by example."*[4]

Many scriptural passages teach congregations to submit to pastors; none teach pastors to submit to the will of the congregation. Although congregations do have some authority, the pastor-teacher (or senior pastor, as he is most often called in North America), preferably with other co-elders, has the God-given role to lead the congregation. The senior pastor's leadership must involve the help and wisdom of co-ministers (elders or deacons).

The pastor-teacher, or 'first-among-equals,' has a significant burden of leading. Furthermore, congregations are given the responsibility to follow his leading. The only time that a congregation is not under such obligation is if and when the pastor is leading the ministry toward a non-biblical stance. However, even in this situation, anarchy is not the answer. A mob mentality is hardly consistent with the spirit of Christ's church.

Such was the response in the peasants' revolt in the time of Martin Luther. Luther was rightly disheartened with the response.[5] In a time when God's people have a right to disagree, and even have strong emotions to-

---

4. Garrett, *Perspectives on Church Government*, 187–88.

5. Kittelson, *Luther the Reformer*, 191–92.

ward a leader they with whom they disagree, they must still remember the teaching of James 1:20, *"for the anger of man does not achieve the righteousness of God."*

Every pastor, at some point, will have to face believers who are sinful in their attitudes toward submission. Some will not submit in peace unless they agree in every detail. These families are usually doomed to wander from congregation to congregation looking for a leader who will allow their disgruntled demeanor or their attempts to run the church from the pew. Pastors must exercise due diligence when accepting members from other churches to avoid a "blow in, blow up and blow out" pattern that can challenge the church's entire ministry.

While Timothy and Titus, as elders or pastor-teachers, were not the same as elders today, the leadership of these apostolic representatives parallels that of elders and pastor-teachers of the modern time. Timothy and Titus did not have inherent apostolic authority. Elders today do not have inherent apostolic authority and yet Paul is clear in his instruction to both Timothy and Titus. These men trained a plurality of elders in each of their congregations. In Titus 2:15, Paul instructs Titus that with the leadership tasks he passes to the elders, he is to teach, encourage and rebuke with all authority. Paul continues, at the beginning of chapter 3, instructing Titus to remind the people to be subject to rulers and authorities. The congregation was not to slander. They were to live peaceably and demonstrate consideration and humility towards all. This would include their relationship with the newly established elders on the Isle of Crete.

AUTHORITY, AS "FIRST AMONG EQUALS"

Many conservative Brethren churches, while holding to a plurality of elders, shy away from a decision-maker who is 'first among equals.' While a senior pastor should make the majority of his decisions in consensus with other leaders, there is evidence of an internal hierarchy that results in what some have called a 'first among equals.'[6] 1 Timothy 5:17 indicates that some elders are worthy of double honor. This does not mean that there is a division within the office of elder/bishop/pastor. The presiding pastor does not have a higher rank. As noted in chapter two he is simply to lead his peers who are equal in rank, but not in the scope of pastoral responsibility.[7]

6. Doran, "The Foundation of the Pastorate," 1–2.

7. Ibid.

Section II: Who Are The Decision-Makers?

The first evidence of this hierarchy appears in 1 Timothy 3:1, where Paul lists the qualifications of the ἐπισκοπῆς (Titus also uses the singular in Titus 1:7). Compare this verse with verse eight, where Paul lists the qualifications of the deacons in the plural (διακόνους).

In contrast to the plural number of deacons is the role demonstrated by James in the Jerusalem Church (second evidence). While James did not lead without the wisdom and leadership of the rest of the elders, he did function as a 'first among equals.' This relationship between James and the other Jerusalem elders is apparent in Acts 15, the occasion of the Jerusalem Council. A similar phenomenon is also seen in Acts 21 in the position of Peter within Paul's report to the Church.

A third evidence of a hierarchy of elders, with one serving as a presiding elder, is the mentioning of the 'angel' (ἀγγέλω) within the context of each of the seven churches of Asia Minor addressed by John.[8]

A fourth evidence appears in the theological discussion of the work and character of God, where one notices that in the other God-ordained institutions an order of authority appears (as found within civil government, Israel, and the family).

A fifth, and perhaps strongest, argument for this internal leader among equals is found in 1 Timothy 5:17. Paul, in this passage, speaks of an elder who receives 'double honor' for his excellent leadership in ruling the congregation. The elder is worthy of this type of honor because of his careful attention to Word and doctrine. This speaks of a special recognition by the congregation at large, especially honoring the presiding pastor-teacher.

A final evidence, while not as authoritative as those coming directly from Scripture, is the witness of the practice of the church for the last two thousand years. Concerning this, Paige Patterson notes:

> ". . .when on February 23, AD 155, Polycarp, the near centenarian pastor of the church in Smyrna, walked to the stake and was burned, the church there had not just suffered the loss of one of its elders; it had lost its pastor. When Chrysostom addressed his parishioners in Saint Sophia's for a final sermon in Constantinople in AD 404, then slipped across the Bosporus under cover of night into exile, the Constantinopolitan church had lost its pastor. The people of London's Metropolitan Tabernacle knew that with the passing of the incomparable Charles Haddon Spurgeon in 1892, they had lost their pastor. On January 10, 2002, when W. A. Criswell loosed from earthly moorings and entered heaven's rest, the saints at First Baptist

8. Ibid.

*Church of Dallas, Texas, lost their pastor even though he had for-
mally retired some years earlier. . .Whether Knox in Edinburgh, Hus
at. . .Prague, Edwards at Northampton, Zwingli in Zurich. . .Boice
in Philadelphia. . .these stellar figures of church history have been by
virtue of calling, gifts, dedication, and what my father termed "moral
ascendance" the acknowledged under-shepherds of their flocks. . ."[9]*

One more point on the function of 'first among equals'—in Luke
22:32, Jesus gives a specific task to the first among equals of his early
apostles. Jesus tells Peter, ". . .strengthen your brothers." The first-among-
equals task at times can be very difficult. It's hard enough to lead a group
of God's children. But leading a group of leaders, even of equal rank, will
place an extra burden on the senior pastor's shoulders. He has an obligation to protect his co-elders. They may be tired and wounded in battle. The
wounds may be the result of these men being loyal to their leader and/
or the body they serve. Especially in those moments, the senior pastor or
pastor/teacher needs to encourage those men who serve with distinction at
his side. No one else will likely know about the struggles they are having.
Even though, dispensationally, Christ's instruction to Peter is not given to
a pastor-teacher today, it serves as a legitimate model for a lead elder, to
demonstrate how to respond with compassion and service to those groups
of men who serve with sacrifice and faithfulness.[10]

Many churches teach that each congregation has only one bishop, but
that there can be other 'elders' in each congregation. That violates the principles of passages like Philippians 1:1 and elsewhere, that indicate that each
congregation, when most healthy, will have a team of bishops who are also
pastors and elders. If the lead pastor has no accountability with the other
elders, then it would be considered a 'third office.' That is not the case, however. Because the lead pastor is accountable to the rest of the elders, then he
is not a distinct entity unto himself. Those that function as a distinct entity,
with assistant pastors, in reality have a *de facto* 'three-office system.'

AUTHORITY OVER HIS TIME

Jesus gives Peter special instruction concerning the shepherding of God's
people in John 21:15–19. Several inferences may be made from this passage. If a pastor is going to shepherd the sheep of Jesus Christ, the shepherd

9. Paige Patterson commenting in Steven Cowen, *Who Runs the Church*, 133.

10. Strauch, *Biblical Eldership*, 46.

will have to be able to make decisions about how he organizes his time on a corporate or individual level. Imposing an 'office-time expectation' such as that found in the secular corporate world steals time from the man of God, time that he could spend with his children and wife, time that he could spend in prayer and devotion, time that he could spend in rest and refreshing his physical and mental needs.

Sadly, though, there are pastors who take advantage of their position and become lazy in shepherding. Fortunately, most pastors seem to be self-drivers and many may actually need to be limited in the number of hours they spend ministering each week. Pastoral leadership is not a 9-to-5 job, nor can a set schedule be imposed on pastors. Congregations are most healthy when they give the pastor(s) the flexibility of schedule that protects the special needs of his calling, his wife and his family. While a lazy or twisted leader is certainly accountable to the body, the lead pastor is to be primarily accountable to God and then secondly to his fellows elder for how he organizes and spends his time in the execution of ministry.

AUTHORITY OVER THE PULPIT

The sense of 1 Timothy 5:17 is that all elders rule. All elders must be able to teach (1 Timothy 3). Those whose job it is to excel in expounding the Scriptures and leading the congregation are worthy of 'double-honor.' It is therefore consistent to see the senior pastor as having control over the pulpit ministry. Added to that is the instruction given to all the elders in the church at Ephesus to preach the whole counsel of God's Word (Acts 20:27). It is legitimate for fellow-elders, deacons or church members to ask the pastor to preach or teach on a certain topic. However, Jesus did not ask Peter to find out what the sheep want and feed them that; He said, "Peter, if you love me, feed my sheep." The senior pastor must have a sense of the congregation's needs and fulfill his responsibility as 'chief feeder.'

Without a doubt, one of the chief decision-making responsibilities that a senior pastor has is the task of preaching God's Word. Paul tells Timothy in 2 Timothy 2:4, "Preach the Word." As Warren Wiersbe notes, "The pastor who is lazy in his study is a disgrace in the pulpit."[11]

The New Testament pastor is called a bishop, an elder and a shepherd (1 Peter 5:1–2). While all three of these functions are paramount to the call of minister, the most important must be the role of shepherding. A

11. Wiersbe, *Be Faithful,* 43.

pastor can get help in the oversight or 'bishoping' of the church by the use of deacons, given by God to the church to free the pastor for 'ministry of prayer and the Word' (Acts 6). The senior pastor is given help in the New Testament by other elders to lead his congregation. But he cannot delegate all of the shepherding. He may not be able to do all of it himself, but he must actively be shepherding God's flock. He must be feeding and nurturing God's people. Without a doubt, this involves one-on-one ministry. However, the most important part of the pastor's shepherding of a congregation is what happens during his personal walk with God and then in his corporate preaching and teaching of God's Word.

AUTHORITY OVER THE STAFF

As noted in chapter two of this book, the pastor is told he must rule or lead the ministry force that God gathers under his leadership. Some churches try to steal this kind of authority and give it to the deacons or some committee in the church. There is no exegetical evidence of a committee or sub-committee of church members giving instructions to James or Paul or other leaders of the early church, as to how the ministry staff would operate, or with whom. Yet, there are congregations all over the world who have the idea that the pastor is to have only the authority to preach, but that the actual leading of the congregation is to be given to another. There is no biblical support for this viewpoint. A congregation may grow to such an extent that a senior pastor will delegate a portion of the staff leadership to a co-pastor of sorts. He may be called an executive pastor or staff pastor. But the average, conservative, Bible-believing church has a membership of less than one hundred. In many of these congregations, there is one senior pastor, aided by elders or deacons.

A pastor does have authority over the staff, but that authority is limited to matters dealing with congregational life. Even in matters of church life, there are limits to his authority. For example, a lead pastor's authority is limited when he wants a specific change in a ministry that would require the volunteer leadership to spend more time than they have available. The lead pastor would be violating his office to instruct the volunteer to spend less time with his family, work or personal schedule to give those hours to the church. The right approach would be to review the desired changes with the volunteer leadership and to consider how the transitions could be accomplished without adding undue burden to those involved.

Section II: Who Are The Decision-Makers?

In matters of personal conviction and liberty, all church leaders should be very careful. If a church member is careless in the way he lives out his liberty, then the issue must be discussed. But that does not give leaders the right to decree, by way of edict, their own personal conscience for the rest of the ministry to follow. Some pastors try to micro-manage the convictions of parents. Some give unsolicited business advice. Sometimes a church leader will take on the role of a surrogate parent. It is scriptural to pastor lovingly with the same tender love of a parent, but it is never right to patronize the congregation as if he is the all-knowing pastor and they are the seldom-knowing parishioners.

There is an important biblical foundation for the precedent of the first-among-equals having a significant role in appointing those on the ministry staff. A number of passages in the New Testament show Paul and Barnabas, or apostolic representatives like Titus and Timothy, being instructed to appoint elders in various cities. The rest of the New Testament text seems to illustrate that these appointments were not made in a vacuum. Based on other passages that have been reviewed, the assembly would be in basic agreement because of their witnessing and affirming the choice made by these apostolic leaders. However, at times Paul simply chose who would be on his staff. An example is when he appointed Timothy in Acts 16:1–3. Paul was staffing his second missionary team and chose to add Timothy along with Silas. On the same trip, Paul added Luke to the team after their ministry in Troas (Acts 16:10).[12]

Titus is told by Paul, in Titus 1:5, to appoint elders in each church that he comes to in the same way he was appointed by Paul. It seems that Titus, while in the fledgling church, would have been a 'first among equals.' The second passage, Acts 15:23, shows Paul and Barnabas as they appointed elders in Lystra, Iconium and Antioch. Many commentators try to prove that the appointments were the action of the congregation. Grammatically, it is Paul and Barnabas that appointed. The passages do not prohibit congregations from aiding in the appointment of rightful individuals, but the pastor or pastor-teacher who serves a team of peers has a biblical precedent to have a significant say and a leadership position with the staff that serve around him.

Sometimes good men will differ on who would or would not make effective ministry companions. An example of this kind of disagreement was the contention that arose between Paul and Barnabas over the ministry

12. MacMillan, *Hiring Excellence: Six Steps to Making Good People Decision,* 6.

of John Mark on the eve of Paul's second missionary journey (Acts 15:39). This parting was used of God. The weight of evidence favors Barnabas' view, and it was not the last time that Paul was short-sighted on a decision. He was warned in Acts 21 not to go to Jerusalem. In 2 Timothy 4:11, Paul, while awaiting execution, admitted that John Mark was helpful to him at this stage of his ministry. While Paul never mentions the role of Barnabas in John Mark's development, the reader can see that Barnabas, accustomed to being an encourager and mentor of leaders, did what he always did. He invested himself in John Mark when Paul had rejected him; he also defended Paul when very few trusted him in Acts 9:26–27.

AUTHORITY OVER THE CALENDAR

In a perfect world, the decision-making role of the senior pastor would never interfere with or overlap that of other elders or deacons or even the congregation. This is not always the case, though. The category of oversight of the church calendar is a good example. While the pastor should have authority over the calendar, he must be open to how the function of other leaders impacts the calendar. Perhaps the youth leaders will want to schedule something with the young people while they are out of school. The calendar will be impacted. Maybe the stay-at-home moms want to take advantage of ministry times while their children are in school. Seasonal events, such as hunting or fishing ministries, will impact the calendar. A senior pastor must learn to juggle missionaries, evangelists, special-emphasis Sundays and other events, and so must have jurisdiction over the calendar. He may choose to delegate much of that oversight to his elders or deacons, but his influence should never be minimized. Leaders must be aware of how last minute changes to the church schedule may discourage volunteer lay-leaders, especially if it is an on-going issue. This can undermine a sense of teamwork.

AUTHORITY OVER DISCIPLINE

Nothing in the life of a church can match the struggle and potential hurt that can happen through the exercise of church discipline. The implication inherent in the instruction of Jesus to Peter in John 21:15–19 regarding shepherding His sheep is that the pastor, if he is going to tend the sheep of Jesus, must mete out discipline to those who stray from the principles of Scripture. This category may at times involve every decision-making group in the local church. The senior pastor will have the responsibility to start the disciplinary process, but may need to bring in elders, deacons and even the congregation in a Matthew 18 type of situation. Each congregant may be faced with the burden of casting a vote concerning the expulsion of disobedient members. One of the passages that speaks to the issue of the pastor having to correct and even on occasion dismiss those that are actively causing division is Titus 3:10. Because he, as pastor, is the shepherd of the one in question, he must be involved in the discipline process.

AUTHORITY OVER INTER-CHURCH RELATIONSHIPS

As we noted earlier, passages such as Acts 20:28 clearly gives the under-shepherd the responsibility to protect the congregation from rogue sheep, false teachers and wolves. Leaders or church members sometimes don't have the information or discernment to ferret out the dangers of 'church-to-church' alliances. Scripture shows that there may be some overlap regarding decisions between sister ministries. Furthermore, the congregation has a right to influence those decisions. However, because God has chiefly endowed the first-among-equals with the responsibility to protect the doctrinal doors of the congregation, the senior pastor must not be left out of ministry-partner decision-making. He is responsible to lead in and be in consensus with any and all inter-church alliances.

Independent churches, especially Baptist churches, have a rich heritage of inter-church relationships and partnerships. Historically, this is how Baptists without a strict denominational identity have been able to leverage the resources of multiple congregations into a single point and project. J. Andrew Kirk describes these kinds of relationships as, ". . .a relationship between churches based on trust, mutual recognition and reciprocal interchange. It rules out completely any notion of 'senior' and 'junior,' 'parent' and 'child' or even 'older' and 'younger'. . ."[13] When one church wants to dominate another, it precludes the ability to have a healthy partnership. Pastors must guard their congregations in how and with whom they relate.

---

13. Johnson, *American Baptist Quarterly*, 3–4.

AUTHORITY OVER SOME MONEY

This is the topic that causes the most excitement. Deacons have a real interest and responsibility in this area of being stewards of resources. The congregation also shares in the decision-making area of finance. There are two areas where a pastor (or senior pastor) should have some control of money. In Acts 6, even after the creation of the office of deacon, elders were given authority over some of the funds of the ministry. Acts 11:29–30 amplifies this. Leaders in Antioch sent resources to the neediest Jewish believers in Judea. The elders sent the money by the hands of Barnabas and Saul (Paul). Undoubtedly, the responsibility should lie mainly with the deacons, but the oversight of pastoral ministry frequently involves directly or indirectly some financial concerns. Biblical principles show that it is equally wrong for a pastor to become the chief financial officer of the congregation as it is for him to run the accounts of the church as if they were his own checking account.

A pastor should have some contact with church monies when he is accomplishing his task outside the needs of his own family. Most churches recognize that, in addition to studying for sermons, evangelizing the lost, disciplining the saved and leading the staff, a pastor occasionally has monetary expenses that impact his calling. For instance, most pastors don't just use their car, they abuse their car. Left to pay for his own gas, a pastor could feasibly burn through a hefty percentage of his food money if not careful. No congregation wants his pastor to have to choose between feeding his family and visiting the sick. Most responsible congregations help their paid pastoral staff with an auto expense account and travel help.

Most congregations allow the pastor time for paid vacations and paid ministry conferences. Pastors who have served for a significant period of time may be allotted ministry-lengthening blessings like a paid sabbatical. It always pays the congregation back in dividends. When a pastor is loved by his congregation to the degree that the congregation gives him an extended season of six or seven weeks off, he will come back to his pulpit with fire, strength and the excitement of a new seminarian.

While most pastors don't receive a sabbatical every year, congregations should do what they can to make sure the pastor is afforded time off for vacation. That presupposes that the pastor is being paid enough to cover not only his regular bills, but any bills that accrue by taking his wife and family away for a time of rest. Even a congregation that is hurting financially can become creative. An occasional love offering is a blessing to the pastor who has to supplement his income with a second job. A surprise paid weekend away is a blessing to a pastoral couple whose wife has no choice but to work to pay bills so that the family can continue to minister in the church where they serve.

Too many congregations are inexcusably ignorant concerning the hidden costs that a pastor encounters in the flow of the ministry. The pastor might be required to take an individual or family out to lunch during the ministry. At times the pastor must entertain a visiting speaker. A wise pastor will be careful not to abuse the privilege of meals paid for by the church. On the other hand, a wise church will do all that they can to financially assist the pastor to reach out to individuals and families in need. This is the personal touch that separates caring pastors from distant ones in the minds of Christian families debating on where they should worship.

AUTHORITY OVER THE DOCTRINAL POSITION OF THE CHURCH

Pastor James held a prominent if not leading role at the Jerusalem Council in Acts 15. James undeniably had a special responsibility for the doctrinal matters that were discussed. However, Acts 15 demonstrates that the other leaders and the brethren themselves also held a stake in the discussion of correct doctrine. This is another potential area of clash among modern congregations, the topic of stewardship in areas other than money. The rest of the elders have a responsibility to keep the pastor in check. The congregation is tasked with making sure that the pastor is teaching truth. The first level of truth is the orthodoxy— the fundamentals or essentials of the faith. These are doctrines that cannot be denied without losing the integrity of the Gospel message. These deal with the nature of Christ; a clear definition of saving faith (including faith and repentance and a view of faith that understands a forensic substitutionary atonement); the authority, accuracy and veracity of Scripture; and the Lord's second coming.

The second level of doctrine is that of belief and practice. This level is where denominational distinctives as Baptists reside. Beyond the fundamental doctrine and denominational beliefs are other doctrinal convictions that, while important, are clearly beyond the baseline of orthodoxy. Denying these doctrines can have implications on the gospel, but do not necessarily distort it. One example is the view of the biblical creationism account of Genesis. The Gap theory and the Day-Age theory are not in fact violating the gospel, but may have implications on how the Scriptures are handled by those who hold to those theories. This difference of opinion doesn't make it to the level of 'fundamental' (and the early fundamentalist movement also did not view this as a fundamental of the faith, as evidence by many of the early fundamentalists who believed in an old earth).

The last level would be other doctrinal beliefs or practices that have incredible diversity among good men, and where such diversity (worship styles, school choice, courting vs. dating, eschatological minutia) does not impact the message of the Gospel. For any congregation to be coherent, they must have a total agreement in the first category, and a majority agreement in the second category. They may, however, have even greater diversity in the third category, as in the issue of Calvinism. Some conservative churches tend to give all beliefs the same level of importance. This is confusing, and further, it's not what is taught in Scripture. If every belief is a fundamental of the faith, then there are really no fundamentals of the faith.[14] The leadership teams of Southeast Valley Baptist over the years have had leaders who hold to a limited atonement while others have not. The topic is a theme of occasional discussion but not division. Why? Because the senior pastor, elders, and congregation believe good and godly men can differ on this theological topic. It is also our conviction that Heaven is dishonored when five-point Calvinists can't work with four-point Calvinists within the same congregation.

In many congregations, the fellowship becomes hostage to one or two vocal, if not influential, 'doctrinal legalists.' A doctrinal legalist is a church member or leader who wants to extend a second- or third-level doctrinal conviction to a (stated or unstated) functional absolute that really must be believed or followed by the entire congregation. These people may be aggressive in trying to convince different church members or leaders that some outside teacher (typically from a para-church ministry with no local church accountability) really has a better understanding of truth than their own pastor and/or leaders and that they must get the leaders to believe this approach or toss them out of their ministries and get someone who believes as they do. Many leaders have lost congregations to mafia-like doctrinal legalists. A leader needs to be aware of any legalistic lifestyle or doctrine. The doctrinal legalists are a slick version of neo-Pharisees, and they need to be checked at the door. A simple phone call to the church that they came from will reveal their true, stealth identity.

14. Bauder, "Thinking About the Gospel," 7:1.

Some doctrine is simply not as clear as an undisputed and universal tenet of orthodoxy. The senior pastor or teaching pastor has the responsibility of leading the discussion and documentation about doctrinal views. Paul encouraged Titus in Titus 1:9, saying that an elder must be able to 'hold fast the faithful Word. . .that he may be able by sound doctrine both to exhort and to convict those who contradict.' In every church, the head pastor must be active in protecting the doctrines that they believe are paramount to the gospel and God's Word. The Scriptures demonstrate that the early elders had access to some of the money to direct at their discretion

AUTHORITY OVER HIS STYLE

God's Word, especially the sections outlining the qualifications of a bishop, addresses a pastor's style. While it is healthy to have a sense of humor, a pastor must have an overall quality of seriousness. He should not have an argumentative style of ministry. The King James Version states that the pastor should be 'grave.' Beyond the teachings of the Scripture, much of a pastor's style in ministry hinges on his God-given personality. The Scriptures can be taught in many different but legitimate ways. We are to be careful to treat God's Word with respect and not take liberties with its meaning, but it is possible to preach and teach in many different ways.

Christ and the Apostles each had their own style of teaching. Jesus used parables to emphasize his thoughts. Luke was educated and experienced as both an historian and a physician and used more technical language to articulate an historical narrative with a matter-of-fact approach. John was a simple fisherman using simple language, and was not as detailed-oriented, but had a broader audience in mind.

In modern times, different teaching/preaching styles may include: 1) exegetical method, in which a pastor teaches his way through a book of the Bible, 2) textual approach, when the major points from a single passage are supported by material from a several different texts, 3) thematic or systematic approach, where a theme (such as God's character) is amplified by studying different passages of Scripture in order to understand who God is.

As with any teaching style, the pastor must be careful not to simply engage in proof-texting. Most theological institutions stress the importance of exegetical care with God's Word. Naïve and untested seminarians may graduate from seminary thinking that any pastor who diagrams a passage or organizes a sermon differently than he was taught is a heretic worthy of 'the death of Servetus.' There are many acceptable teaching and preaching styles that a pastor may employ. In all of them, he should be careful in his methods lest he wreak havoc in his assembly.

A pastor's personality, or temperament, is a facet of his style. A congregation can get used to a particular personality type, and a subsequent pastor can potentially be held in contempt by the congregation because his personality isn't as friendly or as gifted with a quick wit as the preceding pastor. The pastor should be especially sensitive when he makes decisions that impact other leaders under his care. Paul says that in the context of ministry, he was careful not to be heavy-handed. He says, in 1 Thessalonians 2:6–8,

> *". . . nor did we seek glory from men, either from you or from others, even though as apostles of Christ we might have asserted our authority. But we proved to be gentle among you, as a nursing mother tenderly cares for her own children. Having so fond an affection for you, we were well-pleased to impart to you not only the gospel of God but also our own lives, because you had become very dear to us."*

A shepherd must demonstrate love as a mother does for her child. He cannot ignore those who will be most affected by tough decisions.

AUTHORITY OVER HIS PRIORITIES

Closely related to the pastoral authority over style is his authority over his priorities. The list of things that a lead pastor must accomplish is daunting. He must "do" hospitality, pray, study, teach, preach, evangelize, disciple, participate in meetings, correct, plan, lead, coordinate, communicate, counsel, marry, bury, peace-make, worship, encourage, mentor, listen, etc. There is no way a pastor can be expected to be great, or even good, in every area for which he is responsible. Although incredibly unfair, sometimes church members will use the pastor's weaknesses against him. This is especially true if they struggle with jealousy or rebellion.

Sometimes a believer will just know that he can do a job better than the pastor. Others are naïve enough to think that a pastor should be great in every area of ministry. A senior pastor has to be a generalist of sorts. Many leaders who must spend twenty to thirty hours a week in study fail in ministry, because there just is not enough time left over for all of the other details of ministry that must be covered. Others focus all of their attention on people-work. Because they do not protect serious study time, they fail in the pulpit. Something has to give. Too often, that something is family, or rest, or personal time.

In the real world of pastoral ministry, there simply isn't enough time in the day to do everything perfectly. This is one of the reasons why a healthy congregation will utilize the gifts that have been given to each leader and congregant. While one leader may be great at communicating, another may have a different strength. Ask critics if they would be willing to help in the area of which they are critical—a good way to see if their criticism is biblically motivated.

A pastor must manage his time well, based on his knowledge of his own strengths and weaknesses. He must also manage based on his knowledge of leaders around him. Every pastor, though, will have one or two congregants who think that they have a better idea of what the pastor's ministry priorities should be, even if the pastor has support from other elders, deacons and the rest of the congregation. People may complain about the pastor's spending habits, or personal time, or hobbies. At some point in time, God's people will need to be challenged to grow up.

John Maxwell, in his book "21 Laws of Leadership," speaks of the 80/20 rule. The rule states that a competent leader should expect 80 percent of his effectiveness when he is rightly committed to the top 20 percent of his priorities. Maxwell notes,

> *"If you have ten employees, you should give 80 percent of your time and attention to your best two people. If you have one hundred customers, the top twenty will provide you with eighty percent of your business. If your to-do list has ten items on it, the two most important ones will give you an 80 percent return on your time."*[15]

While there are at least a dozen areas for which a pastor is responsible, three of his primary tasks are the work of a bishop (overseer), an elder (leader), and a shepherd (nurturer). A pastor must never pass up these three tasks for competing interruptions.

A pastor must make shepherding his top priority. Peter was asked of Christ, "Do you love me?" God's response to Peter was, "Feed my sheep." God gives a pastor the aid of deacons and co-elders to help with the minutia of administration and leadership. The pastor must never give up his work as shepherd. While it is true that pastors are to 'rule' their congregations in some sense, that does not undermine his main task as pastor or shepherd.

---

15. Maxwell, *The 21 Irrefutable Laws of Leadership*, 177.

The primary concept that a congregation should have of their pastor is not one of a bossy manager, but one of a nurturing teacher.

AUTHORITY BUT LIMITED

Pastor, you are not the mediator of a theocracy! You have but limited authority, inter-related to the authority of others in the congregation, as we have noted. What makes any discussion about authority difficult is the tension in the Scriptures. We are to follow the authority of each other. We are to submit to one another in the fear of God. Some have called this mutual submission. The function of making decisions relies on a legitimate authority. Passages such as 1 Timothy 5:17 show that the pastor literally "stands first" (προιστη). A similar term is found in Hebrews 13:7, 17, 24. The term ἡγέομαι suggests the same type of leadership. This term is used by Paul to the Thessalonians in the sense of 'think,' 'consider,' or 'have regard for.'[16] So a pastor has authority and should be respected and followed by a congregation because of his calling. However, when making decisions, a senior pastor or any leader in the church does not have the same level of authority as God himself. God's authority is unquestioned. God's character is perfect. Man's authority may be called into question. Why? Because man's character and knowledge are not the same as God's.

Additionally, leaders today don't have the same level of leadership that earlier offices in redemptive history have had. No one today has the same level of authority that an Old Testament prophet or priest had. No one today has the same level as an apostle. Even the apostles didn't always use the authority of the office. Paul requested certain actions of Philemon, not based on authority but based on love (Philemon 8–9). As noted by Jeffrey Brown, "He does not command (ἐπιτάσσειν), he appeals (παρακαλῶ)."[17]

The senior pastor has a legitimate decision-making authority, but this is not absolute. He will hurt his credibility if he treats his authority as absolute and unquestioned, on the same level as God speaking to Moses. A pastor's authority is not the same as God's. Gordon Fee says:

> *"Although most Protestants in theory deny apostolic succession to reside in its clergy, de facto it is practiced in vigorous and sometimes devastating ways—in the "one-man show" of many denominational*

16. Lenski, *The Interpretation of St. Paul to the Colossians, to the Thessalonians, to Timothy and to Philemon*, 351.

17. Brown, *Corporate Decision-Making in the Church of the NT*, 87.

churches or in the little dictatorships in other (especially "indepen-dent") churches. And how did such a pluralism of papacies emerge? Basically from two sources (not to mention the fallenness of the clergy whose egos often love such power): (a) from the fact that the local pastor is so often seen (and often sees him/herself) as the au-thoritative interpreter of the "sole authority"—Scripture; (b) from the pastor's functioning in the role of authority, thus assuming the mantle of Paul or of a Timothy or Titus."[18]

When leaders act like their authority is "God-like," it breeds distrust in young people and families. That is one of the reasons that too many churches that have a certain kind of Christian school lose the majority of their young people after high school graduation. Too many of those Christian schools treat their handbook as the sixty-seventh book of the Bible. The students see through this type of hypocrisy and run away, looking for reality somewhere else. Leaders and ministers have to be responsible for how they frame their authority. Les Ollila stressed the differences between institutional guidelines and personal holiness.[19] Northland International University in Dunbar, WI continues to be served by Matt Olson, who holds to the same convictions. Both of these men understood what far too few leaders and ministries have understood: there is a qualitative difference in the kind of authority that exists in heaven from that which exists in the form of man-made institutional guidelines. Both are important, but they are not equally important.

Some pastors have told their congregations that they should do ex-actly what he says in their private lives because the Holy Spirit has revealed to him the exact non-revelatory aspect of God's personal will for their lives. This is not inconsistent with a charismatic ministry, but if the pastor is lead-ing a congregation that believes in the sufficiency of Scripture, the priest-hood of the believer and individual soul liberty, this is a problem. Does the pastor really know the best car for you to drive, or the best school for you to send your children to, or the best person for you to marry?

Nearly as dangerous are the pastors who expect congregants and staff members to follow their leadership and authority as if they were the parent and everyone else the children. Both of these views of pastoral authority are dangerous and in some cases cultic, and any leader that pretends to have such rights, ability or knowledge should be avoided. This kind of leader

18. Fee, *The First Epistle to the Corinthians*, 149.
19. Ollila, *Brothers. . ..but Different*, 3.

is an ecclesiastical fraud and doesn't belong in the pastorate of a Bible-preaching church.

Even when legitimately using strong authority, a pastor must be very careful not to be abusive. Some pastors shout out orders like the church was a branch of the military. While he may have the authority to lead, and there is an aspect of leadership that results in people following his wishes, he should never have the aura of a boss, but rather of a servant-leader. There are Scriptural limits.

There is no possible way for a pastor to know the exact details of God's will for congregants under his care. He probably won't know the details of God's will for his own life, outside of a broad picture. There is a two-pronged approach to pastoral authority called *the Pyramid and the Box.*

The pyramid approach places one man at the top of the pyramid. He directs many resources to a project in order to achieve the goals he has in his mind quickly. In some cases, this one man is the senior pastor; in other cases, he is the chairman of the deacon board. In a few confused situations, these two may fight for top position within the pyramid, straining the entire structure. In any case, the strict pyramid approach identifies one man as the only person who can make the final decision on just about everything. This leader may become such a CEO that he loses touch with the shepherding side of ministry altogether. These ministries and organizations display very centralized leadership.

The pyramid approach may lead to ecclesiastical demagoguery on the part of the leader. Everyone assumes that all decisions must have one individual's approval before they can be implemented. Too often, the assumption is that the chairman or the pastor always knows best, even when the item falls outside of the leader's area of expertise. These leaders can display a harsh and unloving demeanor.[20] While a godly leader might be forceful or show strong emotion, he is to have that energy checked by a personal code of conduct and character that is consistent with 1 Timothy 3 and Titus 1."[21]

This is one of those areas where decision-making is directly tied to polity. Church leaders often make self-claims about polity that in reality is far from accurate. L. Roy Taylor says that many *"large congregations that originate with congregational church government often develop a de facto Episcopal government whereby the senior pastor is the primary decision-maker on*

---

20. Finzel, *Top Ten Mistakes Leaders Make*, 22–35.

21. Greenleaf, *Servant Leadership*, 63.

major issues. While some may regard this as novel, it is actually a replication of the older mono-episcopacy of the second century."[22]

Another common characteristic of the pyramid approach is the development of little pyramids within the big pyramid. It tends to shift the priority away from people toward the expansion of tangible resources. When a ministry leadership team views people as just another resource for the existence, success, and future of the ministry, this signifies the attitude labeled "the box." The box is an approach to ministry that places the tangible existence of buildings, vehicles, bank accounts and other assets above the value of the individuals that these resources theoretically exist to serve.

This box attitude accounts for the ease with which some ministries direct resources towards buildings while withholding adequate compensation from those who depend upon the ministry for their livelihood. When the building or the budget of a ministry becomes more important than adequate support for its servants, then its priority is out of order. One of the more obvious examples of this approach occurs when ministries pay a large salary to one leader, invest heavily in the buildings, but then support the rest of the staff at or below the federal poverty line. Those who labor in these ministries often harm their families by doing without adequate health insurance, clothing, transportation, and other necessities.

The point is not that Christian servants should never make sacrifices. Blame must be laid upon leaders, however, who place an unreasonable burden on ministry staff to live in or near poverty. The problem here is the ease with which certain ministries are willing to ignore the clear responsibility to take care of those who serve full-time. How can such ministries claim the label 'fundamentalist' or 'evangelical' when the teaching of Scripture is that one does not muzzle an ox while it treads out the grain (Deuteronomy 25:4, quoted by Paul in 1 Corinthians 9:9), and that the laborer is worthy of his wages (Luke 10:7, quoted by Paul in 1 Timothy 5:18)?[23] A new generation of leaders is attempting to change this problem and is aggressively putting into place strategies to replace the box. Once a strategy is in place to rectify the financial injustice, local ministries can eventually reverse much of the damage incurred by the box mentality.

There is one final word of warning for those who aspire to the office of lead pastor. One of the realities is that there is a special burden for the first among equals. Even though many of your decisions will be in consensus

22. L. Roy Taylor, commenting in Cowan, *Who Runs the Church?*, 74.
23. MacArthur, *1 Corinthians*, 203.

with other leaders, there will be times that, because of your specific influence, convictions and leadership, there will be families who decide to worship elsewhere. Former British Prime Minister Tony Blair has rightly noted, "*to decide is to divide.*"[24] If a leader has any kind of convictions at all, especially with the result of calling church members to a higher level of personal commitment to the Lordship of Jesus, there will simply be a negative response by some. Jack Hayford mentions the importance of accepting the inevitable losses:

> *Any church leader's decisions will result in some people leaving to seek a less demanding environment of commitment. We feel those losses deeply. To be effective leaders, we must overcome impersonal or insensitive ways and find a place of confidence in the Lord, so that if people are committed to leaving, we can "send them with blessing" rather than being pained or declaring them unreliable or disloyal.*[25]

24. Blair, *A Journey*, 49–50.
25. Hayford, *Leadership Handbook of Management and Administration*, 181.

4

The Decision-Making Role of The Elders

KEY CHAPTER PRINCIPLE:

"Because the elders oversee the spiritual sphere of ministry, and because they will give account for the spiritual health of the body, their decision-making authority in leading the spiritual sphere of the congregation must be protected at all cost."

IMPORTANT DECISIONS AN ELDER TEAM WILL MAKE:

"How to utilize the gifted members of the congregation; the approach to corporate worship the congregation will take; how to integrate the deacons and congregation in key decision-making; ministry goals and priorities; expectations for leaders and congregants; a philosophy of Christian education, missions and outreach; ecclesiastical partnerships."

The last chapter examined the decision-making role of the senior pastor. This chapter will explore decision-making by a group of elders. The lead pastor should be making more decisions in the context of consensus with the elders or deacons than simply making decisions of his own. The late Dr. Richard Weeks, who taught at Maranatha Baptist Bible College in Watertown, WI, said in his Church Management class, "God doesn't just speak to *you*—he also speaks to your deacons!" God not only gives wisdom, leadership and discernment to the lead pastor, but he also gives the same things to the other leaders that serve with that pastor.

Many of the decision-making categories that are placed under the leadership of the senior pastor can also be placed next to the elders as a group. There is tremendous overlap in these decision-making categories. That makes any kind of taxonomy of ecclesiastical decision-making a challenging issue. It is also one of the reasons why there is so much disagreement on this topic.

There is an admonition in Scripture about the advantage of a slate of multiple wise counselors. The other undeniable biblical truth is that the phrase 'Senior Pastor' is never used in the Scriptures. This work has already explored the evidence that there was a first among equals. What is as evident as any fact in the Scriptures is that the pattern for the New Testament church was for single congregations to be led by a plurality of bishops, elders and pastors. To say otherwise is uninformed. The best view of offices for the local church is that today there are two: elders and deacons.

Almost no one has a problem with the view that there was a plurality of deacons in the early church. Yet there is far more evidence of a plurality of elders in each congregation than there is of the *diakonate*. Alexander Strauch notes this oddity:

> "It is strange that people have little difficulty accepting a plurality of deacons, but are almost irrationally frightened by a plurality of overseers that is far more clearly demonstrated in the New Testament. The New Testament informs us that the pastoral oversight of many of the first churches was committed to a council of elders (overseers). This was true of the earliest Jewish congregation in Jerusalem (Acts 11:30; 15:6; 21:18), Judea, and neighboring countries (James 5:14), as well as in many of the first Gentile churches."[1]

To suggest that to hold to a plurality of elders is biblically illiterate because of the evidence of the New Testament is bizarre and baseless. The view that a single leader (without ministry peers for co-labor and accountability) should lead the church of Jesus, just as Moses led the nation of Israel misunderstands both the leadership of Moses and the design of the local church. First of all, Moses was a prophet and had direct access to the voice of God. Second, as noted in chapter two, even Moses was able to share his leadership and oversight with other leaders as a result of the wisdom gained from his father-in-law. Third, prophets in the Old Testament were

---

1. Strauch, *The NT Deacon*, 168.

not priests unless they were of the tribe of Levi. Even then the Holy Spirit of God did not universally guide by way of an internal compass the way the Spirit of God works with New Testament leaders. In that day, Israel needed to hear from Moses, the single leader who had heard from God. Today, in a healthy congregation, believers hear from a variety of elders who hear from God by way of Spirit-guided leadership via God's written Word. Evidence of this is seen in 1 Corinthians 14 when Paul instructs the Corinthian assembly on how to receive God's message from multiple leaders. That would not have been right under Moses.

Some will argue for a single leader position because of a pattern evidenced by other God-given institutions such as the home, government or Israel. This view is reminiscent of the second century development of what is called the "monarchical bishop."[2] In reality, this second century ecclesiology involved three offices: deacons, a council of elders and the bishop. This was the beginning of what we call the Episcopalian system of governance. Some have concluded that because one sees a pattern, this necessitates that each congregation must have a single leader with whom the buck always stops.

As already seen, the New Testament allows for a special leader among leaders, the nature of his office and authority is never like a single, lone leader sitting on top of his own pyramid. Robert Greenleaf says this:

> "To be a lone chief atop a pyramid is abnormal and corrupting. None of us are perfect by ourselves, and all of us need the help and correcting influence of close colleagues. When someone is moved atop a pyramid, that person no longer has colleagues, only subordinates. Even the frankest and bravest of subordinates do not talk with their boss in the same way that they talk with colleagues who are equals, and normal communication patterns become warped."[3]

Dr. Wayne Grudem from Phoenix Seminary makes a similar observation:

> "A common practical problem with a 'single elder' system is either an excessive concentration of power in one person or excessive demands laid upon him. In either case, the temptations to sin are very great, and a lessened degree of accountability makes yielding to temptation more likely."[4]

2. Ibid., 169.

3. Greenleaf, *Servant Leadership*, 63.

4. Grudem, *Systematic Theology: An Introduction to Biblical Doctrine*, 931.

SHARED AUTHORITY

The New Testament data is overwhelming. There ought to be no doubt, because the text of the Scriptures leaves none. From the very beginning of the recorded dealings with the local church, there is clear evidence of multiple elder leadership (note the Jerusalem council of Acts 15). As mentioned earlier when Paul wrote an epistle to Philippi, he greeted "the overseers (plural) and deacons (also plural)." James, as pastor of the Jerusalem assembly, gives a picture into the normative practice of calling 'elders' from the congregation into the private lives of congregants to pray during times of illness and threat. Acts 14:23 seems to be the smoking gun of evidence when it states, "And when they had appointed elders for them in every church, having prayed with fasting, they commended them to the Lord in whom they had believed." Titus 1:5 is a similar passage. As noted by Alexander Strauch concerning the work done by Bruce Stabbert,

> *"It is concluded after examining all the passages which mention local church leadership on the pastoral level, that the New Testament presents a united teaching on this subject and that it is on the side of plurality. This is based on the evidence of the seven clear passages which teach the existence of plural elders in single local assemblies. These passages should be allowed to carry hermeneutical weight over the eight other plural passages which teach neither singularity nor plurality. This is a case where the clear passages must be permitted to set the interpretation for the obscure. Thus, of the eighteen passages which speak of church leadership, fifteen of them are plural. Of these fifteen, seven of them most definitely speak of a single congregation. Only three passages talk about church leadership in singular terms, and in each passage the singular may be seen as fully compatible with plurality. In all these passages, there is not one passage which describes a church being governed by one pastor."*[5]

Without a doubt the issue of the leadership and the decision-making role of the elders is crucial both for the elder himself as well as the congregation he serves. Concerning his own relationship with God, every elder has been given a place of great privilege. As such he will be held accountable for what he does, how he lives, and how he leads (Luke 12:48; James 3:1). The New Testament elder is to the church to a similar degree as were the elders in the Old Testament covenant community.[6] Elders did much in the

5. Stabbert, *The Team Concept*, 25–26, referred to by Strauch, *Biblical Eldership*, 37.
6. Merkle, *40 Questions About Elders and Deacons*, 66–75.

Old Testament.[7] Elders aided Moses in oversight of leading God's people out of Egypt and into the Promised Land (Deuteronomy 27 and Numbers 11). Elders in the Old Testament functioned in decision-making capacities on numerous fronts. They helped with the unraveling of disputes between a Jew and his brother (Deuteronomy 1:9–18). They helped disseminate information to the covenant community as a whole (Exodus 19:7). They oversaw details connected with important occasions of worship such as Passover (Exodus 12:21). Eventually they would hold positions of great authority such as leadership over cities (Ezra 10:14), as well as functioning as governors over tribes and magistrates (Deuteronomy 16:18; 31:28). Elders were also involved in the rebuilding of the Temple after the exile.[8]

SOURCE OF AUTHORITY

What is the source of authority of the elder team? This is an essential question. The source of authority is two-fold, as found in key passages. First, it comes from the congregation who individually and corporately submit to the collective authority of the elder team. Second, there seems to be a sense in 1 Timothy 4:14 where there is a connection between the function and authority of the elders, the call of God and the recognition of agreement by the laying on of hands by the elders themselves from leader to leader. Acts 15 is a pivotal moment in the development of local church ecclesiology.

Three powerful realities stand out about the Jerusalem council. The first is the presence of both apostles and elders. If nothing else, it is significant because the apostles didn't dictate to the elders what should happen. In Philippians 1:1, Paul is interacting with bishops and deacons. In 1 Timothy and Titus, qualifications are given for pastors and deacons. It's clear that James takes a leadership role in the meeting. The second point of interest is that the findings of the leadership are combined with the assent of the congregation. There is a passing on of some kind of leadership authority from the early apostles to the team leadership of elders, and to a lesser degree even to the deacons.[9]

Just as the lead pastor's authority is limited, so is the authority of the pastor team. Some elders quote Hebrews 13:17, emphasizing the portion of

---

7. Van Dam, *The Elder*, 41–95.

8. MacArthur, *Answering the Key Questions About Elders*, 4.

9. Saucy, *Walvoord: A Tribute*, 232–34.

the text that teaches submission to leaders. What is left out are the linguistic details of the word 'obey.' Benjamin L. Merkle says,

> *The word translated 'obey' (peitho) also can mean 'to be persuaded.' The normal word for 'obey' or 'to subject oneself' is hypotasso, which is a stronger word. Although the verb peitho demands obedience, it is the 'obedience that is won through persuasive conversation.' The second command, 'submit' (hypeiko), is found only here in the New Testament and means 'to submit to one's authority.' Similarly Paul encourages the Corinthian believers to submit (hypotasso) to the household of Stephanas, as well as other fellow workers (1 Corinthians 16:15–16; cf. 1 Peter 5:5).*[10]

AUTHORITY OVER SHEPHERDING

The most important function of the pastor-elder-bishop of each congregation is the shepherding of God's flock. Ezekiel 34 is a powerful passage, God's scathing review of Israel's worthless shepherds. God's servant, Ezekiel, speaks prophetically against those who took the title of leader or shepherd. Some of their failures included 'taking care of themselves' (v.2); 'clothing themselves while ignoring the sheep,' (v.3); 'ignoring the sheep that were weak and injured,' (v.4); and 'ruling them harshly and with brutality,' (v.4). God's response to those charlatans is pointed and powerful:

> *Therefore, you shepherds, hear the word of the Lord: "As I live," declares the Lord God, "surely because My flock has become a prey, My flock has even become food for all the beasts of the field for lack of a shepherd, and My shepherds did not search for My flock, but rather the shepherds fed themselves and did not feed My flock; therefore, you shepherds, hear the word of the Lord: 'Thus says the Lord God, "Behold, I am against the shepherds, and I will demand My sheep from them and make them cease from feeding sheep. So the shepherds will not feed themselves anymore, but I will deliver My flock from their mouth, so that they will not be food for them.""* (Ezekiel 34:7–10).

Some pastors propose that as long as they study and present sermons that are theologically accurate and pastorally warm, then they have fulfilled their duties towards the sheep of God's pasture. Others believe that if they effectively oversee and administrate the church as a well-oiled machine,

10. Merkle, *40 Questions About Elders and Deacons*, 96.

then the job will get done. Neither of these views is in keeping with the full counsel of God's Word. In James 5:14, the lead pastor of the church of Jerusalem shows us the core of what shepherding should look like. He says that the sick of the church are to call the pastors (called elders) who will come and pray with oil. In this context, James even mentions the private counsel between elders and those within the assembly. This is a powerful and personal relationship between the under-shepherd and those that are fed by his personal and pastoral touch. To force a form of shepherding that knows nothing of a personal relationship between the pastor and the people to whom he is ministering is to miss the concept of a New Testament pastor. Daniel Doriani in his commentary on James says it well,

> "*The apostles commissioned elders to watch the flock. Peter tells elders to "be shepherds of God's flock that is under your care, serving as overseers" (1 Peter 5:2). As shepherd's, elders come alongside the people to serve. As overseers, they know the needs of the people better than they know themselves. . .Sick men and women call the elders as a group. They do not call those with a gift of healing; rather they call all to pray for healing. James says the prayers of a righteous man are effective. Since the first qualification for an elder is holiness—not social standing or theological acumen—the prayers of elders are effective.*"[11]

Serving as an elder, with a group of elders, is a daunting task. It is rewarding. It is difficult. It can be overwhelming. Tasks abound; time is limited. Relationships must be nurtured—relationships with individual church members; with visitors to the congregation; with believers and non-believers outside the congregation who are being ministered to by the congregation; with deacons, teachers, and other leaders in the congregation; and finally with the other elders. Many things capture the time and attention of an elder, but his mandatory function is to shepherd the flock. Peter could not be any clearer when he writes, in 1 Peter 5:1–2, *Therefore, I exhort the elders among you, as your fellow elder and witness of the sufferings of Christ, and a partaker also of the glory that is to be revealed, 2 shepherd the flock of God among you, exercising oversight not under compulsion, but voluntarily, according to the will of God; and not for sordid gain, but with eagerness.*" That means that in all of his relationships, an elder must have a shepherding aspect to each. To carry out this function, the elders of the congregation must have the authority to shepherd. That is, they must have a

---

11. Doriani, *James*, 193.

free hand to carry out the nurturing ministry to those in the congregation. The deacons, trustees or others in the congregation have no authority to instruct the shepherds on how to shepherd. That matter resides between the Scriptures and the teams of shepherds.

Why would Peter be so emphatic about the importance of the elders shepherding God's flock? Partly because Peter experienced forgiveness after the painful trial of failing our Lord, and received a commissioning for the mission of shepherding Christ's followers. John 18 records the failure of Peter in his denial of Jesus. Three chapters later is the powerful exchange between Jesus and Peter over the question of his supposed love for the Savior. Jesus not only accepted his servant back into the flow of ministry, but gave his servant a priority of ministry. "Peter, if you love me, feed my sheep." Jesus does not say, 'lead my sheep.' Neither does he say, 'discipline my sheep.' Nor does he say, 'indoctrinate my sheep.' Instead, he commands Peter to FEED his sheep. In unquestioned terms of nurture and love, Jesus is concerned that his sheep are fed. This involves leading, guiding, encouraging and discipline, but not at the expense of feeding.

Members, deacons and others in a congregation may have legitimate requests or feelings concerning how the elders are to shepherd the congregation. The Scriptures place the authority of those decisions with those who are held accountable and responsible to see that the shepherding tasks are done. When deacons try to usurp the shepherding task from the group of men who have been placed in authority, they are being irresponsible and rude.

Sometimes a well-intentioned deacon, or group of deacons, will take over a shepherding task that really belongs to the pastor or the elders, because he thinks it's not being accomplished. That, in and of itself, is not inappropriate if the deacon is truly motivated biblically and has the giftedness to help the elders in this kind of ministry. However, it is important that the deacon communicates with the pastor so that the pastor has an understanding of how the deacon is touching the individual in question. This will also give the pastor a chance to explain what has or has not been done with the person in question. The deacon may only know part of the story. The pastor may actually have a good reason why a certain expectation of the deacon has not been accomplished. The deacon may have erroneously arrived at the conclusion that the pastor wasn't doing his job, and instead of having a private discussion with the pastor, simply assumes that he is guilty as charged.

A far better scenario would be for the deacon to have a conversation with the pastor or pastors about whose job it is to nurture. The deacon may also choose to make a biblical appeal to the elder(s) in question. Every church member has a right to express concerns about aspects of the pastoral office that he feels are being neglected. He may find that the pastor is simply overwhelmed, and is doing all that he physically or spiritually can do. At those times, the pastor may ask the questioner to be part of the solution. Those who are biblically motivated in their concerns join in a partnership with the pastor. Elders must be approachable.

There is no scriptural evidence that deacons were given to the local church to maintain checks and balances on the elders. The elders are to oversee each other to make sure the task of shepherding is accomplished. In 1 Peter 5, Peter could have used his apostolic authority to call the *presbyteroi* to *poimen* the church. Instead, Peter appeals to the brothers as a fellow-elder.[12] The application for today is that elders must hold one another accountable as elders. The senior pastor must be very accountable. When a senior pastor refuses to be held accountable, he becomes another Diatrophes, who is discussed by John in his third letter, 3 John.

AUTHORITY OVER DOCTRINE

Nineteenth-century Presbyterian Thomas Murphy wrote about the pastor and his stewardship of the doctrine of the church, especially as it relates to the pulpit ministry:

> "The people should be instructed in reference to all the doctrines, that they may be assisted in maintaining the truth in its never-ending contest with error. The doctrines of the Bible are assailed from every quarter; they are misrepresented either from ignorance or design. . .From the pulpit they should be assisted in preparing to tell why they believe, to explain and to defend the truths of God. Each great doctrine is linked in with every other one, and there must be some knowledge of all in order to have an intelligent comprehension of the whole system. . .If they are not built up in the truth, they will gradually lose their interest and drop off from the nerveless preaching, and it may be, fall a prey to some form of error."[13]

12. Getz, *Elders and Leaders*, 149.

13. Murphy, *Pastoral Theology*, 177–78.

This is another category that has overlap from one decision-making entity to another. In this case, the overlap is between the elders who lead and teach the congregation in areas of doctrine and truth, and the congregation that is to protect against leaders who peddle false doctrine. 1 Timothy 5:17 teaches that double honor goes to the elders who effectively serve the church in leadership and teaching. Titus 1:7–9 goes one step further and stresses the necessity of the elders of the church to both exhort in doctrine as well as to refute those who teach inconsistent doctrine. 1 Timothy 3:2–7 shows that elders are 'apt to teach.' The responsibility of teaching and protecting sound doctrine belongs primarily to the elders. The deacons and the congregation have a significant and legitimate concern for doctrine, but the leadership and stewardship of doctrinal decision-making rests on the shoulders of the elders. This commitment of sound teaching can be traced back to the beginning of the church age in the aftermath of Pentecost. Acts 2:41*ff* shows that the early church and its leadership focused great care and attention in teaching (i.e., doctrine). Right teaching is as important today as it was in the early church.

AUTHORITY OVER CHRISTIAN EDUCATION

It may seem a bit redundant to state that the elders exercise biblical oversight over the Christian education of the assembly. 1 Timothy 3:2 shows that central to the shepherding oversight, the elders are to give the congregation the teaching to understand the Scriptures. Historically, this was a task that most reformed and puritan pastors took to heart. Richard Baxter said,

> *"Having disclosed and lamented our miscarriages and neglects, our duty for the future lies plain before us. God forbid that we should now go on in the sins which we have confessed, as carelessly as we did before. Leaving these things, therefore I shall now proceed to exhort you to the faithful discharge of the great duty which you have undertaken, namely, personal catechizing the instructing everyone in your parishes or congregations that will submit thereto."*[14]

Baxter continues to explain why, in that day, such a commitment to Christian education was important for those called to the eldership:

---

14. Baxter, *The Reformed Pastor,* 172–256.

Section II: Who Are The Decision-Makers?

> *"It is too common for men to think that the work of ministry is nothing but to preach, and to baptize, and to administer the Lord's Supper, and to visit the sick. By this means the people will submit to no more; and too many ministers are such strangers to their own calling, that they will do no more. It hath oft grieved my heart to observe some eminent able preachers, how little they do for the saving of souls, save only in the pulpit; and to how little purpose much of their labor is, by this neglect."*[15]

In many congregations, the issues of curriculum, educational staff and teaching formats are taken out of the hands of the elders and given to others in the congregation. While it is legitimate for the elders to delegate many of the details and decisions connected with Christian education, such delegation should rest in the hands of the elders themselves. There is no evidence that the churches in Jerusalem, Antioch or even Ephesus had committees or sub-committees to dictate to the pastoral leadership of these congregations what the form and function of teaching would be.

1 Timothy 4:13–14 ties the knot between the work of elders and Christian education. It says, "*Until I come, give attention to the public reading of Scripture, to exhortation and teaching. Do not neglect the spiritual gift within you, which was bestowed on you through prophetic utterance with the laying on of hands by the presbytery.*" The function of the elders in verse 13 is public reading and instruction. The third term in verse 13 is the Greek word '*didaskalia*.' This can be translated as either 'doctrine' or 'teaching.' The elders have been given the job of ordaining leaders to this task. Elders may utilize non-elders in the teaching ministry of the church, as long as they don't lose oversight of the ministry. D. Edmond Hiebert writes in his commentary on verse 15,

> *Paul earnestly presses upon Timothy the fulfillment of these duties by means of four present imperatives. The present tense means that he is to continue doing these things as he now is. These imperatives are grouped into two pairs, each pair followed by an explanatory clause. Paul appeals for a wholehearted occupation with "these things," those set forth in verse 12–14. "Be diligent in these things; give thyself wholly to them."*[16]

In verse 16, Paul concludes that careful attention to teaching and living will result in salvation and perseverance not only for himself but also

15. Ibid., 178–79.
16. Hiebert, *First Timothy*, 87–88.

for those whom he leads. Hiebert rightly notes that the passage identifies that salvation, "*is not procured 'by doing' but 'in doing.'*" In other words, faithful action is consistent with the sphere of salvation, and not with the earning of salvation.[17]

AUTHORITY OVER ORDINATION

In his chapter entitled, "Ordination to Pastoral Ministry," Richard L. Mayhue gives this description:

> *The overarching concept of ordination to ministry appears in both the Old and New Testaments. Ordination is the process of godly leaders affirming the call, equipping and maturity of new leaders to serve God's purposes in the next generation. Ordination validates/ authenticates God's will for a fully qualified man to serve God and His people.*[18]

While the Holy Spirit in the New Testament separated out leaders and the congregation concurred with those appointments, it is the spiritual leadership of a congregation that has the responsibility to make sure that those being sent have been tested. Notice again the verse that we just examined under the elders and their responsibility to make sure that Christian education happens in the assembly. In addition to Christian education, 1 Timothy 4:14 demonstrates that the elders are the ones who laid hands on those being sent out into the ministry. The laying on of hands is both a transfer of authority as well as an act of approval. The same thing is shown in Acts 6. The spiritual leaders of the congregation (in Acts 6, that would have been the apostles), demonstrate their approval of the men called out by the laying on of hands. The leadership of the church is elsewhere commanded to '*Do not lay hands upon anyone too hastily*' (1 Timothy 5:22). On comparison of Acts 6 with other key passages (1 Timothy 3:1–7 and Titus 1:5–9, for instance), we find that there is a role for the congregation at large to approve and send out men from amongst those who have been called for ministry. There is also a function for the spiritual leaders. Implicit in these passages and others is a time of observation of the man in question,

17. Ibid., 89.

18. Mayhue, *Pastoral Ministry,* 108.

searching for the qualities in him of both internal and subjective realities as well as external and objective aspects that demonstrate a call for ministry.[19]

AUTHORITY OVER MANAGEMENT

1 Timothy 5:17 states that elders who rule well are worthy of double honor. The word for 'rule' literally means 'to stand first.' Elders are to manage or rule the congregation. This rulership must be with a servant's spirit. Many congregations in countries with a democratic tradition of governance will often try to strip away the managerial authority of the elders in order to maintain a "democratic" balance of power. Such a balance is not found in the New Testament. While there is a sphere of leadership and responsibility that rests on the shoulders of the deacons and congregation, rulership cannot legitimately be taken from the elders and remain a biblical model.

One of the terms used for pastor is *episkopos*. This word speaks to the issue of administration and management. Some believe that each congregation could have multiple elders and multiple pastors but only one bishop. Those that take this view typically refer to the single use of 'bishop' in 1 Timothy 3 as compared to the plural use of the word 'deacons' in the same chapter. But the context of 1 Timothy 3 hardly lends itself to setting a pattern of singular bishops with plural deacons. Philippians 1:1 demonstrates that a plurality of bishops and deacons was the pattern of the gentile church, especially as experienced by the Apostle Paul.

What needs to be managed in the local church? This is where other offices of the local assembly overlap and come under the leadership of the elders.[20] Acts 6 makes clear that the office of deacon was established to aid and assist the elders with the large task of management. While the elders cannot pass off the job of nurturing, they may seek the aid of deacons to help with various aspects of management. The first group of deacons aided the early church in the oversight of 'tables.' Overseeing tables seems to have involved two tasks. First, it included the oversight and management of the real needs of widows (aided later by deaconesses such as Phoebe in Romans 16:1). Second, it involved administration of the finances incurred by the care of the local church life. The deacons aid the elders in the stewardship of the physical and financial sphere of ministry. The deacons do not sit in jurisdiction over the eldership. Rather, the deacons serve (hence the

19. MacArthur, *Pastoral Ministry*, 110–112.
20. Merkle, *40 Questions About Elders and Deacons*, 244–48.

meaning of deacon—*diakonete*) the elders and the congregation by use of co-managing certain logistical and managerial tasks. This allows the elders to spend more of their time on the important function of spiritual nurture.

Biblical elders will care how their decisions impact the deacons and the congregation as a whole.[21] An elder or elder team that leads without caring about how their decisions impact the congregation or the deacons is misguided. Godly elders will do all they can to lead with responsibility in such a way as to not add any unnecessary burden to the deacons who serve typically with a self-sacrificial attitude. The elders, while having the authority to lead the congregation, must always keep in mind the importance of how their decisions impact individuals in the congregation to avoid unknowingly causing harm.

Myron Rush, in his book outlining the essence of ministry management, discusses the role of staffing. He says that *"people are an organization's most valuable resource."*[22] The family-oriented ministry would agree, but the institutional-oriented ministry would probably say that the most valuable resource might be the donors, the bank account, or the PPE (plant, property and equipment).

The foundational problem with many who want the elders to allow them a role in ministry is not that they have a strong desire to serve, but that they are not able to work effectively in a team setting. As Rush points out,

> *When recruiting team members, many managers make the mistake of looking at an individual's skills and abilities without considering his personal goals (agenda). Having talent and ability needed by the group does not guarantee an individual could—or should—serve on the team.*[23]

Many potential leaders do well on their own when they can organize and execute a process as they want. However, when they are placed in a team setting, they haven't learned how to let go of certain expectations in order to come to a consensus with the key ministry goals of the group. This is common for those who have served in an executive capacity in the secular world, or in some other ministry, and now are asked to serve under the leadership of someone else. They may be motivated for a few months. In fact, because they have data and information at their disposal, they may be

21. Van Dam, *The Elder*, 143.
22. Rush, *Management: A Biblical Approach*, 20.
23. Ibid., 56.

viewed by the pastor or elder team as influential. But before long, their desire to influence the direction of the church or the leadership, or their commitment to help begins to wane and they will disappear from the church, often vocally and critically.

AUTHORITY OVER SOME MONEY

As was noted previously, the elders should have a clear measure of authority with the finances of the congregation. This does not strip away the fiscal stewardship that the New Testament gives to the deacons. In Acts 11:30, the elders in the church of Antioch determined the size and nature of the gift. Then they commissioned Paul and Barnabas to take the gift to the Jerusalem Church. While it is true that the deacons have been given to the local congregation in part to relieve the elders of the weight of money management, it is also true that for the elders to fulfill all that the New Testament commands them to do, they will need to have access to some ministry dollars. When godly men fill both the offices of elder and deacon, there will be harmony over the use of the church's finances. If an elder cannot be trusted to manage ministry money wisely, he probably has no business being placed into a leadership position in the church.

AUTHORITY OVER THE PRACTICAL

While deacons are to protect the elders' ability to focus on the ministry of prayer and the Word, they must not shield the elders from meeting some of the practical needs of the saints. In Acts 20:35, the Ephesian elders are instructed to 'help the weak.' Strauch writes,

> "As shepherds of the flock, the elders must be available to meet whatever needs the sheep have. This means visiting the sick, comforting the bereaved, strengthening the weak, praying for all the sheep, even those who are difficult; visiting new members, providing counsel for couples who are engaged, married, or divorcing; and managing the many day-to-day details for the inner life of the congregation."[24]

The idea that the elders' decision-making never interacts with the practical concerns of the New Testament church is foreign to the New Testament. They cannot totally divorce themselves from the lives of the

24. Strauch, *Biblical Eldership*, 29.

congregants. This is especially true when meeting these kinds of needs is directly connected to discipleship.

AUTHORITY OVER ECCLESIASTICAL RELATIONSHIPS

The issue of ecclesiastical relationships is so important to a congregation that it will be addressed in two separate chapters of this book. Acts 13 describes how the church in Antioch sent Barnabas and Paul (with the help of John Mark) to reach out to the cities that would be part of Paul's first missionary journey. Paul and Barnabas carried with them the authority of the congregation and leaders of the church in Antioch. In Acts 15, the believers from Antioch reached out to the believers in Judea and they jointly dealt with the question of requiring Old Testament practices such as circumcision to be part of the salvation-expectation for the Gentile believers.

Today, the issue of ecclesiastical relationships is important to fundamentalist and evangelical churches alike. A strength of protestant fundamentalism throughout the years has been its practice of ecclesiastical separation, but many fundamentalist congregations have crossed the line from being correctly separated to being incorrectly isolated from other believers and ministries for personal reasons vis-à-vis Biblical ones. This has caused increasing angst and division among fundamentalist congregations. On the other hand, too many evangelical congregations are not willing to take a firm stand on biblical separation at all. They fall on the other side of the line from the incorrectly isolated fundamentalists—they join in an ecumenicalism that repudiates any kind of ecclesiastical and theological discernment.

Within the last decade, a growing coalition of balanced fundamentalists has reached out to a growing group of militant evangelicals who are taking a stand for the gospel, and they are ordering their ministries in such a way as to protect biblical co-ministry while building appropriate walls to keep the wolves of false faith and false religion from stealing the purity of the Lord's body. This development is known as "Type B fundamentalism," "the emergent middle" or "young fundamentalism." This growing coalition is in stark contrast to the ministries that are characterized by the far right of hyper-fundamentalism as well as the far left of ecumenical evangelicalism.[25]

25. Joel Tetreau, Lines in the Sand Redux: A Plea to Type A Fundamentalists (http://sharperiron.org/article/lines-sand-redux-plea-to-type-fundamentalists), February 29, 2012. Also see Bob Bixby, The "Emerging Middle" (http://bobbixby.wordpress.com/2007/08/04/the-emerging-middle), August 2007.

Embedded with the instruction for elders to lead Christ's church is the issue of protecting it from the threats outside and inside the body. Warnings about false teaching from outside the church and attempted theological 'coup' within the church are common. Almost every New Testament epistle at some point speaks to the importance of guarding against these errors and the propagators that peddle them. Jesus tells his followers to *'beware of false prophets'* (Matthew 7:15). His warning was not a new one. Deuteronomy 13 talks about the false teachers of Moses' time. In Romans 16:17–18, elders of a congregation are exhorted to not only be on guard against false teachers, but also to be on guard against those leaders who are self-serving and whose actions demonstrate that they are schismatic and divisive. This makes the issue of internal and external ecclesiastical relationships of paramount importance in the task of leading Christ's church.

AUTHORITY BY AGREEMENT

If the elders lead by way of the same Spirit, there ought to be an experienced unity and consensus in decision-making. The New Testament gives no evidence that the first century church led by way of a majority. Where there is uncertainty among the elders, there ought to be a dedicated season of prayer and study until a unity and consensus is achieved. Not only should this pattern exist with the elders, but it should be followed by the deacons and other segments of the congregation as well. When at all possible, there ought to be a willingness to work through disagreement, not around or over them by using power and authority to avoid the painful work of coming to an agreement about differences and concerns the believers might have. The key to effective decision-making is to make sure that no undue pressure is exerted on anyone to cast their vote in a specific way.[26]

What happens when an elder no longer seems to fit within the scope of the elder team? Sometimes an elder will be burdened to take on the role of the pastor-teacher or senior pastor. This usually corresponds to an increase in passion and conviction about philosophy of leadership. It is their time to move up to a church where they can do the majority of the point-preaching and the leading of the leaders. Sometimes an elder will struggle to the point that he is no longer profitable as an elder. That doesn't mean he is spiritually unqualified, but simply because of new life challenges in his family or secular job, he can no longer help the elder team as he wishes to

---

26. Getz, *Elders and Leaders*, 308.

or as he has in the past. It is his time to step down and address his personal issues. Sometimes when an elder struggles with the rest of the elder team, it is because of his own attitude. He may need to find a position in a church with philosophical similarities where he can serve. If he leaves one church and doesn't continue to minister somewhere, it may be that the philosophical incompatibility was really an attitude problem. Even if the Lord doesn't open a new position for that elder to minister, if the man is truly called of God to shepherd, he will shepherd. It is part of his nature and call. His faithfulness in ministering legitimizes his calling, his previous ministry and his future service.

Using a thumbs-up, thumbs-down, thumbs-sideways approach to unity and consensus will help forge balanced and cohesive decisions without a feeling of forced agreement. A majority of thumbs up indicates agreement and excitement for a certain direction. Thumbs sideways should signal the necessity to reexamine the issue to see if there is a better way to implement the desired effect. If the majority signals thumbs down, a red flag has been raised for the leaders to stop the action and address the concerns. A prior agreement that no one uses the thumbs-down vote unless there is a biblical or ethical reason to do so will prevent abuse of the veto.

5

The Decision-Making Role of The Deacons

KEY CHAPTER PRINCIPLE:

"Because the principle role of the deacons is to serve the body in the physical and benevolent sphere of ministry under the supervision of the elders, their decision-making tasks in these areas need to be protected and honored at all costs."

IMPORTANT DECISIONS A DEACON TEAM WILL MAKE:

"How to protect the pastors from unfair expectations from the congregation; protecting the elders from having to deal with anything that takes away from the spiritual sphere of ministry; the physical and plant priorities for the particular ministry; wise financial policy; understanding the right approach to a debt; safe approach to the ministry of mercy, benevolence and widows; keeping the congregation safe from unnecessary legal risk."

Consider the remarkable function of a deacon.[1] He has a decision-making role in the New Testament church. While the Scriptures give no explicit or specific list of decision-making categories for the deacons, what does it teach about the *diakonate*? Are there discernible patterns that can show universal or normative principles that might impact the deacon as a decision-maker today?

1. Foshee, *The Ministry of the Deacon,* 20–21.

The source of the deacon's authority and role differs from that of the elder's. Strauch says that the deacon's source of decision-making authority comes from the deacon's call 'to serve.'[2] The elder's source of decision-making authority comes from the elder's call 'to lead.' This call to serve is heightened by the impact that this service has on the church's health and God's glory. Paul, in 1 Timothy 3:13, says, "For those who have served well as deacons obtain for themselves a high standing and great confidence in the faith that is in Christ Jesus." Donald Guthrie says that of the three possible basic interpretations of this passage, the best one sees this standing as a deacon's testimony within the Christian community. It may also represent the deacon's place before God.[3]

The New Testament office of deacon is challenging. The epistles and the book of Acts state that the character of a deacon must be worthy of respect, and he must be full of wisdom. John Calvin states,

> *It is necessary for them to be provided not only with the other graces of the Spirit, but also certainly with wisdom, for without it that task cannot be properly carried out. They may thus be on their guard not only against the impostures and frauds of those who are far too inclined to begging, and suck up what was needed for the brethren who were in extreme poverty, but also against the calumnies [slanders] of those who are constantly making disparaging remarks, even if there is no occasion for doing so. For as well as being full of difficulties that office is also exposed to unjustified complaints.*[4]

The Greek term for deacon literally means 'servant.' That means that the heart of this office is not primarily leadership, but service. The early church was instructed to appoint seven men in Acts 6 who would take the physical and benevolent weight of ministry from the spiritual leaders of the congregation. During that time, the spiritual leadership resided with the apostles.[5] Today, the spiritual care of the congregation has been placed with the elders, led by the first among equals.

The ultimate source of authority for the office of deacon and elder is God. However, in the mediatorial sense, the source of authority for the elders comes from the congregation. Based on Acts 6, the source of authority

2. Strauch, *The NT Deacon*, 75.

3. Guthrie, *The Pastoral Epistles*, 85–86.

4. Calvin, *Acts*, 1:162.

5. Nichols, *The Work of the Deacon and Deaconess*, 9.

for the deacons, humanly speaking, comes from spiritual leadership of the congregation.

The point of Acts 6 was that the deacons, the 'ministers of mercy,' would serve the congregation and the apostles so that the spiritual leaders of the congregation could spend the time needed in the Word and in prayer. In some of today's churches, the office of deacon has degenerated into a "board of the corporation" mentality. The deacon no longer functions as a legitimate *diakonate* and the congregation with whom they are connected is probably no longer a biblically ordered congregation. In other cases, because leaders fear a *diakonate* that runs amok, the leadership boards and pastors are unwilling to share the physical sphere of ministry with them.

In what ways do deacons serve? Sometimes deacons look at their function as being a 'check and balance' on the pastor's authority. Some deacons see their job as being a buffer between the pastor and the congregation. Some deacons feel that their job is to be the pastor's personal assistant. None of these is truly the design that God gave in his Word for his church. The early deacons were men who served God and others privately, and that private devotion resulted in a public ministry. Today, a congregation would be wise to find men who are already serving before publically naming them as deacons.

SERVANTS WITH BISHOPS

Nowhere in Scripture are the deacons asked to serve as the balance of power with the pastor. If the Scriptures teach anything, it is that a plurality of elders is to serve as a countercheck to each other, to hold each other accountable. In return, the congregation makes sure that the elders are teaching and leading with biblical integrity. The view that the deacons serve as a balance of power is politically-inspired, not scripturally derived. There are times, though, when a pastor or team of elders should submit to the wisdom of godly deacons. While this may seem inconsistent, the Scriptures teach a type of submission that is supra-gender and beyond the issue of office. There are times when any believer can benefit from the biblical wisdom discerned from other believers (male or female, pastor or deacon, congregation or congregant). This does not undermine the teaching of male headship seen in 1 Corinthians.

The extreme that places the authority of the deacon over the authority of the pastor is a twisting of what the Scriptures teach. Benjamin Merkle writes,

> *There are a number of factors in Scripture that indicate that the office of deacon is, in one sense, a lesser office than that of the elder. First, the function of the deacons is to provide support for the elders so that they can continue their work without being distracted by other matters. . .Second, the office of deacons is mentioned after the office of elder/overseer. There are two examples in the New Testament. In Philippians 1:1, Paul not only greets the entire congregation (as was his normal practice), but he also greets "the overseers and deacons." Later when Paul lists the needed qualifications for overseers and deacons in 1 Timothy 3, the qualifications for overseers are listed first. . .Third, references to the office of deacon are far less frequent than reference to the office of elder. . .Fourth, elders were appointed to new churches before deacons were. The early church in Jerusalem had elders before deacons were. . .Paul commands Titus to appoint elders in every city on the island of Crete (Titus 1:5), but he says nothing about deacons.*[6]

Another extreme is the over-reaction against a heavy-handed *diakonete*. The end result is the advent of congregations who do not have deacons. Some of these churches take the view that the office of deacon is a 'vestigial remain' from the apostolic church. Some have been so traumatized by lay leaders or deacons that they hesitate to jump into appointing new deacons when the previous ones have left or been dismissed.

One of the most devastating occurrences in the Lord's work is the loss of friendships because of disagreements in decision-making. Countless times, pastors and deacons have found their personal friendships ended because of disagreements over decisions. Paul says, in Philippians 1:1, "Paul and Timothy, bond-servants of Christ Jesus, To all the saints in Christ Jesus who are in Philippi, including the overseers and deacons:" This verse speaks strongly to the existence of teamwork between the two offices, at least in the Apostle Paul's mind. As he considers the congregation in Philippi, he speaks of unity. When he addresses the two offices, the words are organized in such a way as to suggest a oneness of spirit. The church was 'together.' More specifically, the church was together with the elders and deacons. If the congregation is not together with the elders and deacons, perhaps it is because there is no togetherness with the deacons and elders. Conflict

---

6. Merkle, *40 Questions About Elders and Deacons*, 244–45.

between the two offices leads to disunity in the church. This ought not to be.

Outside of the unity that characterizes the elder team, there is no more important unity than that fostered between the elders and deacons. When there is unity between the leaders in these two offices, a great amount of work can be accomplished, and a sense of camaraderie will dominate the congregation. When there is a concrete spirit of unity between the elders and deacons of a church, a meaningful church split will be difficult to accomplish. A split may result in loss of a clique, but the majority of the leadership will stay with the church. When there is unity of spirit between the two offices, any loss of members is likely due to an irreconcilable difference of philosophy or frankly pride on the part of those members demonstrated by an unwillingness to submit to the wisdom and leadership found within the two leadership teams of the church.

What does it take to build up a ministry? The fruit of the Spirit. A willingness to roll up the sleeves and work hard without complaint. Unity of spirit.

In the opening verses of Philippians, Paul sends his greetings to the church of Philippi. At the end of the first verse, he places the believers within the care of the two offices, bishops and deacons. He didn't specify one or two names. He placed the care of the congregation into the hands of a group of men from the two offices. Opponents of a plurality of elders wonder why there has been a resurgence of the view of the plurality in church leadership. The quick answer is that the churches have returned to an emphasis on exegesis of Scripture over the last two decades. This would include even many "baptist-like" leaders who on the one hand hold to a congregational-based polity, while on the other hand continue to also hold to an active plurality of eldership. Some leaders are under the impression that if you emphasize an elders-led authority structure, you eliminate either a special leader-among-leaders or you threaten a congregational-based authority. However, it is possible to have both a congregationalism and an active and real plurality in spiritual leadership.

Another viewpoint says that the plurality-of-elders leadership can take a congregation much further than one man alone can. An understanding of plural leadership comes through reading the New Testament. It is not biblical illiteracy that feeds this but faithful exegesis (Philippians 4:15). In addition, some extra-biblical documents also support the plurality. The external source of a letter from Polycarp shows that there was a single congregation in Philippi, indicating that single congregations were served by a plurality of elders and a plurality of deacons.[7]

These two offices were so significant that they each warranted their own mention. If the office of deacon was not significant, why did Paul mention it separately? When compared with Acts 6, the picture of the office of deacons is that the office works with and not against the spiritual leaders of the church.

Many ministries are led by a single man who is afraid to let go of power and has difficulty sharing ministry decision-making with other leaders that may perform ministry a little differently than he would. Tension between the pastor and deacons in decision-making often indicates that there is a misunderstanding of the biblical role or function of either the elder or the deacons. Sometimes the pastor is trying to dictate the conscience of the deacons. Or perhaps the deacons are attempting to throttle the leadership of the pastor. In any case, if one office is undermining God's pattern of the two offices working in unity, chaos results. When done biblically, the balance of work results in pastors having the time and resources they need to effectively shepherd the congregation while the deacons have the time and resources to effectively serve the assembly.

The office of deacon is really a hands-on ministry. The deacon, by fulfilling his ministry in the area of finances, mercy and physical details, protects the time and energy of the pastor so that he can give himself to the task of shepherding. In order for the relationship to work, the two offices must respect and submit to one another. The elders don't give up a measure of their leadership, but will submit to the wisdom of biblical deacons when deacons lead and serve the church with care and stewardship. The deacons will submit to the wishes of the elders in doing all that they can to make the vision of the church a reality as the elders lead. If a congregation has self-centered elders or self-centered deacons, this relationship will obviously not work.

SERVANTS UNDER BISHOPS

There is no biblical evidence that pastors serve under the authority of deacons. There is much evidence that deacons serve under the leadership and authority of the senior pastor, aided by other co-elders. Yet, in many congregations, the reverse is true, although not confined to our day and age.

7. Strauch, *The NT Deacon*, 168.

Section II: Who Are The Decision-Makers?

Alexander Strauch shows us a number of historical notations about this misunderstanding.[8] He also offers a critique:

> In many churches, deacons act more like corporate executives than ministering servants. In direct contradiction to the explicit teaching of the New Testament and the very meaning of the name deacon, which is 'servant' (diakonos), deacons have been made the governing officials of the church. Even more troublesome is the fact that deacons are often placed into a competitive field with the shepherds of the local church. This practice is a proven formula for prolonged church warfare.[9]

Dr. James Barnett, a noted Episcopalian historian, notes that "*the deacons seem often to have overshadowed the presbyters in their importance and influence.*"[10] Philip Schaff wrote that Jerome (c. A.D. 345–419) wrote a letter to a leader named Evangelus refuting the move of making the office of deacon a higher office than that of the elders. Jerome responds, "*I am told that someone has been mad enough to put deacons before presbyters, that is before bishops* (Jerome knew that presbyters and bishops were originally the same)."[11] In A.D. 325, at the council of Nicea, the gathered bishops took this issue head on. Canon eighteen states, "*Let the deacons remain within their own bounds, knowing that they are the ministers of the bishop and the inferiors of the presbyters. . .And if, after the decree, any one shall refuse to obey, let him be deposed from the diaconate.*"[12]

Today, there may be legitimate reasons why deacons accrue natural authority. In some congregations, the pastoral turnover is significant, especially in rural settings where the faithful deacons of the congregation have served for year after year, decade after decade, while at the same time a never-ending rotation of pastors continues. In the words of many deacons, "Long after the pastor leaves, I'll still be here holding the bag." It may be that the stranglehold of the deacons makes it impossible for a new pastor to breath, let alone lead. A tough-minded pastor may need to come into such a church and clean out the deacon team with the blessing of the congregation.

---

8. Strauch, *The NT Deacon*, 162.

9. Ibid., 9.

10. Barnett, *The Diaconate, A Full and Equal Order*, 67.

11. Schaff, "Letters," 6:288.

12. "The Seven Ecumenical Councils," in *Nicene and Post-Nicene Fathers*, 14:38.

SERVANTS OF FINANCE

Deacons are to be servants of finance, not tycoons of resources. The deacons in the early church were responsible to oversee the business of finance. The Greek term 'tables' in Acts 6 probably refers to tables used to count and deal with finances. A good translation of Acts 6:2 is: "It is not right for us to neglect the preaching of God's Word in order to handle finances." This also seems consistent when one considers the context of Acts 4:34–35. These first deacons (sometimes called proto-deacons) demonstrated oversight of the finances by:

1. Collecting money and goods contributed to the needy (Acts 4:34, 35, 37; 5:2).

2. Distributing the money or goods to the needy (Acts 4:35).

3. Ensuring that the church justly and fairly distributed the money (Acts 6).

4. Coordinating the church's overall financial affairs and ministries of mercy (Acts 6).[13]

How should deacons help pastors and congregations in the sphere of church finances today? Keeping to the spirit of Acts 6, deacons serve congregations by giving a detailed look at and management of funds and other physical resources so that the church can execute the ministry and serve its members responsibly. They minister to the physical and financial needs of church members, not as a welfare society for lazy people (warned about by Paul in 2 Thessalonians 3), but as a failsafe for those who cannot take care of themselves, such as widows or orphans who have no living or immediate family members to care for them.

Congregations have a responsibility to care for pastors who depend on the ministry for their livelihood. This is a not a commentary against ministers that choose to be bi-vocational. For those churches that have determined to enable their pastor to dedicate all of his time to the shepherding of the congregation, deacons aid those congregations by ensuring that the pastor's financial needs are being met. In Acts 6, the deacons were given, in part, to protect the spiritual leadership so that they could continue to devote needed time for prayer and ministry of the Word. Deacons must be available to free the elders from the details that would otherwise bog them down and keep them from active shepherding.

---

13. Strauch, NT Deacon, 33

SERVANTS OF MERCY

Why was the office of deacon created? Acts 6 shows that the widows needed to be protected and cared for. The terms *diakonia* and *diakonos* (see Acts 11:29; 12:25; Romans 15:31b; 2 Corinthians 8:4; 2 Corinthians 9:1) show that the heart of the office is the corporate response of mercy to the needy. In the words of F.J.A. Hort,

> *"It can hardly be doubted that the officers of the Ephesian ecclesia [church], who in 1 Timothy are called 'diakonoi,' had for their work. . .chiefly, perhaps even exclusively, the help of a material kind which the poorer or more helpless members of the body received from the community at large. It is difficult to account for the word, used thus absolutely, in any other way. They would share with the elders the honor and blessing of being recognized ministers of the Ecclesia. But that would be nothing distinctive. Ministration to the bodily wants of its needy members would be distinctive, and would obviously tally with the associations most familiar to Greek ears in connection with the word."*[14]

Combining the view of the deacon from the pages of Scripture with the observations from history, a picture of the deacon as the mediator of charity is revealed. The deacons of the congregation have the opportunity to represent the arms of the congregation in extending the love of Christ to those who have real need, both in and outside of the congregation. When deacons take on the persona of 'boss of the church,' they miss the biblical and historical sense of what it means to be a deacon. According to Charles W. Deweese, the deacons in the historical church

> *". . .visited martyrs who were in prison, clothed and buried the dead, looked after the excommunicated with the hope of restoring them, provided the needs of widows and orphans, and visited the sick and those who were otherwise in distress. In a plague that struck Alexandria about A.D. 259, deacons were described by an eyewitness as those 'who visited the sick fearlessly,' 'ministered to them continually,' and 'died with them most joyfully.'"*[15]

14. Hort, *The Christian Ecclesia*, 209.
15. Deweese, *The Emerging Role of Deacons*, 12–13.

SERVANT OF WIDOWS AND THE QUESTION OF 'DEACONESS'

The point of Acts 6 was that the widows of the early church needed to be cared for. In the context of the passage, a specific group of widows, namely the Grecian Jewish widows, were being neglected while the needs of the Palestinian Jewish widows were being attended to. The apostles had been responsible for the watch of widows. This may have been inaugurated by our Lord Himself when he passed the care of his mother to John the Beloved (John 19:25–27). Very few sections of Scripture carry the vibrato of familial emotion as these passion passages between Jesus, Mary and John.

By combining what is written in Acts 6 with the actions of a deaconess called Phoebe in Romans 16:1, and also considering what 1 Timothy 3:11 says, a comprehensive approach to taking care of widows becomes apparent. This care seems to bring together the oversight of the elders, the deacons and a group (named and unnamed) of women that may have been called 'deaconesses.' In addition to Phoebe, many believe that 'wives of deacons' in 1 Timothy 3:11 can be understood as an official group of women leaders who specifically took care of certain special 'gender-specific' needs of the widows. These needs would have been the kind that elders and deacons could not really take care of. Some Bible teachers believe that these women may have been the wives of both the elders and deacons of the congregation. If indeed there was a group of women who functioned as female deacons, they would have avoided the two restrictions that the Scriptures place on women and ministry, namely that they not usurp authority over men, and that they cannot serve in an executive theological role of leadership within the congregation.[16]

The plot of the contemporary widow in the time of Christ is seen in Luke 21. The widow woman in this story had virtually nothing. Her strong faith was all that she possessed. Jesus had a special affection for such individuals because of their sacrifice and faith. Most healthy congregations today have a group of women that functions with or without the official title of deaconesses. The title of deaconess is not as important as the commitment on the part of female servant-leaders who step up and partner with the elders and deacons to reach out to the specific needs of widows. Connected with this is the responsibility of the elders and deacons to make sure that those who are truly needy receive the help that they need. Congregations

16. Nichols, *The Work of the Deacon and Deaconess*, 11–14.

often have to deal with immature believers, or even non-believers masquerading as believers, who develop a sense of entitlement. These lazy women begin to rely on the help of others to the extent that they become rebellious, gluttonous and disobedient in the area of a personal work ethic. They become gossips and complainers. Connected with this 'women-to-women' ministry is the instruction found in Titus 2:3–5. Here, older women are to be taught and then they are to teach the younger women Christian values and family disciplines.

6

The Decision-Making Role of The Congregation

KEY CHAPTER PRINCIPLE:

"Because the church is the body of Christ and because Jesus is her head, there must be a corporate commitment on the part of the congregation to allow the will of Christ to lead us. As a body of 'believer-priests,' God will often move through the collective assent of His church."

IMPORTANT DECISIONS A CONGREGATION WILL MAKE:

The doctrinal convictions of the congregation; Who will serve as executive leaders of the church in the office of elder and deacon; Church discipline matters that concern the congregation as a whole; An agreement with the elders as to what philosophical shape the congregation will take.

Methodist pastor Daniel Nehrbass wrote in his thesis paper, "A Biblical Model of Church Decision-Making," about an incident that took place in what he calls a 'democratic, committee-driven United Methodist Church':

The first controversy came within two months of my arrival at the church. We had no phone in the church building, so a few committed chairmen suggested at our board meeting that we get one. Someone even offered to pay the phone bill. But when it became evident that there was a great deal of resistance to the idea, the discussion was tabled for a month. Over the next thirty days two strong factions arose: one pro-phone, and the other anti-phone. At the next meeting the discussion of the phone topic went for an hour. We heard arguments such as: "We never needed a phone before." "But what if someone gets hurt, and we need to call an ambulance?" "But the youth will be calling China!" "But a phone would make the pastor's job easier." Finally, when the ballots were counted the phone was turned down by one vote. After this meeting I had to ask, "Isn't there a better way?"[1]

Ask someone in a Westernized country what a church looks like and they are likely to use descriptors like 'foyer,' 'pews,' 'choir loft,' 'piano/instruments.' There are fellowships of Christians throughout the world; some meet in buildings, some in homes, and still others in huts or lean-tos, or even under shade trees. Typically, whatever God's people lack by way of resources, they seem to make up in pure, God-praising joy! This reflects the common phrase, "The church is the people, not the building." So when the church 'does church,' what role or part should they have as a collective on the decisions of the congregation?

Even if a congregation does not believe that it is the final court of appeal, the New Testament Scriptures demonstrate that congregations should be involved in decisions, including disciplining members (Matthew 18:15–17; 1 Corinthians 5:1–5); sending out missionaries (Acts 13); nominating and electing certain leaders (Acts 6:1–6, possibly Acts 14:23); providing accountability in some ministry efforts (Acts 14:27); determining the amounts of gifts that are given in congregational relief efforts (1 Corinthians 16:3); and sending representatives for specific tasks (2 Corinthians 8:19), including working in consensus with the theological leadership of other congregations (1 Corinthians 16:3, Acts 15).[2] While protecting the doctrinal position of a church is a part of the pastor's function, the New Testament church bears a congregational responsibility to make sure the Scriptures are accurately understood and followed (Acts 15). Samuel Waldron lists a number of occasions where the Scriptures instruct the congregation separately from its leaders.[3]

Every form of polity seems to have its own special and unique challenges. Congregationalism is one such challenge, especially in the area of

1. Nehrbass, *A Biblical Model of Church Decision-Making*, 8.
2. Moritz, *Congregational Church Government*, 10–11.
3. Waldron, *Who Runs the Church?*, 119.

the merging of the decision-making authority of the leaders with that of the congregation. This balance of leadership and accountability is often tense, even in a spiritually healthy congregation. Daniel Akin, a friend to the single-elder-led Congregational Church says,

> *Single-pastor Congregationalism is often a sight to behold. It is not necessarily a pretty one. A somewhat paranoid autocrat as a pastor, monthly business meetings dedicated to senseless issues that only eat up time, a committee structure that looks like the Department of Education and is about as effective, and a deacon board that functions like a carnal corporate board. . .(this) is not what the Bible teaches about Congregational church government. What we discover in God's Word is altogether different.*[4]

While it may be true that the authority of the congregation and that of its leaders can sometimes overlap, that does not mean that all-out conflict must erupt. A look at the New Testament will demonstrate that the congregation's authority and the authority of its leaders actually worked well together in the primitive church. Much rises and falls on having a humble and responsible Christ-like attitude that is more interested in servant hood than in seeking one's rights.

When congregationalism goes wrong, it's usually because those congregations misunderstand their authority. God never intended the authority of the congregation to override or undermine the authority of the elders or even the deacons where the Scriptures give clear authority to the leaders of a congregation. Two specific groups, when allowed to override the wisdom and leadership of the God-ordained male leadership of the church, can cause chaos. The first is the women of the church. The second is a group of wrong executives, male or female, who have not been appointed as deacons or elders, especially when they are devoid of the biblical qualifications for either office.

EVANGELICAL FEMINISM

Many professing evangelical churches are dealing with the issue of evangelical feminism. Scripture limits the leadership roles that are available to women.[5] Evangelical feminism tries to explain away or simply ignores the

4. Akin, *Perspectives on Church Government*, 25.
5. Grudem, *Evangelical Feminism & Biblical Truth*, 62–101.

teachings of Scripture on decision-making and executive corporate church leadership. Several verses construct the limitation to women from interfering with the executive decision-making of the assembly.

In 1 Timothy 2:11–15, Paul instructs Timothy:

> "*A woman must quietly receive instruction with entire submissiveness. But I do not allow a woman to teach or exercise authority over a man, but to remain quiet. For it was Adam who was first created, and then Eve. And it was not Adam who was deceived, but the woman being deceived, fell into transgression. But women will be preserved through the bearing of children if they continue in faith and love and sanctity with self-restraint.*"

The context of this limitation is in the gathered assembly. A few verses earlier, Paul addresses the issue of praying with 'holy hands' in a corporate setting. He also speaks to the issue of women and modesty. Even earlier, Paul speaks to the issues of church corporate officers. The result of the setting of this limitation of women teaching men is in the context of the corporate gathering of the local church. One other set of passages that blocks a woman from serving in the executive theological leadership of the church would be 1 Corinthians 11:4–5 and 14:33–35. Both of these passages bring implication as far as women giving or even correcting congregation-wide biblical instruction or direction. The New Testament explains that there is a headship principle that is to be applied in both the institution of the church and the institution of the home. Paul says that since Eve was deceived by Satan, even Christian women, in their fleshly nature, have had a problem with authority.[6]

Having a few limitations on women and leadership in the local church does not mean that women are second class citizens in the church or in God's Kingdom. It simply means that they may not legitimately serve in executive leadership (officially or by way of stealth). In many churches, small but crafty groups of women undermine the pastor's authority. There are the power-brokers, or as the Apostle Paul calls them, 'busybodies.' Sometimes older women of the church think that the scriptural teaching about gossip doesn't apply to them. They may need to be confronted and disciplined with church discipline, which sometimes is a problem because these women may be some of the major financial backers of the ministry. A pastor may find himself facing the challenge of following the Scriptures or keeping his financial base. A Christian woman may offer an opinion

6. Ibid.

within congregational church life, but when the women of the church take on a stealthy or an openly defiant attitude against the male leaders of the congregation, the church is dying or may already be dead.[7]

Sometimes the pastor's or deacon's wife may feel she must run the church through her husband. This may be by constant nagging or by being contentious. Men who cannot lead their wives toward a greater degree of righteousness are not qualified to lead or serve the church of Jesus. Ministry wives must remember that their primary call is one of wife or mother, not assistant pastor or the chief ecclesiastical consultant of the church. This may be hard for the wife of a leader who is sacrificing much for her husband's ministry. She needs to feel valued and part of the team, but she must not cross the biblical line.

IMMATURE BELIEVERS

The second group of people that often abuses a healthy congregationalism is composed of men or women who would never be allowed to chart a direction for the church as an elder or serve as a deacon (or deaconess) because their lives are devoid of the biblical qualifications needed to serve in office. Every congregation has believers who, while being sincere in their faith, are naïve in the areas of church leadership because they are young in the faith or are careless or worldly in their lifestyle. Daniel Akin:

> "Should a babe in Christ have an equal voice and vote as, say, the pastor? This seems foreign to the spirit of the New Testament and reads more into the doctrine of the priesthood of all believers than is justified. That 'part of the maturing process can be participation in the decision-making of the congregation' is true. However an 'equal voice' to the spiritual leadership of the church 'across the board' is both unscriptural and unwise. It is at this very point that Congregationalism has been abused and rightly criticized."[8]

These may be men or women who have leadership functions in the secular field and because of some secular success, they are self-deceived into thinking that they might know a better way to lead the church than the pastor or deacons. Many churches have allowed themselves to be hijacked by one or the other of these two groups (women and men not mature enough

---

7. Van Dam, *The Elder*, 207–26.

8. Brand and Norman, *Perspectives on Church Government*, 196–97.

to handle leadership at home with their wife or leadership at church with the malcontents). Whatever the right role of the congregation's authority, it was never given by God to allow an immature or carnal group of women or men to undermine the leadership and direction of godly men. When a congregant persistently complains that the pastor or deacon always gets his way, it's a demonstration of a lack of their understanding of Scriptures and a lack of a sweet and submissive spirit when it comes to following authority, especially pastoral leadership.

CONGREGATIONS DETERMINE WHO IS ACCEPTED INTO MEMBERSHIP

Galatians 1:8–9 was a strong warning given for the entire Galatian church. In his commentary on Galatians, Martin Luther noted, "Here Paul casteth out very flames of fire, and his zeal is so fervent that he beginneth almost to curse the angels, and himself."[9] At the very least, this passage says something about the collective stewardship of the membership. Paul cares deeply about congregations not allowing teachers or members to remain within the congregation who teach or represent a different gospel.[10] When Galatians 1 is compared to Matthew 18 and 1 Corinthians 5, the conclusion must be that congregations have the final authority and responsibility for the makeup and identity of its membership. Throughout the New Testament, and specifically the book of Acts, congregations were given the charge to accept only regenerate believers into the membership. Furthermore, God has given the local church as the guardians of the ordinances. The congregation has the responsibility to protect the membership and the ordinances from being shared with non-believers. The Apostle Paul charges the early congregations to mark, and if necessary, put out from amongst themselves those who would pollute the local body. The leadership has an important role in the accepting of members, but ultimately it is the responsibility of the congregation itself to discern who is genuine and edifying in their faith, worthy to be part of congregational church life.

9. Luther, *Galatians*, 25.
10. Ibid., 25–26.

CONGREGATIONS DETERMINE EXECUTIVE SERVANT-LEADERS

As noted before, healthy decision-making is not the purview of just one approach to polity. Congregationalists will appreciate the thoughts of early Reformers who saw a legitimate role on the part of the congregation to be involved in the issue of who would lead them. In the final analysis, the overwhelming majority of the Continental Reformers, as well as the majority of British-born Puritans, would not have appreciated the typical congregational-oriented ecclesiology found in most North American independent and conservative churches today.

Jeffrey Brown, in his PhD dissertation, wrote that

> *"Luther was one of the first in modern times to extend this discerning ability of Christians to their right to choose teachers. He did so by combining the teaching of 1 John 2 with John 10:1ff and Matthew 7:15. For Luther, the ability to understand the Scriptures and the ability to choose pastors went hand-in-hand.*[11]

In Acts 6:2 and 6:5, the Apostles' request for deacons pleased the multitudes and they chose. The apostles laid hands on those appointed by the congregation of early saints. The congregation elected, with the apostles' approval, those who would be their leaders. Some see a congregational involvement in ordaining of elders by Paul and Barnabas in Acts 14:23. In both Timothy and Titus, Paul gives oversight concerning characteristics of both bishops and deacons. The biblical practice of congregations voting, ordaining and following biblical leadership is attached to wisdom. In the New Testament epistles of 1 Timothy and Titus, congregations are given instruction concerning the kind of character that those who would serve the church as either pastor or deacon must display. 3 John gives instructions to help believers determine the difference between excellent leaders (Gaius) and dangerous leaders (Diatrophes).

Including Acts 14, there are ten New Testament passages which describe corporate decision-making in choosing leaders or representatives: Acts 1:15–16; Acts 6:1–6; Acts 8:14–17; Acts 11:19–22; Acts 13:1–3; Acts 14:21–23; Acts 15:36–41; 1 Corinthians 16:3–4 and 2 Corinthians 8:18–19.[12]

Acts 1 shows a proto-ecclesiastical congregationalism in the choosing of corporate leadership. Judas was lost both in body and soul. The early

11. Brown, *Corporate Decision-Making in the Church of the New Testament*, 100.

12. Ibid., 116.

corporate identity of the disciples of Jesus determined that, for the sake of mission, a successor to Judas was needed. Even with the presence of powerful apostolic leadership, the determination of the successor not only fell to the casting of lots, but came down to the determination of the group. Brown notes:

> "Luke identifies the assembled group as the eleven apostles (whom he names, v. 13), the women ('Mary Magdalene, Joanna, Susanna, and many others'). Mary the mother of Jesus, and the brothers of Jesus (James, Joseph, Simon and Judas—Matthew 13:55). . .The whole group is simply called 'the brothers'. . .Luke is therefore relating that at this juncture in the life of the Jesus Movement, a group of about 120 persons participated in the replacement of Judas."[13]

While eventually the Roman Church did away with the congregational involvement in the choosing and electing of executive church leaders, the first three centuries demonstrated a consistent pattern of congregational involvement. Everett Ferguson says that during the first three centuries of the church, leaders universally were chosen and placed into power by the whole body.13 Edwin Hatch makes the case that *"there was always, in the case of. . .bishops, presbyter, deacon and elder, either the reality or the semblance of an election."*[14]

CONGREGATIONS TAKE PART IN "SENDING OUT"

The beginning of a pattern takes place in the book of Acts. The local congregation identified and sent out those who would serve the body of Christ away from the congregation. There is evidence that at times the leaders of a church sent out other leaders for the sake of ministry. In Acts 8:14, the apostles heard of the effect of ministry in Samaria where they had sent Peter and John. Later in Acts (11:22), when the church at Jerusalem heard of the effective result of ministry from those who had been scattered, the congregation chose Barnabas and commissioned him to go to Antioch for the sake of the ministry and for encouragement. In Acts 13, the local assembly sent out Paul and Barnabas. Technically it was the Holy Spirit that called out these servants, but it was the collective act of the congregation in recognizing the special call from God.

13. Ibid., 132–33.

14. Ferguson, *The Free Church and the Early Church*, 134.

Since 1792, Baptists in particular have formed agencies to send out missionaries. These missionaries go with the authority of the congregation, not the mission board.[15] This approach has a biblical basis. Philip acted under the authority of the church at Jerusalem when he baptized the eunuch from Africa in Acts 8:38. 2 Corinthians 8:18–19 serves as a foundation for this kind of missionary partnership. Within a year of finishing the first epistle to the Corinthians, Paul had to deal with the issue of financial giving for the sake of the hurting church in Jerusalem.[16] He made new arrangements for the transfer of funds. Unlike the year earlier when Paul was accompanied by representatives from the church of Corinth, this time Paul and Timothy sent a brother who had been appointed by a group of congregations to help Titus. A group of churches sent out a representative to aid the apostles for the sake of ministry.

CONGREGATIONS TAKE PART IN "PLACING OUT"

The local assembly has the final authority in the final discipline of its members as demonstrated in Matthew 18:15–17. Jesus gave his disciples a four-step approach to handling discipline in the church: 1) personal confrontation (v. 15); 2) confrontation by two or three witnesses (v. 16); 3) confrontation by the entire body (v. 17) and 4) expulsion from the corporate fellowship if there was still no repentance (v. 17–18). The end of this gospel instruction is powerful: if need be, 'tell it to the church.' Mark Dever says,

> "Notice to whom one finally appeals in such situations. What court has the final word? It is not a bishop, a pope, or a presbytery; it is not an assembly, a synod, a convention, or a conference. It is not even a pastor or a board of elders, a board of deacons or a church committee. It is, quite simply, the church—that is, the assembly of those individual believers who are the church."[17]

This is an example of how God holds congregations collectively accountable for failing to handle disciplinary issues. In 1 Corinthians 5:1–7, God exposes and confronts the Corinthian congregation for not dealing with an open sin issue. Individuals in the leadership and the membership of a congregation have significant roles in confrontation. A congregation

15. Hatch, *A Dictionary of Christian Antiquities,* 2:1504.
16. Moritz, "Congregational Church Government," 11.
17. Dever, *Nine Marks of a Healthy Church,* 221.

should not be privy to the details of a disciplinary issue until the stages of Matthew 18 have been concluded, preferably initiated simultaneously by multiple brothers and sisters who are alarmed by a disobedient lifestyle. The Scriptures indicate that final discipline is to be a collective act of the congregation for the purpose of love and restoration. In 2 Corinthians 2:5–11, the brother that was disciplined in 1 Corinthians was to be restored. Paul gave further clarification that the purpose of the discipline was not simply punitive, but rather restorative. The decision was made by a majority consensus. 2 Corinthians 2:6 says that the offender had been placed out by the act of a majority.

CONGREGATIONS SUBMIT TO EACH OTHER INTERNALLY

The congregation is to submit to the elders in the area of spiritual leadership and church ministry (Hebrews 13:7, 17). Furthermore, the congregation submits to the deacons in the areas of the physical and benevolent spheres of ministry. Finally, the congregation is to submit to lay leaders who are leading in the areas of their ministry strengths and gifts (Ephesians 5:21— Paul teaches mutual submission as an evidence of being Spirit-filled). One of the implications of 2 Corinthians 2:6 is that when a congregation makes a decision on behalf of the body, it is right for individuals to submit not only to the decision by way of church life, but they also should alter their personal life in such a way as to not undermine the determination of the assembly as a unit.

Strong passions or emotions in the life of the church are not wrong. Romans 14 shows that there may even be certain freedoms or practices that some of God's children feel should be curtailed. Paul emphasizes that believers are to have a Spirit-fed conscience in areas that some believers feel are "righteousness" but which others count as "sin." The dynamic is not an easy one. It means that the congregation needs to be careful not to wound the fragile consciences of some believers while at the same time guarding against those same believers undermining the freedom of the assembly. Congregations that are characterized by humility and love will have a high degree of charity between individual believers and the congregation as a whole.

CONGREGATIONS REACH OUT TO OTHER CONGREGATIONS EXTERNALLY

Acts 15 shows a council between two autonomous congregations, two assemblies that worked together mutually for a specific purpose. In that case, the purpose was doctrinal in scope. Page Patterson notes, ". . .*congregations related to each other through a loose confederation based on common commitment to Christ, and to the doctrine of the apostles.*"[18] In Acts 18:27, one congregation wrote to another congregation approving the ministry of one brother for the new assembly. This reaching out often included a financial aspect of ministry from the congregation as a whole. Such was the case in Philippians 4:15. Paul commended the Philippian congregation for their collective support early in his ministry. He mentioned that no other congregation during this Macedonian season of his ministry partnered with him like the Philippians did.[19]

Another campaign involving funds is found in 1 Corinthians 16:1–4. Again, representatives from the congregation were taking a specific ministry gift. This was a pattern even in the early days of the New Testament church, as seen when Paul mentions that he had also given this kind of instruction to the church in Galatia. In Colossians 4:16, Paul instructs the assembly in Colossi to read and then exchange with a congregation in Laodicea letters that he had written. This speaks to the relationship congregations can have with other congregations.[20] An implication here is that often much insight can be gained by one congregation seeking out the experience and wisdom from a sister church who has faced similar issues. Often the data shared can seriously help in working through especially tricky corporate decisions.

CONGREGATIONS PROTECT RIGHT DOCTRINE AND PRACTICE

In Romans 16:17–18, Titus 3:10 and several other sections in the New Testament, the local assembly is warned concerning the dangers of being deceived by false teachers. In 1 Corinthians 11, the Corinthian church is strongly rebuked by Paul because of the various mistreatments of the Lord's Supper. This doctrinal commitment should at its core protect the gospel.

18. Patterson, *Who Runs the Church?*, 133.

19. Boice, *Philippians*, 251–52.

20. Wright, *Colossians and Philemon*, 160.

Section II: Who Are The Decision-Makers?

Galatians 1:8–9 is pointed: if anyone tries to pollute the gospel, not only is he to be rejected from the congregation, he is to be considered '*anathema*' (literally, 'let him be damned'). Individual believers have the responsibility to make sure that the Scriptures are being taught accurately. When the church is gathered, there is a corporate share in the responsibility of protecting the pulpit. Parallel to right doctrine is right order. In 1 Corinthians 14:39–40, the entire church in Corinth was challenged to 'let all things be done decently and in order.'

CONGREGATIONS ACT BY A MAJORITY WITH A MIND TOWARD CONSENSUS

According to internal textual evidence, it appears that congregations worked toward consensus by a majority. At the same time, it appears as if the spiritual leadership of the early church (comprised of either apostles and elders, or later elders and deacons) made decisions based on a commitment to consensus that may have had as its root the practice of the elders in the covenant community of Israel.

There are three responses to the question of agreement: 1) yes, I agree; 2) I would do it differently, but I trust you; and 3) I am convinced that this is wrong. When an elder responds with the third response, it is time to stop and prayerfully reconsider based on the concern of the leader in question. However, if the leader consistently has the third response, there could be a significant problem, perhaps an unqualified leader who is self-centered and won't work with a team, or possibly he is the only discerning leader and the rest are not following Scripture on some level. It may be that the nay-sayer is just not philosophically in tune with the rest of the team.

In 2 Corinthians 2:6, an interesting thing happens. Paul mentions that the sinning brother of 1 Corinthians 5 had been disciplined by 'the more.' The word comes from the Greek phrase *hupo ton pleionon,* which is translated as 'the majority.' This holds two implications for decision-making. It demonstrates that at the congregational level, decision-making can go forward with a majority consensus. The biblical wisdom here protects against several threats. It combats the ability of a rogue leader (such as the dangerous Diatrophes of 3 John) from hijacking a congregation. It protects the membership from the wolves that internally pretend to be sheep. It also protects from the occasional bad decision-making of even a good man (such as Peter or Barnabas).

It also shows the commitment on the part of the individual to personally follow the action of the congregation as a unit. When an individual believer attending a congregation ignores the body decision to place outside the membership a rebellious and unrepentant member, the inconsistency of that decision undermines the effectiveness and even the integrity of the congregational decision. An exegetical source to this kind of commitment is apparent in the events that happened during the Jerusalem Council and Acts 15. In 2 Corinthians 2:6, Paul makes mention of the fact that the Corinthian assembly responded to the sinning brother from 1 Corinthians 5 by way of the majority. The local church is a bit of a decision-making clash. On the one hand, decisions are to be made by elders in consensus with other elders. There will be times when a single leader will need to act with decisiveness. Congregations sometimes act by way of majority. This shows the ability of churches to be committed to 'situational decision-making.'[21]

Technically a congregation is not under the constraint of a pure consensus, but there ought to be a desire on the part of leadership and congregants toward that end. Leaders and believers must seek each other out and do all that they can in a loving manner to understand the concerns of each other. When a majority of a congregation decides on a course of action, the majority should seek out the minority to make sure that the dissenting portion of the fellowship understands that they are loved and valued. This is often a difficult thing to do.

21. Dever, *Polity*, 21.

7

The Decision-Making Role of
The Church Member

KEY CHAPTER PRINCIPLE:

"Because each converted church member is a believer-priest, and has been fitted for body-life with specific spiritual gifts, and whereas the clear teaching of the text of Scripture is that believers submit one to another especially based on spiritual wisdom and placement in the body, it is consistent to conclude that each believer will at some point in time be the best qualified to make certain decisions in the context of his or her ministry.

IMPORTANT DECISIONS A CONGREGANT WILL MAKE:

The theological and practical non-negotiables of the church you will belong to; an understanding as to your unique giftedness and ministry abilities; the level of commitment that will be given to the congregation; how to best bring your personal resources to add to the effectiveness of the collective ministry of the congregation; how to handle inevitable differences with fellow-congregants and congregational leadership.

One way of teaching the role of each individual in the local assembly is through the acrostic "SHAPE," a method popularized by Rick Warren.[1] 'S'

---

1. Warren, *The Purpose Driven Church,* 370.

stands for spirituals gifts that the individual receives from the Holy Spirit at the time of salvation; 'H' is for heart, what the individual is passionate about; 'A' is for ability, the natural abilities that a person is born with; 'P' stands for personality; 'E' is for experiences—family, educational, vocational, faith. Scriptures show that God has ordained this SHAPE. Passages such as 1 Corinthians 12:12–31 show that an assembly is healthiest when its members are serving based on their individual God-given SHAPE.

FOUNDATIONAL VIEW OF AUTHORITY AND DECISION-MAKING

Consistent with this individual ministry that God desires of each of his children is that they be able to minister with their hands free, and with the decision-making ability that they need to accomplish the task that they've been handed. The assumption is one of trust. We trust that each believer can function in ministry without looking over their shoulder every second of the day. The only time leadership should really limit the decision-making scope of a church member is when the sphere of those decisions demand greater accountability because of the nature of those decisions.

A foundational view of decision-making as it relates to the individual church members in the congregation is important. The principle is to give as much authority to those who are directly involved in each ministry as possible. If someone has been given the spiritual gift necessary for an effective ministry in a particular area, they should be allowed as much authority as they need to accomplish the task. Nothing is as discouraging or counterproductive as giving someone a task without giving them the decision-making authority to fulfill that task. Ephesians 5:21 addresses this. At some level, we are to submit one to another. This aspect of mutual submission to one another in the body-life of the church is a manifestation of the filling of the Spirit of God.

Passages such as 1 Corinthians 12 show the unmistakable presence of an 'every member' ministry. From the huddled gathering of an initial group of a hundred or so followers of Jesus, to the ecclesiastical Big Bang of Pentecost, to the impressive team of the Apostle Paul, there is a division of power, leadership and decision-making found with the gatherings of true worshippers of Christ. In Mark 10:42–43, Jesus states that those who demand exclusive power have more in common with power-hungry Gentiles than with him.

Section II: Who Are The Decision-Makers?

There must be a decentralized decision-making present in the local assembly. A church must be clear-headed about when to rely on the expert opinion of one of the congregants who may be especially talented or gifted to give leadership, and when it's right to seek a determination from the body. Robert Saucy notes that the *". . .truth that each member of the church is equipped for ministry by the Lord through the Spirit would point again to a certain diffusion of authority throughout the entire church."*[2]

A common fallacy in the teaching of individual decision-making capacity in the church is that the church can either have equality within or else a stated structure of authority. Both are possible, though. Jeffrey Brown discusses how this view of equality and team work in ministry affected even the approach of the Apostle Paul towards others.

> *Paul's view of his authority is demonstrated in his interactions with his co-workers. Paul names over one hundred assistants in his mission work, and his comments about them demonstrate a concept of shared authority (Philippians 2:29; 1 Timothy 4:12; Titus 1:5). . .Various terms Paul uses show that he holds his co-workers to be on a common plane with himself, such as fellow worker (thirteen times), fellow traveler (once), fellow soldier (twice), yoke fellow (once), partner (once), fellow slave (twice).*[3]

Paul's teaching about the body of Christ in passages such as 1 Corinthians 12 show that it is natural to see other church members as competent to be able to contribute to the congregational decision-making, both as an individual and as part of the assembly as a whole. While not every member is competent in every decision and sub-ministry in the church, Scripture reveals that all believers are gifted in some way to encourage and move the assembly forward. It should be the natural response of the pastor or deacon to assume that the individual who ministers with them is competent to make ministry decisions, especially in the areas of ministry where they are involved. It is incumbent on the one fulfilling the ministry to demonstrate a level of maturity and responsibility consistent with good stewardship and spirituality.

Whatever is said about the role and privileges of personal decision-making by individual church members, the collection of those rights must never override the Scripture's teaching on the importance of protecting the health and unity of the church. The New Testament is not silent about the

2. Saucy, *Walvoord: A Tribute*, 228.

3. Brown, *Corporate Decision-Making in the Church of the New Testament*, 87–88.

command of protecting the unity of a congregation. *"Be diligent to preserve the unity of the Spirit in the bond of peace"* (Ephesians 4:3). *". . . being of the same mind, maintain the same love, united in spirit, intent on one purpose."* (Philippians 2:2). *"Standing firm in one spirit, with one mine striving together for the faith of the gospel;"* (Philippians 1:27). *"All of you be harmonious, sympathetic, brotherly, kindhearted, and humble in spirit; (1 Peter 3:8)."* *"That together you may [unanimously] with united hearts and one voice. . ."* (Romans 15:6). All of these reflect the Old Testament sentiment of Psalm 133:1, *"Behold, how good and how pleasant it is for brethren to dwell together in unity."*

The church member must remember that disagreements never cause division; people cause division. Conflict is not necessarily a bad thing. According to Dr. David Smith, *"Conflict, if managed well, can spur a church on to greater unity and ministry excellence."*[4] There are times, though, when disagreements within a congregation, even if managed, are so deep that a determination must be made to go in separate directions. That is why it may be right for an individual believer to quietly and gently leave a congregation instead of staying and splitting a church when the leadership and the bulk of the congregation agree with the present direction of a congregation. The responsibility of keeping the unity of the body that Christ has brought to his church is laid at the feet of each believer (Romans 12:18). The job does not belong exclusively to the pastor, the deacons or any other group within the local fellowship, but because of the priesthood privilege that each believer has, protecting the unity of the church is ultimately each individual's responsibility.

DECISION-MAKING OVER SUBMITTING TO THE PULPIT MINISTRY

While any church member has a responsibility to exercise care and discernment regarding the preaching and teaching ministry of a church, the head of the household carries a considerable weight. Not only must he exercise wisdom for his own spiritual growth, but he must take great care that he doesn't place his spouse or children under the careless communication and proclamation of God's Word. 1 Thessalonians 5:21 challenges each believer to *"test all things; hold fast what is good."* Jude 1 commands the individual believer to *"contend earnestly for the faith."* John 4:1 instructs each believer

---

4. Smith, *Pastor Revisited*, 105.

to *"test the spirits whether they are of God."* At the very least, each believer has the responsibility to ensure that they are sitting under a faithful pulpit.

There was a time when believers had confidence that the pulpit ministry in the average church could be characterized by a gospel-centered zeal, a Christ-centered view and a Bible-centered accuracy. Those days are long gone. Too much of fundamentalism has become a hotbed of secondary issues which have stolen the focus of militancy away from the core of the faith and have given its vigor to man-made standards of holiness. At the same time, too much of evangelicalism has lost its ability to be militant at all, even with the gospel itself. It is doubly important now that each believer, especially heads of households, weighs carefully the preaching and teaching ministry of a congregation.

As long as the preacher is preaching the Bible and honoring both the text and application of the Word, a congregation should lovingly receive and follow his ministry. The relationship between the church member and the pastor is similar to the authority relationship between a husband and wife. A wife submits to her husband as an equal. Colossians 3:18 uses the Greek word, *"hupotasso."* This is literally "subject yourself."[5] When Scripture teaches children to submit to parents such as is found in Colossians 3:20, the reader finds a different word (*"hupakouo"*). This second term of submission carries with it the idea of the submission of an inferior to a superior. In a similar way, church members submit to their pastor (Hebrews 13:7, 17). The church member and the pastor are equal in priesthood and essence, but not in function and authority. Too many church members believe that they only must submit to their pastor when they agree with the pastor. That is not submission. That is a vote! It is sad how often church members will leave a church out of protest because of a single decision of disagreement with a pastor who loves them and will one day give account. The sheer volume of evangelical churches in North America make it easy for many self-absorbed believers to rotate from church to church.

It is a different story when one finds themselves in congregation where the preacher consistently preaches his own thoughts and is not careful in the pulpit. In a case like that it is time for the family to move on. It is far better to be in a congregation where the pastor teaches and honors God's Word and where an every-member ministry flows. Once in that place of worship, it is incumbent upon every member to follow the leadership of

5. Harris, *Colossians & Philemon*, 177–80.

that church, even if you occasionally disagree with an individual decision a pastor makes.

DECISION-MAKING OVER THE GIVING AND RECEIVING OF MUTUAL EDIFICATION

Colossians 3:16 indicates that every believer has the right and the ability to minister to others in the congregation by way of teaching and admonishing. Interestingly enough, the stated primary way that this is accomplished is through participation in singing and corporate worship. The same concept is spelled out in 1 Corinthians 14:26, *"What is the outcome then, brethren? When you assemble, each one has a psalm, has a teaching, has a revelation, has a tongue, has an interpretation. Let all things be done for edification."* David Lowery says,

> *"Paul addressed the Christian community in Corinth as brothers, a general term including both sexes. When the church met, anyone was free to participate by contributing a hymn, or a word of instruction (cf. 1 Corinthians 14:6; probably a lesson based on the Old Testament), a revelation from one gifted in prophecy (cf. vv. 6, 29–32), or a word from one gifted in a tongue followed by an interpretation of what was said. The controlling principle in this free participation was the rule of love. All that was said and done was to have as its goal the need of strengthening others."*[6]

Galatians 6:1 addresses the restoration of each other in love and with gentleness. This is a decision that can be made by any individual church member toward any other church member. Within the official teaching of the church, a woman may not instruct a man. However, in the private relationship between believers, women can encourage men and even challenge a brother in Christ as long as it's done with respect and in keeping within the headship principle. 1 Corinthians 13 implies that it is better for a brother in Christ to challenge another brother in Christ, and a sister in Christ to challenge a sister in Christ.

Many North American Christian fellowships are lacking in the skill set of the giving and receiving of an appeal. In today's culture, protest is likely when there is a disagreement, rather than appeal. Unless a sin has occurred in the open, believers should not assume guilt toward any other believer, especially toward leadership. This is why passages such as 1 Timothy

6. Lowry, "I Corinthians," 2:540.

5:19 forbid the open accusation of leadership unless it has been verified with multiple witnesses (of the infraction). However, because believers are brothers and sisters in Jesus, there should be some ability—especially in the church family context—for men and women, in a healthy relationship, to allow the occasional giving and receiving of an appeal. An example is when Aquilla and Priscilla taught Apollos, *"explained to him the way of God more accurately"* in the privacy of their own home (Acts 18:26).

A side application is the decision of individual believers in the giving of tithes and gifts. Acts 11:29 says that every man, according to his ability and conscience, sent relief gifts to the believers in Judea that needed help.

DECISION-MAKING OVER PERSONAL CONSCIENCE

Acts 11:29 is evidence of decision-making for the individual believer. 2 Corinthians 9:7 says that each believer is to give as dictated by his heart. The question of giving is not set by some leader, but the Holy Spirit leads with conviction for each believer. Other passages speak of the understanding of financial partnership for the Church age. At least a portion of the issue of giving is a personal one between the believer and his God.

Diotrophes demonstrated the spirit of twisted leadership in 3 John. The Apostle Paul was very clear in Romans 14 concerning the eating of meat and the meeting of certain days with the instruction, *"Each person must be fully convinced in his own mind."* Concerning the limitation of a congregation's authority over the conscience of each believer, Edward Hiscox says:

> *". . .the liberty of a Church is limited by the terms of the great Commission, and by its divine institution, to the pursuits and the purposes contemplated in the Gospel. . .The Church cannot dictate what a member shall eat or drink or wear; what shall be his business or his pleasure. But if, in any of these matters, questions of morals and religion come to be involved to the reproach of truth and the Christian profession then the Church has the right to interpose."*[7]

Diotrophes simply removed from the fellowship those he couldn't control. Christian leaders too often try to dictate the personal standards of Christian brothers and sisters in specific areas where there is no obvious teaching in the Scriptures or where finding a clearly-stated position is at

7. Hiscox, *Principles and Practices for Baptist Churches*, 152.

least challenging (if not impossible). Pastors and ministries that cross the line not only demonstrate a twisted leadership, but they also run the risk of institutional hypocrisy. It is pure arrogance for a Christian leader to tell a parishioner that God's will for his life is something particular (apart from the Scriptures).

The issue of standards in a ministry can be a difficult one. If a church is to have a standard, there must be vigilant against hypocrisy. A pastor telling his parishioners that attending the movie theater is wrong, and then slipping off to the nearest Harkins is pharisaic. If that isn't bad enough imagine the damage done when the same leader tags his "no movie" policy as binding as the Ten Commandments! Many conservative ministries that had Christian schools in the 1970's and 1980's are missing too many of their former students from that era in large part because the students saw through this kind of hypocrisy and spiritual abuse that this approach to authority and decision-making too often breeds. Too many students coming out of that kind of environment have either ran headlong into the world, or have become twice the Pharisee that their leaders were. How tragic! However, it is possible to honor certain standards of holiness because one loves God and as a result, he feels he must or must not do certain things. That kind of holiness is pure and God-honoring and much more attractive than other forms of standards.

DECISION-MAKING OVER A STYLE OF EXPRESSION

The body of Christ is a rich tapestry of believers. Some have a deep love that is introspective and serious. Some have a faith that, while just as real, results in external forms of worship. Some believers will close their eyes while they sing. Others will openly weep over the heart-felt lyrics of a theologically sound hymn. Some will raise their hands in worship toward the heavens. Corporate worship in the Scriptures is both reverential and celebratory. Who should dictate to each believer how they will worship individually within the congregation? The Holy Spirit should dictate and the rest of the congregation should allow them that freedom.

Unfortunately, in today's "worship-wars" environment, it is easier to build a large traditional, legalistically-oriented church or a contemporary, entertainment-oriented church than it is to build a truly blended congregation that embraces Spirit-filled believers, some of whom are traditional and others who are more contemporary in their personal taste. Each believer has the right to determine how he relates to God through prayer and worship. Whether a believer is more or less expressive, those around him are not to judge or become intrusive in his worship.

DECISION-MAKING OVER PERSONAL CHOICES

A similar issue is the issue of personal conscience. God gives the individual church member the freedom to make personal choices, some of which may impact the local body. For instance, a single believer has the right to marry anyone that the Scriptures would not condemn. 1 Corinthians 7 says that they are free to marry one who is 'in the Lord' (v. 39). The Apostle Paul goes on to suggest that those who are single and wish to make a difference in the service of the Lord remain unmarried. Even though Paul was an apostle, he does not give his own opinion as authority. He recognizes the right of the individual single believer to choose whether or not they should marry.

Men and women in ministry sometimes are fired from their ministry positions because of emotional or health issues. It's understandable if the ministry has to let someone go who can no longer minister in the area of agreement because of these challenges, but if the ministry is ordered correctly, it will do all that it can to financially help that brother or sister or at least investigate other ministry opportunities for the person. If the person cannot stay, at the very least the ministry should do all it can to help them find a new ministry. A family-oriented church will do all it can to help in a situation like this. An institutional church will ultimately need to cut its losses so that the machinery of ministry can continue.

God's ministers and lay families need to be careful about partnering with a ministry that chooses buildings and budgets over servant-leaders.

DECISION-MAKING OVER THE LEVEL OF INVOLVEMENT

This particular category of personal decision-making is a bit controversial. There are two common views. The first is that if you are a member of a congregation, you should essentially be at the church every time the door is open. On the other end of the spectrum is the view that congregants should be able to come and go whenever they please without a certain expectation from leadership. To be clear, the latter view has no support from Scripture. Joshua Harris, in his short but pointed book, "*Stop Dating the Church*," identifies the telling signs of what he calls 'church daters':

"First, our attitude toward church tends to be me-centered. We go for what we get—social interaction, programs and activities. The driving question is, "What can church do for me?" A second sign of a church-dater is being independent. We go to church because that's what Christians are supposed to do—but we're careful to avoid getting involved too much, especially with people. . .Most essentially, a church-dater tends to be critical. We are short on allegiance and quick to find fault in our church. We treat church with a consumer mentality—looking for the best product for the price of our Sunday morning. As a result, we're fickle and not invested for the long-term, like a lover with a wandering eye, always on the hunt for something better."[8]

There is an alarming rate of unfaithfulness even in the lives of young leaders preparing for church vocational ministry. Asking a young seminarian who was barely noticed in church life during the formative seminary years to lead one's congregation seems like as smart an idea as a CPA firm turning over the reins of the corporation to a post grad student who has never actually worked a 9-to-5 job handling corporate money. What is even more unrealistic than unfaithful leaders thinking that they can successfully lead a ministry is the number of ministries that have actually hired the unfaithful seminarian in spite of their woeful record in real-life ministry.

The idea that believers can simply come and go in and out of church life at their convenience is alien to the New Testament. This doesn't mean that individual believers or congregations should place so much of the week's time into the corporate body that there is nothing left over for one's personal or family time. Some churches have church on Sunday, post-high school Bible education on Monday night, AWANA on Tuesday night, prayer meeting on Wednesday night, visitation on Thursday night, youth activities on Friday night, and a men's or women's prayer breakfast on Saturday morning. It would start all over again on Sunday. Not all churches that offer a week-long ministry schedule put pressure on families to be at everything. However, too many ministries do. The attitude coming from the pulpit frequently is 'to the degree that you are here at church is the same degree that you are spiritual.' Many of the leaders who were at church all the time, now a decade or two later have lost their spouse to divorce or their children to unbelief. Many ministries feel trapped. They can't see themselves doing ministry any other way, because their tradition dictates that this approach is acceptable.

8. Harris, *Stop Dating the Church,* 16–17.

The Scriptures demonstrate that there ought to be a visible commitment on the part of the believer to be with his brothers and sisters in the church life. The amount of co-ministry and one-another ministry in the New Testament seem to indicate that an obedient commitment to church life will result in believers that not only are faithful in church attendance on Sunday, but are committed to believers throughout the week. Sunday attendance ought to be a priority. If you belong to a congregation that believes, for the sake of the health of the congregation, that they ought to have Sunday ministry in both the morning and evening, a consistent application of the New Testament text is that you should strive to be with your brothers and sisters as often as you can. To pit your personal family against your church family is illegitimate, especially when you as a family are out multiple nights doing other things when you could use that rest time so you can be faithful in God's house and to God's family. Too many congregants look at the ministry services as a buffet, choosing one thing and leaving another.

The best approach is to encourage all believers to be faithful to the times of corporate worship and teaching. Those that allow other distractions to undermine their faithfulness demonstrate a lack of maturity and reveal that they are limited in their ability to lead and serve. The congregation must agree to hold those who serve in ministry to certain expectations. In the clash of congregational authority and individual authority, the individual needs to understand that because he or she has chosen not to be as faithful in ministry as others, they will miss out on some opportunities that would otherwise be available to them.

DECISION-MAKING OVER GIVING AND REVIEWING OF FINANCIAL RECORDS OF A CHURCH

Some church leaders personally challenge couples about giving of their tithe, and even go further by instructing and extorting parishioners to give the amount that the leaders demand. It's not unknown for a senior pastor to even negotiate the amount of the Christmas gift that he expects from the church. This is spiritual abuse; New Testament teaching says that giving should not be done by compulsion. Paul says, in 2 Corinthians 9:7, "*Each man should give what he has decided in his heart to give, not reluctantly or under compulsion, for God loves a cheerful giver*" (NIV).

Perhaps with the exception of reviewing what people give, any member should be able to review the financial books of the church if he so wishes. Everything needs to be open for fair review for any member that wants to understand some aspect of the church's financial statement. If a congregation will not allow its books to be open, the legitimate concern is that something is being kept from public knowledge. Opening the books doesn't mean that every bit of financial information is fair game. The combined pastor and deacon leadership of a church may determine that a specific part of the financial picture needs to be kept private because of ministry or personal sensitivity. However, other than these kinds of exceptions, the main policy and spending patterns of a congregation should be open to the members for review. Not allowing the congregation to know what is owed or how the monies are spent is not only unethical, but in some cases may be illegal.[9]

Some congregations reject the open book policy because of the belief that not all the members are trustworthy. If a church member is not trusted, this should not result in a closed-book policy, but in an occasion for personal discipleship for the church member in question. If a church member is not faithful enough to be deemed responsible to look at the books, it may indicate that the church needs to review what it means to be a member. Churches that will not allow members to examine the general financial records generally have leadership with a wrong view of the financial freedoms of the leadership to make decisions on behalf of the membership without a commitment to full disclosure.

REALITY FROM THE ROAD: YOUR CHURCH WILL BE LIKE YOU. . .NOT PERFECT!

Many Christians leave churches too quickly or too frequently, based on reasons that are not scriptural (i.e., taste in music, mild theological differences, personality clashes). There are few legitimate reasons to leave a congregation where there are 1) Biblical leaders who are men of character; 2) The gospel of Jesus Christ is faithfully preached and there is a real intent on the part of the membership and the congregation to submit to Jesus as the true head of the church; 3) The Bible is viewed as the accurate and authoritative standard for life and godliness. As long as these three characteristics are true, either one starts a congregation that is more in agreement

9. Elson, O'Callaghan, and Walker, "*Corporate governance in religious organizations: a study of current practices in the local church,*" (http://findarticles.com/p/articles/mi hb618/is 1 11/ai n28565876). January 2007.

with particular convictions, or one must stand whole-heartedly behind the particular congregation and its leadership and do the best they can to encourage biblical consistency. If a particular geographical area has multiple God-honoring churches, pick one and settle in!

PART III

How Do We Make Decisions?

8

How to Recover from Bad Decision-Making

KEY CHAPTER PRINCIPLE:

Because God is a God of second chances, and because sanctification in all areas is a process, it is the responsibility of every decision-maker in a local church to learn from those occasions of bad decision-making and to use them as lessons for the future rather than to be destroyed by their failures.

The catalogue of missed steps for many of us can grow to epic proportions. The list of things I've said and done on accident are legendary within the circles of family and close friends. There was the occasion I was thanking a friend and his sweet wife for their hospitality in hosting a small group of us during a leadership conference I had spoken at in Pennsylvania. As my friends and I were leaving I turned to the dear couple and explained that their sacrificial hospitality reminded me of . . .well I wanted to say "Aquilla and Priscilla." What I said (much to the surprise of everyone present) was "Ananias and Sapphira." My friend Bob Bixby put his hand on my shoulder and whispered loud in my ear so that all could here, "*uh—Joel. . .God killed those people!*"

The more serious mistakes common to all who serve in pastoral leadership are unfortunately also legendary. Dr. Richard Mayhue of Master's Seminary wrote a chapter entitled, "*All-Too-Frequent Mistakes of Rookie Pastors or Pastors Who Did Not Learn from Their Rookie Mistakes,*" a list of common *faux pas* among pastors.[1] Some of these include exhibiting impatience; trying to make your first church an exact replica of another well-known church; studying too much, to the exclusion of significant shepherding; failing to realize one must earn respect as a pastor by being a pastor; and quitting too soon.[2]

An area pastor was once asked by an older member of his congregation to take a stool sample to the hospital for analysis. A staff member who served for many years with distinction was once mooned by a woman in the hospital who wanted to show the pastor exactly what her medical condition was. Another pastor was asked by a new convert to help him stash some of his "pills" somewhere safe on the church property, assuring the pastor that it was for medicinal purposes only. In the Lord's work, truth can be stranger than fiction. Because so much of the unexpected is tossed the pastor's way, the ministry makes for a breeding ground of bad decision-making.

Sometimes the decision isn't bad, but the PR from a legitimate decision that other leaders or parishioners disagree with gives that impression. Opinions are formed by the amount of information that is available to the congregation. The mature believer will assume that there is more information behind the scene. The immature believer will fill in the blanks; human nature being what it is, the assumptions will be less than flattering. Disseminating as much information as possible, as quickly and efficiently (and accurately) as possible will nip this process in the bud.

Previous chapters have examined the roles of elders, deacons and others in the church in the area of decision-making. This chapter will examine the issue of surviving and even thriving in the face of bad decision-making. Everyone in ministry has made a bad decision at some point in his or her life. The issue isn't the decision per se; the issue is getting back up after making a bad decision. A man of God has to have lived and ministered a fair amount of time before he is proficient at leadership. Ministry has so many nuances that it may take years to master it. There is good reason that most Old Testament covenant community elders really were elders, in years as well as experience.

Success is often built on the rubble of failure. It is not possible to lead without failure. Studies have found that the average successful business leaders have suffered through at least two business ventures that have failed

1. Mayhue at *http:audio.gracechurch.org/sc/2005notes/MayhueWhyPastorsFail.pdf*, 6–8.

2. Ibid.

before finally succeeding at one. They failed twice as often as they succeeded, but were finally successful on the third try. Mark Tetreau, successful in several businesses in Prescott, AZ, said, "I've never met a businessman who hasn't made at least one bad investment." Young men just entering ministry need to hear this—ministry is a difficult road and you need to have a clear sense of your calling if you hope to succeed. You must also be humble before God or your congregation will help you achieve humility.

The Old Testament book of Nehemiah shows many aspects of wise decision-making that can be applied by New Testament believers. At the very beginning, Nehemiah calmly and truthfully explained to King Artexerxes and his queen Damaspia how his heart was heavy because Jerusalem was in ruins. He told them that he was burdened to see the gates and walls rebuilt. He didn't try to sell himself or his plan. He simply explained his passion.[3] Nehemiah was obviously a responsible leader, because he found immediate favor in the eyes of Artexerxes. The king provided what was needed and sent Nehemiah to accomplish his task. Nothing about this decision seemed forced. If ministry decisions are consistent with our character and God's timing, the support for those decisions will come about naturally.[4]

Nehemiah worked with the leadership families of post-exilic Jerusalem, taking the rubble of what was once a proud city and using it to rebuild the walls, gates, homes and even the Temple itself. Throughout the job, the leaders and workers were being ridiculed by friend and foe alike. In Nehemiah chapter 6, he wrote that it took those courageous Jews fifty-two days to rebuild the walls.[5] The decisions that Nehemiah had to make are similar to the types of decisions that a congregation today faces. Nehemiah, in the first half of his book, recorded the challenges of the rebuilding. The last half of the book shows the issues surrounding people, religious leadership, practice of worship and how to foster an ongoing relationship with God. New Testament leaders can learn much about planning, executing the plan, neutralizing threats and handling internal discipline issues just from this one single book. Just as Jerusalem was rebuilt after a period of devastation, so today's ministries can survive and become stronger by learning from the destructive decisions of the past.

The English poet Alexander Pope said, "To err is human, to forgive divine." Both parts of the quote connect with the issue of decision-making

3. Fensham, *The Books Of Ezra And Nehemiah*, 161–62.

4. Dale, *Pastoral Leadership*, 66–69.

5. Young, *An Introduction to the Old Testament*, 410.

in the church. Every decision-maker in the course of church life will have to occasionally admit that a decision was the wrong one. Furthermore, every decision-maker in every congregation will have to make the decision to forgive the failures of others in their decision-making. Pope, in another work, observed, *"A man should never be ashamed to own that he is wrong, which is but saying in other words that he is wiser today than he was yesterday."* Two popular sayings sum this up: 1) There is a God. You are not him. 2) I work for God, but I am not God. In other words, it's important to remember that believers still bear the marks of sin and imperfection and as such, will make errors in judgment.

The list of reasons for failure is long and arduous. We are sinners saved by grace. We are too often influenced by our depraved flesh that will shade our walk until it's bound by the presence of our resurrected Lord. In his presence, we will no longer have to endure a body that is raked with the presence of sin, failure and curse. Sometimes we make wrong decisions because we are human. That doesn't mean we sinned in making the decision, except for the effects of original sin, but that we just made a mistake or were limited in our understanding. Dr. Rolland McCune notes, *"Man is a finite creature. This means, among other things, that his mind partakes of limitations."*[6] His point is that one has limits on knowing God fully. God is incomprehensible and cannot be fully known by our finite minds. The same condition affects our judgments and decisions as leaders. We will never have all the data and all the knowledge that God has when we make decisions.[7]

A big reason why some err in decision-making is because they grew up in homes or prepared for ministry with bad examples of how to make decisions. Another reason is because they think that decisions should be made and followed as if they were a military outfit or a corporation. The higher rank is always the higher rank. The army doesn't believe that a general should follow the orders of a major. Corporations don't tell their vice-presidents to submit to shift managers. However, there are times when a pastor will submit to the godly wisdom of a janitor. If the autocratic approach is all one knows, that person may end up as either a benevolent dictator or a schizophrenic one.

One more dynamic in ecclesiastical decision-making often results in bad decisions. Humans are creatures of the pendulum. Although it may be

6. McCune, *A Systematic Theology,* 1:29.
7. Ibid.

subconscious, people have the tendency to go to one extreme or the other. Pastors, deacons and congregations may either make decisions based on the idealist end of reality, or on the opposite extreme, they may make decisions based on the pragmatic side. The idea that ministries must choose between that which is effective or that which is right is a fallacy. It is very possible, and preferable, to pursue that which is both effective and right.

The context of a decision is almost always fluid, not static. A decision may be right initially, but as time goes on, circumstances or the environment change and the initial decision becomes obsolete. The United States government announced that it will no longer use the five color alert system to notify the public of increased or decreased terrorist threats. Initially, in the aftermath of 9/11, the system made sense. Now, a decade later, the government believes that the context of the decision has changed to such a degree that the system needs to be replaced. Church leaders sometimes have difficulty letting go of decisions that were important years or months ago, but have lost their relevancy in the meantime. Instead of being committed to the decision, a wise leader will be able to say that the decision is no longer the right one because the context has changed.

Some leaders don't give decisions the weight of importance that they deserve, or they may overestimate the importance of those decisions. They must ask themselves, "What is the life-span of this decision? Is it for the long term, or is it with a short-term goal in mind?" If we are not clear on those aspects of a decision, wide-spread confusion will result.

COMMON FAILURES

Decision-making in a church is like a Swiss watch, with hundreds of small moving pieces all rotating at the same time but in different directions. It may be that a decision is not the wrong one per se, but because one part of the process was out of order, the decision was wrong as a result. There is literally no way to catalog all the process failures that could occur within a decision-making process in a local New Testament church. Some, though, are common:

1. The failure of the pastor's priorities: Thom Ranier, president and CEO of *LifeWay Christian Resources,* made a pointed statement of what he would do differently with his own priority as a pastor if he could go back nearly four decades in ministry and do it all over again. With refreshing candor, Rainer admitted that he would "spend more time in

the Word and prayer," "give the family more time," "spend more time sharing my faith," "love the community where I lived more," "lead the church to focus more on the nations," "focus less on critics," and finally, "accept the reality that I can't be omnipresent."[8]

When the list is unbalanced, two major parties are guilty. First, the pastor has to take responsibility because God has given it to him by way of gifts of the body and by delegation, especially to other leaders. This is a difficult concept for some. Delegation may open the leader to being misunderstood or misused, but there really is no other choice. Ministry is tough and those that lead in ministry must be tough-minded, while still being tender-hearted. In most North American congregations, the senior pastor is the major decision-maker because of time and training. His decisions most often make the largest impact on a congregation. When his priorities are not in line with heaven's wisdom, the entire congregation suffers. Second, congregations that expect the pastor to live on a shoe-string salary and spend all of his work time and spare time at the church office need to readjust their priorities lest they share in the accountability for the failure of the ministry.

2. The failure of picking up an illegitimate offense because of differences: This category might also be called "the failure of correctly giving and receiving of an appeal." In many instances, when believers leave their church and transfer to another, it is because they have sinfully responded to a difference of opinion with the leadership and/or the congregation they are leaving. Should you really leave the church because you were asked to sing your song with another brother or sister who could accompany you with his musical gifts? Should you really leave because you can't get along with one family in the church? Should you really leave the church because your daughter was confronted about sinful attitudes? Of course congregations can always improve in the area of Matthew 18, but the church is a family, and as such deserves the respect and love of its members.

3. The failure of being paralyzed by fear: Theodore Roosevelt once noted, *"Far better it is to dare mighty things, to win glorious triumphs even though checkered by failure, than to rank with those poor spirits who neither enjoy nor suffer much because they live in the grey twilight*

8. Rainer, *Seven Ministry Mistakes.*

that knows neither victory nor defeat."[9] Fear is a common reason for failure in decision-making. We can't make the decision we need to in a timely manner because of the paralysis of fear. When this happens, Roosevelt's vision of fearless leadership evaporates from the church. 2 Timothy 1:7 addresses this issue—*"For God has not given us a spirit of timidity, but of power and love and discipline."*

While it is true that the general word for 'fear' (φοβος) is not used in 2 Timothy 1:7, the word that is used essentially means 'cowardice' (δειλιας). Paul is challenging Timothy not to be timid in the face of the real dangers of doing gospel work. The point to Timothy should be the same as to us: that kind of fear doesn't come from God and it most certainly does not help with decision-making. Olan Hendrix says that "to make decisions involves risk."[10] He also notes,

> *"If you are in a place of leadership you have to make decisions. Hesitancy in deciding will breed demoralization and frustration among your subordinates. The longer it takes a person to get a decision from you, the more encumbered he or she is, and the more you are saying, 'Your time and activities are of minimal importance.'"*[11]

Go back to the verse. Is there anything here to indicate that we are God-prepared to make wise decisions? Notice at the end where Timothy is told by Paul that God has equipped him with 'a sound mind.' Why would God's servant need a sound mind? In order to execute decision-making with wisdom. We are not to rely primarily on our own thinking for decisions. Solomon states it this way, *"Trust in the Lord with all your heart and do not lean on your own understanding. In all your ways acknowledge Him and He will make your paths straight."* (Proverbs 3:5–6). Abraham, in Genesis 24, is a good example of this. After being directed to Isaac's future wife, the servant's testimony is powerful. In the King James Version, it reads, *"I being in the way, the Lord led me."* The servant of Abraham was led to the right decision through a process. The same will happen to leaders today who are not controlled by fear that makes them unable to follow God through a process of fluid decision-making.

9. Roosevelt, *The Strenuous Life.*
10. Hendrix, *Management for Christian Leaders,* 104.
11. Ibid.

4. The failure of mishandling of the data: Two of the biggest blunders in modern military history were the invasion of Russia by Napoleon Bonaparte and his 'Grand Armee' in 1812 and then, a century later by Hitler and his much-feared 'Wermacht.'[12] On both occasions, leadership failed to take in all of the necessary data for a successful military campaign. What made Germany's failure even more noteworthy was that history had already demonstrated the futility of invading Russia in the winter.

Another example of data-fumbling would be the ignoring of data. On the other end of the spectrum, you can make too much of the data. You can misinterpret the data. The Scriptures teach that there is wisdom in counting the cost before launching into a decision or project that will impact those on both the working end and the receiving end. Specifically, in Luke 14:28, Jesus made use of the typical response to building a tower. In Bible times, a tower would be built near a home or in a field for protection. Prior to building such a tower, the owner would have to dig the needed footings and would have to make sure that money and supplies were sufficient for the entire project. Jesus said that wisdom dictates that one consider the cost of a project before launching into the task. He used this as an analogy for counting the cost of discipleship.

Many congregations fail to consider the data before making a decision, thinking that the exercise violates the spirit of Proverbs 3:5–6. However, God never intended for us to ignore what resources we have. The difference, at the end of the day, is whether we've trusted the resources or the God of the resources. Can God give us more resources later? Yes, but has he already given us more than we need right now? No. Wisdom says, "We have a finite amount of resources, we can exercise stewardship over this amount. If the Lord provides more later, hallelujah. Until then, we will be responsible for what we do have." There is a difference between biblical faith and blind faith. A biblical response to faith is consistent with review. In every aspect of church life, regardless of teaching, leading, building or even planning, we are encouraged in 1 Thessalonians 5:21 to "examine everything carefully." John MacArthur, in his work "Reckless Faith," says this:

12. Whitelaw, *History's Biggest Blunders: And The People Who Made Them*, 102, 149–53.

The Greek text is by no means complex. The word "carefully" has been added by the translators to make the sense clear. If we translate the phrase literally, we find it simply says, "Examine everything." But the idea conveyed by our word carefully is included in the Greek word translated "examine," dokimazo. . .Elsewhere it is translated, "analyze," "test," or "prove." It refers to the process of testing something to see that it is genuine, to distinguish between the true and the false. . .In other words, he wants us to examine everything critically.[13]

To make a decision about a certain doctrinal or practical church matter and then to refuse a careful examination of that decision in the name of faith violates the biblical concept of discernment and faith. Any time leaders refuse to demonstrate the reasonableness of a decision consistent with data is a sure sign that decision-makers have misunderstood what biblical faith looks like in the day-by-day operation of the ministry.

5. The failure of favoritism: There are some forms of favoritism that are healthy and natural. A pastor's child running into the pastor's office, jumping into his lap and reaching into his candy dish is an appropriate form of favoritism. There is almost nothing in ministry, though, that undermines one's credibility and effectiveness like being guilty of favoritism or nepotism. There are situations where a father brings a son onto the ministry staff of a specific organization even though the son was not the best qualified candidate, and the organization knew it. Sometimes leaders level discipline against wayward children in the church, but ignore or even actively block the same type of accountability for their own children. A pastor may allow his wife to be an unofficial assistant pastor, controlling things behind the scenes. These covert or overt acts of nepotism are ministry killers.

6. The failure of sharing too much information: A pastor should understand the sacred trust between himself and congregants that share deep and personal pain or failure. Only if the law requires it or if a Matthew 18 church discipline process requires the sharing of information should a pastor share what's been told to him in confidence. Some pastors, immediately upon hearing the dirt of another believer's struggle, feel the right and necessity of sharing the items with people who have no business knowing. Furthermore, when a leader or a group of leaders makes a decision in connection with a discipleship or

13. MacArthur, *Reckless Faith,* 69–73.

discipline issue, that information must remain private. Galatians 6:1 says that those who are spiritual or mature should be involved in the rescuing of other believers who struggle. That means that information needs to stay with those mature believers who are individually responsible for the spiritual rescue of errant brothers. When leaders are careless about the protection of that information, great damage to the body of Christ occurs, undermining the advance of discipleship that should be the desire of all believers.

7. The failure of not sharing enough information: Information that relates to personal matters is to be kept as private as possible. Information that relates to corporate matters is just the opposite. Calendar items, ministry activities, the ministry philosophy, future building plans, present ministry issues such as financial challenges or staffing issues need to be widely disseminated. Hans Finzel wrote a book entitled, "Top Ten Mistakes Leaders Make." In the chapter entitled, "Communication Chaos," Hans introduces his discussion on the role of communication with four points of consideration: (a) Never assume that anyone knows anything. (b) The bigger the group, the more attention must be given to communication. (c) When left in the dark, people tend to dream up wild rumors. (d) Communication must be the passionate obsession of effective leadership.[14] Hans shares in this chapter why he had to change his approach to decision-making. He recalls how, in the early days of his ministry, when the staff was very small, the group could make an informed decision together on a coffee break or while jogging together in the woods outside of Vienna. Once the group grew to beyond sixty, 'hallway decision-making' was no longer effective. As the group gets larger, communication has to be a priority.

8. The failure of being unclear on vision and mission: When we are not clear as to our vision and mission, we will not be clear on which decisions are the ones we need to make. When this happens, we begin to sacrifice the future with decisions we make today because we have no sense of where we want to go in the future. At the same time, we sacrifice today with decisions we think we might make tomorrow because we have no clear vision of what we're doing other than simply maintaining what we've always done. A good review and exercise is to read through the ministry vision, mission, objectives and goals

14. Finzel, *The Top Ten Mistakes Leaders Make,* 129.

periodically. Do they represent the present heartbeat of God for your ministry? Are the leaders and the congregation on board with the strategic picture? The acid test is whether the average church attendee in the congregation can vocalize the same vision and mission in their own words to match the understanding of the person sitting next to them.

9. The failure of being too many things to too many people: Most in ministry have a heart for people. That is a mixed bag of blessing and curse. The positive part is that those in ministry will reach out through sacrifice for the sake of ministry and healing. The negative part is that they can actually be taken over by ecclesiastical pragmatics. In the 1990's the push was to be all things to unchurched people. The two well-known pastors behind the market-driven, or what is sometimes called the church growth model were Rick Warren (Saddleback Community Church of Mission Viejo, CA) and Bill Hybles (Willow Creek Community Church of South Barrington, IL). A third leader, George Barna, rounds out what might be called the 'trinity of church growth gurus.'[15]

The essential thought behind this approach is this: the church should be formed in such a way as to culturally attract the lost so that they can hear the gospel and make a decision for Christ. On the surface, such a strategy sounds redeeming, if not redemptive. The central problem is that it's rather impossible to shape a congregation to make a non-believer who is in rebellion against God comfortable enough to worship his Maker in such a way as to bring glory to Jesus and edification to the heart of the believer, who is sitting in the same service. Those things that please God and the God-fearer are not going to please the God-hater. The Scriptures make it clear that when there is a doxological approach to ministry that aims to bring glory to God, there will still be occasional tares mixed in with the wheat. In the marketing approach to ministry, we have the opposite composition, namely a few wheat sheaves mixed in with the tares. One of the many results of all of this is a total neglect of a real local church membership and what that means Biblically if not practically.[16]

Invite the lost, of course. Love the lost, without a doubt. Share the gospel with the lost, absolutely. Organize your church to make the

---

15. Barna, *A Step-by-Step Guide to Church Marketing*, 13.
16. Leeman, *The Church and the Surprising Offense of God's Love*, 31–32.

lost feel comfortable? The ultimate way that God is glorified in the local assembly is through the corporate worship of him in spirit and in truth.[17] Non-believers cannot worship God in spirit and in truth. They can hear the gospel, but they cannot share in its ministry because they have not been redeemed and indwelt and gifted for the purpose of mutual ministry. Only believers have been gifted for New Testament ministry. The local church primarily glorifies God by the corporate worship, biblical discipleship and then mutual ministry of born-again believers. It is not wrong to have an aggressive approach to sharing the gospel, but building the church around the central focus of watering the gospel down in the name of cultural relevance so it's palatable to those who hate God is in fact damaging to the gospel itself. With very few exceptions, the congregation that chooses to keep the Bible-preaching at such a level so as not to repel the non-believer simply is not going to be able to feed the believer to the level that he needs. This is what the cults, Catholics, and postmodern-evangelicals who peddle their sports stadium feel-good sermons, masquerading as essential biblical teaching do. Gathering a large crowd is hardly the same as the Holy Spirit's creating a real church with real disciples and a real church life.

If the main focus of the congregation is to build the ministry around the culture, wishes, or likes of the non-believer, the congregation will make decisions differently than the ministry whose primary focus is the building up of the saints in their most holy faith.

10. The failure of being a weak and careless administrative steward of the congregation: The most important task of a pastor/elder/bishop is to be a shepherd. A second function that is close, if not equal in importance is the giving of consistent strong leadership that engenders trust and gratitude in the hearts of the parishioners. This is Moses-type leadership.

When delegating ministry to others in the church, leaders must be aware of some common stewardship failures:

a) Giving too much authority to those who have not proven themselves to be loyal to the direction and philosophy of the ministry.

b) Not dealing quickly with unfair expectations from disgruntled leaders and church members.

17. MacArthur, *Worship*, 10.

c) Not dealing quickly with leaders and church members guilty of gossip and undermining ministry leadership within the church.

d) Giving leadership authority to those who are not officially leaders in the church.

e) Giving leadership responsibility to individuals only because they have experience.

f) Giving leadership responsibility to individuals based on friendship.

g) Misreading honest questions from or sincere hurts of parishioners and turning those back on them as if church leadership is being attacked.

h) Ignoring talented believers and their gifts, experience and ability and over-using paid staff while under-using volunteer staff, in part because of past situations.

i) Becoming apathetic on how decisions negatively impact the ministry of volunteer lay leadership in the congregation.

j) Assuming that gracious leadership is the same as soft leadership.

k) Moving too quickly after internal disruption of a congregation. Church leadership needs to understand that after a disruption, they will need to do some "post-hurricane" cleanup before moving on.

Typically, God wants his leadership to stay, not run. A recent study suggests that when a pastor leaves a church because of opposition, it is usually because of eight disgruntled church members.[18] Rather than the pastor leaving, a better course of action might be to warn each of the eight, individually and collectively, to stop causing division or find another congregation. Frequently, a congregation isn't able to move past a controversy because of the eight theoretical members. The congregation needs someone of strong character to pick up the pieces and clean up the mess. Sometimes, though, the leader needs to move on because a congregation doesn't know how to be loyal to God's leadership. And occasionally the eight theoretical members are legitimately wounded and hurting and the pastor needs to repent and

18. McDonald, *Vertical Church Seminar.*

change or move on to a congregation that has a philosophy closer to what he believes.

In moving forward, be patient. It may take a while for the remnants of the disgruntled congregants to have either their attitudes or their membership changed. One pastor whose congregation went through a tough time told his church that a certain Sunday was "Stay-or-Go Sunday." Those that had issues and weren't really committed could move on with no questions asked. Those that stayed after that Sunday were assumed to be committed to the progress of the work.

It's usually best to forgive those who have left. They may have left behind a feeling of betrayal, but it is death for a leader to allow the failures and disloyalties of past parishioners to choke out his joy in the presence of the Lord. A congregation can have nothing worse than a leader who is full of bitterness because of past hurt relationships. Some families become a blessing just by leaving and taking their negative attitudes with them. Other families may be a blessing overall, but have a different philosophy of ministry and so feel the need to move on. Finally, there are families who leave for petty or irresponsible reasons, who should have stayed. Rather than angst on the part of the pastor, he should demonstrate the attitude of the father of the prodigal son, praying for reconciliation, and then hugging their necks and embracing them in full forgiveness when the reconciliation happens.

It is useless to spend time defending yourself. If you must defend yourself for the sake of the ministry, spend the least amount of time focused on yourself and the majority of your time and energy focused on the Lord's work and ministry. In the end, it is your character that will defend or condemn you. God's people will trust what they see, not what they hear or are told. Simply respond to critics by reminding them of Paul's admonition in 1Timothy 5:19, "*Do not receive an accusation against an elder except on the basis of two or three witnesses.*" If there are not two or three witnesses who have all seen or observed the failure in question, the combined leadership of the church must confront the accuser and defend the elder. If the accuser doesn't drop the accusation, he is now open to Matthew 18 for due process of church discipline.

At times it may be appropriate to confront any pockets of resistance or angst. Before doing so, there must be cohesion at the leadership level. There are three options open to the dissenters:

A. If they agree with the church leadership enough to stay, but not enough to serve, let them step down from any leadership positions with the understanding that by staying, they will not undermine those who lead.

B. They may agree with the leadership enough to stay and continue serving.

C. If the disagreement is sufficient enough to concern the leadership (i.e., if the presence of the individual in question threatens the unity of the congregation), the leaders would be within their rights to ask the family in question to move on to another fellowship. In doing so, they must make sure that the leaving family understands that they take with them the love and appreciation of the former congregation for past service, and for leaving the congregation with integrity and love. Paul and Barnabas agreed to disagree, and sometimes good people must do the same in order to protect the unity and cohesion of a congregation's ministry and vision.

A leader can't be so proud in his leadership that he won't admit that he has failed in some degree. In admitting to the rest of the leadership team (and sometimes to the entire ministry) that he missed a significant call, he begins the healing necessary to keep the ministry afloat, especially when the failed decision deeply wounded the ministry. The best apologies include not only an admission of failure, but also lessons that were learned from the failure and steps that are being taken to avoid the same pitfalls in the future. Some leaders shy away from these kinds of public expressions because they fear that such move will be interpreted as weakness on their part. In reality, these expressions actually communicate the opposite—biblical leadership.

When bad decision-making causes corporate discouragement, the key to a reversal in the spirit of the congregation is to have a group of committed leaders stand shoulder-to-shoulder with the point leader, determined to be faithful and committed to the emotional and organizational healing of the congregation.

A congregation will heal most quickly when it focuses on its outward ministry. If the congregation is fixated on their inward issues, they will remain discouraged. Gathering the energy, focus and direction of God's people back to the mission will stimulate the excitement needed to reach the lost and to minister in outreach to other brothers and sisters.

If those who have left the congregation become abusive and subversive, they may need to be officially contacted and warned by the leadership of the congregation. If that is not effective, the leadership may call an official, special meeting to "mark those who are causing division" (Romans 16:17). Those individuals have become wolves, and as such should be avoided in the area of Christian fellowship. They are not to be hated, but to be loved primarily through prayer. If they contact the leadership, they should be reminded and encouraged to respond rightly instead of sowing seeds of discontent.

11. The failure of fighting the wrong battle: Not every hill is worth dying for. A ministry leader is simply not going to be able to do everything that he wants to do, when he wants to do it. Jesus frequently commended the ability to be careful in one's dealings. Sometimes a leader must accept the fact that he can't accomplish more than a small percentage of what he wants to do. But if he is patient and careful, he can steer his congregational 'ship' through a sea of icebergs and the congregants will follow him because they know that he is not acting without thinking, but is deliberate in his course. One of the common failures among ministry leaders is that they don't count the cost before making a particular decision. Their pride pushes them into an all-or-nothing attitude about a decision that really isn't critical. With patience, listening and mutual respect, a compromise can usually be worked out. If the leader makes every decision a hill to die on, eventually he will die on some hill. And after his 'funeral,' the ministry will do what they wanted to do anyway. But if the leader will patiently preach and teach biblical principles, other leaders will come to the right conclusion and in God's time the change will be made.

Turning back to the annals of armed conflict, in February of 1836, Santa Ana, the Napoleon of the West, decided to force his will against a small and determined band of fort defenders at a small obscure adobe mission in the middle of the Texas prairie.[19] Primarily because of the general's pride, the entire Mexican army spent valuable days attacking this little outpost with its courageous small group of defenders, including Davy Crockett. No doubt some low-ranking Mexican soldier probably grumbled about why they couldn't just bypass that

19. Whitelaw, *History's Biggest Blunder: And The People Who Made Them,* 112–16.

pesky little outpost. The delay because of battle gave Sam Houston and the army of Texas time to gather their forces and eventually catch an overconfident Santa Ana at the Battle of San Jacinto. While the Mexican leader won the battle of the Alamo, it was the wrong fight, which resulted in him losing not only the war, but he also lost Texas. A common failure among church leaders is that they fight the wrong battles.[20]

IT'S RARELY TOO LATE

Leaders will often say when they are emotionally tired, "it's too late!" but that is usually not even close to the truth. Many leaders just need to stand up privately before God and publically before their congregations and admit that they've made a mistake. This will be an almost instant act of credibility, and will in many cases have an immediate calming effect on his ministry. The congregation needs to know that their leader is human and can make mistakes. They will show an outpouring of love and understanding that will heal the hearts and hurts of believers who love their pastor but who have been discouraged by the shortcomings or oversights of a good leader. Many pastors won't admit failure or normalcy to the congregation for fear that the congregation has an unhealthy or unfair expectation of their leader and his ministry. On the other hand, if there are unfair expectations, the leader has to be able to say to other leaders or to the congregation that the expectations are irresponsible.

When the FAA investigates a plane crash, they frequently find that a string of bad decisions ultimately led to the crash and loss of life. In the area of ministry, even if the leaders have made one or two bad decisions in a specific area, it's almost always possible to break the pattern before the ministry crashes. A cruise ship doesn't sail from New York harbor to a port in Europe without a number of course corrections. Likewise, a ministry must make corrections in its course over time to avoid sinking. And even if the ship of ministry sinks, it doesn't follow that loss of life (spiritual) necessarily must ensue.

One more thing that the FAA usually finds is a glitch in the management of the flight. Management of the local church belongs especially to the bishops (overseers) of the church. It also applies to the function of deacon.

20. Ibid.

LIGHTEN UP

Church leaders who can't laugh at themselves are boring. Leaders who can't enjoy life are dangerous. Ronald Reagan was a favorite of many people. He exhibited a confidence in God, himself and his team. That confidence was most evident when he would use self-effacing humor. Not long after the assassination attempt by John Hinckley, Reagan said, "Honey, I forgot to duck." To the surgeons he quipped, "I hope you're all Republicans." While humor is important, it doesn't change the fact that God's work is serious business. It demands the best that we can give. At the end of the day, God will accomplish his purpose. Someone said, "If you take yourself too seriously, no one else will." Enjoy the journey and learn to laugh at your mistakes and shortcomings. No one is perfect; most have had to learn that the hard way once or twice.

A Spirit-controlled man of God will not lose control in the midst of a bad decision. It's embarrassing to all involved when members or leaders lose control over a difference of opinion they might have with a decision the leadership or a leader has made.[21] A calming voice in the midst of a calamity can help defuse the tension in the air. Conversely, a volatile response makes everything worse. If it was a bad decision, the best response is to patiently and lovingly point that out. It may take time before the other decision-makers in question will understand that. However, a patient attitude will help others to see that the decision in question was bad. But a rude and imbalanced attitude will so dominate the conversation that logic will be lost.

RESPONDING TO CHURCH MEMBERS WHO GO AWOL

What should a leader's response be when families, for very petty or self-centered reasons (in the opinion of the leaders), leave the congregation? The best thing to say to them is, "I don't think this is the right decision, but we love you in the Lord. If at some point in time you find that perhaps you shouldn't have left, please know that you're welcome to come back." Sometimes it takes an unbiblical exit to reveal the poison that was being spread from them to other believers. Although the exit may be hard at first, it may be better in the long run for the health of the body of believers.

21. Lutzer, *Managing Your Emotions*, 92–103.

When Paul and Barnabas split, the Lord used the presence of two ministry teams for the sake of the Gospel and the early church. Sometimes, the differences and expectations of disgruntled members toward the leaders were so great that their departure was inevitable. Sometimes, believers need to be disciplined because of an unbiblical attitude during an unbiblical exit. Congregations must exercise caution when accepting members from other congregations. They should investigate the cause of the exit and how the other congregation dealt with it. Church discipline must honor the spirit and teaching of passages such as Matthew 18. Sometimes, Scripture will have the new congregation siding with the incoming wounded member, but most often the previous congregation was in the right and the leaving church member departed for unbiblical reasons and with an unbiblical spirit.

GOD'S PURPOSES FOR OUR FAILURES

God allows us to fail for a reason. Imagine how self-sufficient we would tend to be if we rarely failed at decision-making. In allowing us to fail, God shapes us in humility and purpose. Not only do we benefit from mistakes in decision-making, but if others are teachable and open, they too can gain benefit from our failures. As leaders, we must all do something that is unsavory for us. That is, we need to take the particular failure out of the closet or wherever it is buried and dust it off and look at it squarely and in all honesty. We need to do a postmortem on the failure. That is painful; we would rather pretend it doesn't exist or didn't happen. That approach will simply lead to its twin, and we don't want to meet its twin. Once is enough. We really need to look at the failure in question closely to see what we can learn from it. The decision may have been based on sound thinking. It may be that the decision was right technically-speaking, but the timing or execution was off. A valuable lesson can be learned when we open ourselves up to admit failure and communicate a willingness to learn and improve. If you are a leader and you've made a failure in decision-making, God's desire for you is to not quit. Proverbs 24:16 says, *"For a righteous man falls seven times, and rises again, But the wicked stumble in time of calamity.* A characteristic of righteous leadership is that even when there is failure, there should be a resolute determination to get up and do it right.

The majority of this chapter has looked at responding to bad decisions that we personally or corporately make. This only covers part of the story. Sometimes we not only have to recover from bad decisions that we ourselves make, but we also have to respond to the bad decisions that others make. How should we respond to another believer or leader, who is connected to us by way of ministry, when they make a bad decision?

The first responsibility that we have is to make sure that we fully understand what was done. When leaders respond to the decisions of others, they don't always have all of the needed information. They are tempted to respond to what they see, which is frequently only a part of the whole story. The second issue of concern that should guide us is a commitment to assuming the best. Third, there needs to be a baseline of compassion. Is there more going on than meets the eye? Individuals that have made a bad decision may be frustrated or confused. They may feel compelled to make some kind of change or some kind of decision.

Fourth, after a failure, the co-leaders need to be challenged to do better. Real leadership does not turn a blind eye to the failures of friends to whom they are ministering. Confrontation is difficult. Moses, in Exodus 32:21–24, confronted and rebuked his brother Aaron for failed leadership in giving in to the peoples' idolatry while Moses was on the mountain receiving the Ten Commandments from God. At the other end of the leadership spectrum was Eli, shown in 1Samuel 2. God was angry toward Eli because of his sons, who were violating the women of Israel in the sacred place of worship while Eli did nothing to stop it. The result was the deaths of Eli, his sons and the loss of the Ark of the Covenant to the enemies of Israel. What are the implications for today's church leaders? Real leaders confront co-leaders even when they may be close friends in the ministry. Encouragement of co-leaders, especially those who have failed at some kind of decision, is important. They need to understand ramifications of their poor decisions, deal with them and move on.

Proverbs 14:16 says that a righteous man will fall, but he doesn't stay down. He rises up to accomplish the task that has been laid at his feet. Failure only becomes permanent when we cement that failure with a refusal to move on in faith. Consider one final thought from Mark Noll reflecting on decision-making failures of the church over the centuries, ". . .*where in retrospect it appears that Christians have blundered badly in their decisions, the Lord of the church has not abandoned them to their folly but, despite their misbegotten efforts, has remained to sustain his own.*"[22]

22. Noll, *Turning Points*, 8.

9

Conclusion

The Decision-Making Process in A Local New Testament Church

KEY CHAPTER PRINCIPLE:

Because executing decision-making is as important in the body of Christ as making the right decisions, congregations must be careful to match their own approach to decision-making to that which is found in the teachings of the Scriptures.

To recap the information presented so far in this book, we've examined the scriptural data regarding decision-making in the early church and how it applies to today's congregations. We've answered the question of *what* decision-making in the church is, along with *who* should make what types of decisions. Now we'll look at *how* those decisions should be made in order to honor the spirit and text of God's Word.

Does God really care about how decision-making happens in His church? Acts 15, speaking of the Jerusalem council, demonstrates that yes, God cares not just about the decisions that are made, but he cares about how those decisions are made. The entire chapter presents principles of decision-making in the church, illustrating the importance of having clarity and honesty between different points of view. Discussions over points of doctrinal decision were spearheaded by strong leaders who stayed connected with the multitude of believers in Jerusalem. They took time to make the correct decisions. They prayed. One congregation sought guidance and help from another congregation during their time of crisis. In verses 13–18, James, first among equals in the church at Jerusalem, took charge and led the conversation to the conclusion that was warranted by God's Word and Spirit.[1]

Psalm 37:23 states, "*The steps of a man are established by the Lord, And He delights in his way.*" God wants us to be careful and purposeful on how we implement decision-making steps as a spiritual body. No matter who a local church determines is responsible for the decision, Scripture indicates by way of command and example how decision-making should proceed. Those involved must commit to several principles and procedures.

Some decisions in the church ultimately belong to one person. Other decisions will belong to a group of believers. Some of the following principles may apply better to one than the other.

1) FIVE LAWS OF DIRECTION

God has a pattern in communicating his will for his children. This was true in the Old Testament with his nation Israel, and it is true today with the church of Jesus. While corporate decision-making is often more complex than individual decision-making, the same five laws of direction apply.

A) Law of the Word

The Psalmist wrote, "*Your Word is a lamp to my feet and a light to my path.*" (Psalm 119:105). When individual believers seek out God's direction for their life, they must start off with the only inspired and complete source of revelation that the believer has, the Scriptures. God's Word is the source of sanctification and growth in Christ (John 17:17). God's Word is sufficient but is not alone when God's people make decisions. Some will preach that God's Word is sufficient but then will ignore the elements of prayer; seeking God's opening; heeding the wisdom of others. Sometimes they will

---

1. Harrison, *Interpreting Acts*, 241–55.

minimize the issue of God's peace by way of the Holy Spirit. This would be a gross misunderstanding of the sufficiency of Scripture.

B) Law of Prayer

In James 1:5, James, says, *"But if any of you lacks wisdom, let him ask of God, who gives to all generously and without reproach, and it will be given to him."* At the crucial time of decision-making. God's children should give themselves over to seasons of prayer and fasting. God's plans are eternal. Prayer does change things, but mostly it changes the one doing the praying. Decision-making requires a clear mind and receptive spirit, and when this doesn't happen, the attitude may be one of the decision-maker thinking he knows best. If important decisions are made hastily without prayer, the results could be tragic. It shows a spirit of pride instead of humility, and indicates a dangerous view of our own abilities. David demonstrated the combination of prayer and the Word in Psalm 119:136, *"Direct my footsteps according your Word" (NIV).* Elsewhere, the psalmist cries out to God, *"Make me know your ways, O LORD: teach me Your paths"* (Psalm 25:4).

C) Law of the Open Door

Pastor Gary Davis who serves with us at Southeast Valley Baptist Church has a saying: "If you have to kick a door in, it's probably not God's will!" God opens doors for his children. Revelation 3:8 says, *"'I know your deeds. Behold, I have put before you an open door which no one can shut, because you have a little power, and have kept My word, and have not denied My name."* This is a powerful verse. The promise, while specific to the church of Philadelphia (one of the congregations in Asia Minor), can be applied to decision-making by both individuals and churches. God opens and closes doors of opportunities. Paul's scheduling decisions during his missionary trip to Ephesus were affected because of God opening a door of opportunity for him. However, 1 Corinthians 16:9 shows that just because God opened a door for him, there was still opposition. Just because some oppose a decision doesn't necessarily make it the wrong decision.

D) Law of Wisdom of Others

Some people think that they don't need outside wisdom. This may be due to an incomplete view of themselves, others or even God, and they rush into a decision without taking the time to listen to the wisdom and experiences of others. Scripture says, *"The way of a fool is right in his own eyes, But a wise man is he who listens to counsel."* (Proverbs 12:15); *"Without consultation, plans are frustrated, But with many counselors they succeed"* (Proverbs 15:22; *"Listen to counsel and accept discipline, that you may be wise the rest of your days"* (Proverbs 19:20). God never intended us to charge into decision-making armed only with our own experiences and viewpoint. A leader who does not listen to the wisdom of others is foolish and shows that he is not a true leader.

E) Law of the Peace of the Spirit

Many independent non-Pentecostal churches have overreacted against what they see as a misunderstanding of the role of the Holy Spirit in general, and in decision-making in particular. The result is an almost wholesale rejection of the legitimate role of the Holy Spirit and his sometimes subjective work in decision-making. Jesus said, *"I will send you a comforter."* That means that part of the Holy Spirit's purpose is to give the individual believer a sense of comfort. Colossians 3:15 says that the peace of Christ is to rule the believer's heart. Philippians 4:7 says that in any circumstance where we find ourselves praying, God's response will be to give us peace. Although feelings can be misleading, the Holy Spirit's subjective peace is nonetheless a biblical teaching. After a believer has considered the Bible's teaching on a matter, followed by a time of prayer, engaging wise counselors and waiting for God's opening of the door of opportunity, the end of the process will be the sense that God is blessing a specific decision. To suggest otherwise is to hold an incomplete view of decision-making. Those who do this may need to consider the direct challenge of the Apostle Paul in Galatians 3:3–4: *"Are you so foolish? Having begun by the Spirit, are you now being perfected by the flesh? Did you suffer so many things in vain—if indeed it was in vain?*

This is not defending a kind of spiritual mysticism that by-passes the spiritual disciplines of study, prayer and meditation. A dear mentor of mine used to say, "anything that bi-passes the mind is dangerous." No doubt that is true. However this is a subjective sense of peace that comes as a result of the objective Word of God. Arguments against the subjective work of the Spirit of God don't hold up against the normative teaching of the New Testament and its universal application for all believers in the age of grace. This view is largely an overreaction against the Pentecostal and the neo-Pentecostal movements.

2) A CORPORATE AND INDIVIDUAL COMMITMENT TO THE MISSION AND VISION OF THE CHURCH

Understanding and accepting the mission and vision of a congregation is not just an exercise in philosophical futility. Leaders are challenged in finding ways to keep the mission and vision of the church fresh before the congregation. Kennon L. Callahan, in his book, *"Twelve Keys to an Effective Church,"* makes the following observation:

> *The decision-making process is solid when the decisions demonstrate wisdom, a sense of priorities and character. First, the most effective decision-making process is one that contributes to the development of wise decisions and thoughtful directions for the life and mission of a congregation.*[2]

He continues with three different occasions when churches make poor decisions, including decisions that are faddish, immature or stupid:

> *Sometimes a congregation develops decisions that are simply fad-dish—that is, they reflect some popular fad among churches across the country. Sometimes churches develop decisions that are im-mature—that is, decisions that are hastily reached on the spur of the moment and reflect an adolescent rather than an adult sense of judgment and discernment. Sometimes churches develop decisions that are simply stupid—that is, the decisions reflect neither wisdom nor common sense. Frequently, such decisions are made because someone has sold that church a 'bill of goods.'*[3]

When a congregation or leadership has clarity on the overall purpose and goals of their ministry, the decision-making becomes more precise. A lack of purpose results in decisions that devolve from a corporate analysis to an individual one, thus leading to a lack of unity. Leaders begin to focus

---

2. Callahan, *Twelve Keys to an Effective Church,* 55.
3. Ibid., 55.

on their own beliefs and values as opposed to those of the church. Polity intersects directly with decision-making in this instance.

— The leader's vision vs. our vision

When a single leader is dictating the vision and mission, the process is easy. What does the boss believe about this? The Episcopalian model (which may also be used in a sacramental church or even a Baptist church) demands that the leader's ways are the ways of the congregation. A different model, where a group of leaders—or the congregation as a whole—are invited to be part of the mission- and vision-making process shows that the congregation will recognize that this is a corporate representation of who they are and where they are headed. Glenn Daman says,

> "*The body of Christ needs to make wise decisions regarding its priorities, programs and resources. Without a clear vision of ministry, the church will not have a clear basis for making those decisions. Vision enables the church to distinguish between what's good and bad for the organization and what is worthwhile to achieve. In light of all the unlimited options and needs confronting the church, without a vision, making decisions becomes a matter of personal preference rather than wise judgment.*"[4]

One of the potential sources of disagreement in decision-making is found in the mission or vision of the church. Each Bible-believing congregation, while believing in the authority of Scripture, will probably have a different emphasis on their mission. Some congregations place heavy emphasis on teaching; others have as their hub an aggressive outreach or missions focus. A third may organize itself into a church-wide small group system, emphasizing the importance of edification. Which is right? In the final analysis, they all may be. Just as there is acceptable variety between leaders, there is also acceptable variety between churches. If one congregation's major focus is on preaching or teaching, their budget decisions will be different from the church that is primarily focused on missions. The former church might allocate significant expenditure to the purchase of a pulpit, or to Sunday school equipment and materiel, or even to bringing on extra teaching staff. The latter church might opt to send a percentage of its income to the mission field. The differences in the decisions of these types

---

4. Damon, *Shepherding the Small Church*, 220.

of congregations may be better understood as mission and focus rather than as right or wrong.

3) A CORPORATE AND INDIVIDUAL COMMITMENT TO THE IDEA THAT THE WILL OF CHRIST IS TO BE PREEMINENT IN THE LOCAL CHURCH

Paul is clear in Colossians 1 that Christ is preeminent in the church because of His work of creation and redemption. John warns the readers of 3 John about a church leader by the name of Diotrephes, for "he loves to have the preeminence among them. . ." Every layman, deacon and pastor must be willing to submit his will to the will of God. If and when a believer (no matter his function in a local assembly) is more concerned about his own will than to follow God's, he becomes an idol. This idolatry seems especially criminal when such a one uses his so-called God-given authority as a cloak to set his own agenda without considering God's will and direction. In the *law of prayer*, the opposite attitude is demonstrated when individual leaders as well as groups of leaders fall on their faces before God and ask him for his mercy and guidance.

One important point is that God sometimes desires to choose one option over another. Then there are times when several choices may be legitimate. If the desire is to truly know the heart of God, he will speak through his Word, through wisdom and through circumstances. Those making the decision must strive to make the wise and appropriate choice by remembering that Scriptures give a providential view. Even a poor decision (humanly speaking) can be used by God to move his church toward fulfillment of His plan.[5]

4) A CORPORATE AND INDIVIDUAL COMMITMENT TO THE PROCESS OF CONSENSUS

A majority decision in a congregation, while legitimate, does not diminish the desire for unity and consensus with Christ's body as frequently as possible.[6] Furthermore, the God-ordained idea of plurality of leadership must be allowed to function as illustrated in the New Testament (notice

5. Hayhurst, *How to Interpret History,* 54–74.
6. Richards and Hoeldtke, *Church Leadership,* 307–8.

the Jerusalem council of Acts 15). God's men worked and prayed through a debated spiritual issue until they arrived at what they understood was God's answer and their consensus.

In order for true consensus to be achieved, there must be a commitment to biblical listening. This does not mean approaching a decision with a mind that's already made up, insensitive to the concerns of others, closed to the wisdom that they may be exhibiting. The Lord uses wise counsel to bring attention to aspects of decisions that may have been missed. A 'thumbs-down' on a decision is not a bad thing, because the concern may be valid. When that concern is taken into consideration, the final consensus will be stronger than it was before.

5) A CORPORATE AND INDIVIDUAL COMMITMENT TO A PROCESS OF APPROVAL AND IMPLEMENTATION

Leaders who are action-oriented may have a problem with this principle. They may not be interested in taking the days, weeks, or even months necessary to make a decision through a process of approval. The three stages of a decision are the inception stage, the endorsement stage and the implementation stage.[7] There are seven steps to a good decision-making apparatus:

a) Understand and state the vision or essence of the decision.

b) Understand and state the desired effect of the decision.

c) Communicate with the portion of the leadership that the decision will affect.

d) Allow for consensus and agreement to form.

e) Communicate the decision with the congregation.

f) Implement the decision.

g) Track the effectiveness of the decision.[8]

Why the last step? Because from time to time, even after a prayerfully made decision, later circumstances may show that a better decision might have been made. A deficient decision doesn't mean that it has to be the final decision. This is important because of the common misunderstanding that a decision made in the past negates any new or different information

---

7. Schaller, The Decision-Maker, 43.

8. Ibid.

or circumstances that may occur in the future. Lyle E. Schaller, in his book entitled "The Decision-Makers," tells an all-too familiar story:

> *"'Last fall we voted against going to two worship services on Sunday morning. Therefore the alternative is closed. About the only alternative left for us is to build,' explained a trustee of the Oak Grove Church. He was describing the problem before the congregation. . .(which) had begun to increase in size and. . .(which now) filled up the 'new' building (entirely). . .(the trustee) was arguing that since a proposal to go to two services had been voted down earlier, he believed they should begin to plan an addition to the church building."[9]*

Schaller explained that another leader suggested to the trustee that just because the congregation had voted it down before did not mean that a two-service structure might not be right now (even though it was voted down before). The trustee replied,

> *"'I'm afraid you don't understand,' he said. 'The vote against going to two services was about 19 to 8. That door is closed.'"[10]*

Schaller rightly points out that every year hundreds of churches that at one point in time had voted down a merger, went ahead with the merger at a later time. Hundreds of churches that at one point in time had voted down a relocation subsequently went ahead with a relocation. His point is painfully obvious to everyone except the poor trustee who doesn't understand. We are all fallible! It is very possible that when the vote was taken the year before, the church made the wrong decision. When the vote came in at 19 to 8, just like when Israel decided to side with the ten spies instead of with Joshua and Caleb, once again God's children missed the best choice. A poor choice last year doesn't mean that the congregation has to be stuck with that decision this year.[11]

6) A CORPORATE AND INDIVIDUAL COMMITMENT TO ASSUMING THE BEST

Closely related to the issue of consensus being achieved in part by biblical listening is the corollary of biblical love of assuming the best. A great

9. Schaller, *The Decision-Makers,* 19–22.

10. Ibid.

11. MacArthur, *The Book on Leadership,* 81–83.

deal of emotion gets released in the midst of local church decision-making. This is especially true when congregations wrestle through differences and conflict, no matter how intense. When people have differences of opinion on an issue, instead of assuming the best about each other, they assume the worst. When Paul was teaching the Corinthians about what true love looks like, he states that love 'hopes all things' and 'trusts all things.' This is another way of saying that love assumes the best of each other. This applies to pastors not only in regard to the sheep of his congregation, but in regard to former pastors. Homer Kent Sr. notes:

> "Every pastor should make it a strict policy to refrain from speaking disparagingly of his predecessor. Failure at this point is bound to react unfavorably on the present pastor sooner or later. No matter how adverse his opinion of the former pastor, the latter in all probability has some friends in the congregation. Why incur their enmity at the start when no possible good can result from uncomplimentary remarks? Individuals in the office of pastor fail at times, but the office is one of honor, and to disparage the person of one who holds it or who had held it is likely to dishonor the office. Failure here gives evidence of a lack of the fruit of the Spirit (Gal. 5:22). Criticism can easily degenerate into the evil of gossip from which the minister, of all personas, should be separate.[12]

This does not mean that confrontation is dismissed. It means that when confrontation occurs, we don't assume foul play on the part of the other. We assume that the brother or sister in Christ is trying to honor God and do what's best for the congregation. If and when it becomes obvious that this is not the case, then is the time to pursue biblical reconciliation (Matthew 18). This is in stark contrast with leaders who assume that those who disagree with them are either not as spiritual or are simply moronic.

7) A CORPORATE AND INDIVIDUAL COMMITMENT TO MUTUAL SUBMISSION

When a congregation is healthy, believers will be submitting to one another in the flow of church life. At times, the leadership and congregation will be submitting to the decision of a senior pastor. At times, the pastor will need to submit to the wisdom of other elders or deacons. At times, the leadership must submit to the will of the congregation. At times, the pastors and

12. Kent, Sr., *The Pastor and His Work*, 53.

congregation will submit to the insights of the deacons. Finally, at times, individual church members will submit to their brothers and sisters because of the specific giftedness and calling that God has given them. This can only be achieved in a sub-culture and whole-hearted commitment to mutual submission. The idea of mutual submission is nearly non-existent. The key verse related to this concept is Ephesians 5:21, *"and be subject to one another in the fear of Christ."* Just a few verses earlier Paul explains that mutual ministry is also experienced as we edify one another in corporate worship.

Mutual submission flows naturally out of mutual respect. This can be very difficult for a generation that grew up with a 'top-down' approach to management. In secular and sacred work, it was generally expected that the boss on top didn't have to respect his subordinates and the subordinates didn't have to like the boss. Mutual submission and mutual respect means that in a sense the boss and subordinates are equal, and because of that they owe each other a hearing and the assumption that the other is not incompetent because they have a different understanding of the decision. More importantly, if the leader really doesn't believe in mutual submission, who will have the right to confront him on sin? C. J. Mahaney writes in his book, "Humility,"

> *"John Owen observed that although each of us display competence in a variety of areas, this is never so in respect to discerning our sin. On our own, you and I will never develop a competency for recognizing our sin. We'll always need help. Never forget that others see what you do not. Where you're blind to sin, their vision is often twenty-twenty. And by God's grace they can impart clarity to help protect you from the hardening effects of sin. Others can exhort you, encourage you, and correct you. They are a gift from God in your battle against sin. . .And don't be put off when a friend's observations may not be 100 percent accurate. I've found that there's truth to be gleaned at times even from an enemy's critique. Humility doesn't demand mathematical precision from another's impute; humility postures itself to receive God's grace from any avenue possible."*[13]

---

13. Mahaney, *Humility*, 133.

8) A CORPORATE AND INDIVIDUAL COMMITMENT TO HUMILITY.

John Ruskin said, ". . .*the first test of a truly great man is his humility. I don't mean by humility, doubt of his power. But really great men have a curious feeling that the greatness is not of them, but through them. And they see something divine in every other man and are endlessly, foolishly, incredibly merciful.*"[14] When two godly men, who love the gospel, love the Word and love the brotherhood have a different view of a matter, when there is a spirit of humility present, both—in an attitude of mercy—will assume that neither of them have this completely perfect. The assumption ought to be that by combining the views of the two men, and together taking that before God in prayer and other peers for an analysis of wisdom, we will look for God to reveal the best approach.

When biblically qualified men differ, the best answer to the approach almost always will be partly from the wisdom of the first brother and partly from the wisdom of the second, and partly from a third source that God reveals. Why can we assume that none of us will have it entirely correct based on our own discretion? Because we understand that our view is rarely 100% accurate. We are blinded by our own prejudices. We may also be swayed by emotions that we may not even know are lurking in the background.

Many of the power struggles that are recorded in the Gospels between the apostles were due in part from a prideful spirit. Christ had to take time out of his ministry to rebuke his disciples for such attitudes on more than one occasion. When a leadership team is working through a decision, all of the participants must have a teachable, approachable and humble attitude. In Matthew 20:28, Jesus said, "*just as the Son of Man did not come to be served, but to serve, and to give His life a ransom for many.*" That should also be true of servant leaders. The Apostle Paul says in Philippians 2:4 that in all we do we should look out for the interest of others, no matter how that affects our own interests. This principle has a direct bearing on decision-making in leadership. How often have leaders, out of pride, made a decision because that decision was in the best interest of the leader and not in the best interest of the congregation? It is impossible for a man of God to continually have a non-teachable and stubborn attitude and at the same time be biblically qualified for either the office of pastor or deacon.

14. Ruskin, The Quotation Page, http://www.quotationspage.com/quote/8560.html.

When a leader has a baseline of humility, it will be evident in the tone of his decision-making. Humility does not mean that one is without theological or philosophical conviction. Too much of postmodern evangelism has fallen to this idea that if one is strong in conviction then he is somehow less than humble. This confusion of what humility is and isn't goes back quite far. John Piper, in his work "Brother, We are Not Professionals," quotes an observation of G.K. Chesterton's about this confusion as early as 1908:

> *"What we suffer from today is humility in the wrong place. Modesty has moved from the organ of ambition. Modesty has settled upon the organ of conviction, where it was never meant to be. A man was meant to be doubtful about himself, but undoubting about the truth, this has been exactly the part he ought not to assert—himself. The part he doubts is exactly the part he ought not to doubt—the Divine Reason."*[15]

John 3:30 says, *"He must increase, but I must decrease."* Paul states it another way in Philippians 2:5, *"Have this attitude in yourselves which was also in Christ Jesus. . ."* In our interactions with others, we must have a base of humility. When we speak the truth in love and humility, the Holy Spirit will show up and bless the endeavor. If, on the other hand, we become impassioned with each other and lead from a base of demand vs. humility, the Holy Spirit cannot bless that approach. It simply will not result in a sense of family and unity but rather a kind of power-dominance. Again, John MacArthur says that the church leader must *"remain gentle, compassionate, empathetic, and humble. If he becomes resentful, repressive, or ruthless in his treatment of his people, he will lose his effectiveness as a leader."*[16]

This is a plea for leaders and congregations to prayerfully consider this issue of humility. No matter what view of polity one takes, this fruit of the Spirit must be present in large quantities for the Spirit of God to bless the efforts of ministry. Even if the congregation is viewed as the final court of appeal, the congregation must have a humble spirit in accepting wisdom from the elders, even if the congregation may not at first understand. The elders ought to show restraint and respect when one in their midst dissents from the majority because of conscience's sake. A pastor needs to be willing to put away his pride and listen with humility when a deacon team vocalizes a struggle with a certain direction or decision. In short, the body must respond to the other parts of the body with grace and humility and

15. Piper, *Brothers, We are Not Professionals*, 162.
16. MacArthur, *The Book on Leadership*, 86.

together prayerfully consider what the best course of action may be. This will be impossible without a Spirit-filled congregation and leadership team.

9) A CORPORATE AND INDIVIDUAL COMMITMENT TO DIVISION OF LABOR.

This commitment is connected closely with the previous category. This is sometimes called the Moses Principle or the Jethro Principle.[17] Moses was running himself into an early grave when his father-in-law, Jethro, pulled him aside and said, "What are you doing?" Exodus 18 tells the rest of the story. Moses divided up leaders who would give judgment and leadership over the vast majority of the corporate issues. Amongst a number of leadership principles that can be derived from this passage, one is the principle of division of labor. Another Old Testament example of this is seen as God gives certain abilities to different craftsmen when the Temple was being constructed (Exodus 36:1) as well as the use of musicians for the purposes of corporate worship of Israel (1 Chronicles 15:22; 25:6–7). Because this was not a time-bound principle limited to the Mosaic Law period, New Testament churches can rightly conclude that this part of Old Testament corporate life may be applied to them. We have the same sense from 1 Corinthians 12. The church universal is a body with many parts. However, the Scriptures place emphasis on participation in a local body. John Stott, in his work, "Basic Christianity," says,

> *"The Christian life is not just a private affair of your own. If we are born again into God's family, not only has he become our Father but every other believer in the word, whatever his nation or denominations, has become our brother or sister in Christ. One of the commonest names for Christians in the New Testament is 'brethren.' This is a glorious truth. But it is not good supposing that membership of the universal church of Christ is enough; we must belong to some local branch of it. . .Every Christian's place is in a local church, sharing in its worship, fellowship and witness."*[18]

Other passages of Scripture, such as Romans 12 and Ephesians 4, shed even more light on the role that spiritual gifts have in the body. At the very least, it means that a spiritual entity such as a church can have a number of decision-makers just as there are a number of leaders. It simply does

17. George and Logan, *Leading and Managing Your Church*, 113–15.
18. Stott, *Basic Christianity*, 139.

not make sense that any one part of the body would make all the decisions for the rest of the body, especially when every believer is an individual believer-priest. The only exception, of course, would be the head, which the New Testament names as Jesus. He is preeminent in the church.

No matter at what level of spiritual discernment a believer is, God has a place for them to serve in his church. If a church does not have enough ministry spots for everyone to serve, that is a sign that the parent congregation needs to start a daughter church. God never intended for believers to show up, tithe and go home. Some leaders are very restrictive in allowing others to serve, but these individuals also have their own imperfections and immaturity. If the body of Christ used the same measuring stick for the ministry as these leaders do, even those leaders would be unfit for service.

10) A CORPORATE AND INDIVIDUAL COMMITMENT TO PATIENCE IN COMMUNICATION

One of the constant challenges in any organization is a commitment to maintaining the flow of communication. When a church is dealing with significant decisions made by a segment of the leadership, decisions made by one part of the body must be communicated to the congregation as a whole. The more data that can be released, the better the body at large can understand the motives, reasons and logic behind the decisions. Sometimes leaders become frustrated after a decision is made, because although he knows of the months and many meetings that went into making the decision, the congregation does not, and questions will arise. The leader may think that the congregation or church member that questions the decision is doing so out of mistrust of the leaders involved. That may not be the case; it may just be that the member doesn't understand or have access to the data that was available to the leaders when they were making the decision. Whatever decisions are shared with the congregation, the best approach may be to present the information and allow for sufficient time for the assembly to digest the data and ask any questions that they may have. This commitment to patience in communication parallels the next category, remaining loving in communication.

11) A CORPORATE AND INDIVIDUAL COMMITMENT TO SPEAKING THE TRUTH IN LOVE

In Ephesians 4:15, Paul links the speaking of truth in love with the growth in maturity and success of the body. James Boice notes the contrast with verse 14, "Children are delightful little creatures to have around but they do have their limitations. Two are instability and naïveté."[19] Boice continues, ". . .children may be easily fooled. . .However it is an unfortunate thing when those same characteristics hang on into adult life, wakening a person's character and limiting his or her usefulness."[20] One of the amazing characteristics of Scripture is not only its inherency, authority and sufficiency, but also its efficiency. In other words, it is practical. This commitment may be the most practical rule for decision-making in a social teamwork environment. It is not only applicable to the church setting, but is also effective at home, work or in any organization.

The sad reality is that non-believers often do a better job of being loving in the midst of disagreements than God's children are. Some believers are of the opinion that if they have a disagreement with the leadership, they will tell them so. That person may be truthful, but then again, he might be a fool. Proverbs 29:11 says, "*A fool uttereth all his mind, but a wise (man) keepeth it till afterwards"(KJV)*. Mature Christian decision-making is a mixture of truth and love. When love is not balanced with a mutual commitment to truth, decision-making becomes a component of 'sloppy-agape.' On the other hand, if truth is not balanced with love, the ministry will leave many behind that feel used and abused. Like in a water molecule, the oxygen alone does not make water; it makes oxygen that can be breathed, but doesn't quench thirst. The hydrogen molecule likewise cannot make water by itself; it is an explosive gas when touched by flame. Love without truth is like the oxygen, truth without love is like hydrogen. It presents the nasty reality of failure without the gentle presence of mercy.

12) A CORPORATE AND INDIVIDUAL COMMITMENT TO TRUST

Proverbs 16:9 is powerful. The passage reads, "*The mind of man plans his way, But the Lord directs his steps."* Ultimately, the believer must trust

19. Boice, *Ephesians*, 149.
20. Ibid., 149–50.

that God is working his will. That does not give license to be lazy or ir-responsible. Even when decision-making is difficult because of the nature of those decisions, the believer must trust that God is at work and that he will continue to grow his church one way or another. This practical and corporate commitment is important. Unnecessary pressure and stress are relieved when the congregation and leaders believe that God will ultimately lead them at every level. Either Proverbs 3:5 is right or it's not. Psalm 16:11 reveals David's confidence in God's continual protection and leadership in the "paths of life." There is one more aspect of trust. The congregation needs to trust its biblically-qualified leaders because of their integrity. There may be, from time to time, a leader who has a hidden agenda and is waiting for a chance to spring a trap, but if the local assembly has been careful about 'laying hands suddenly on no man' (1 Timothy 5:22), such unpleasant ex-periences should be the exception rather than the rule. It is a bad sign if a congregation goes into a meeting trusting a brother, but as soon as the brother takes an opposing view the trust is gone. That signifies that there is a skewed approach to trust somewhere, that trust is conditional upon agreement. That is not trust.

A powerful example of this is how the early church trusted each other with ministry through leaders like Paul and his team. Even though each missionary team came from a different church (Paul and Silas from An-tioch—Acts 15:40, Timothy from Lystra—1 Timothy 4:14), the churches allowed each team to make decisions about agenda, destinations, travel ar-rangements and more. There was no micro-managing of these men. Acts 15:40—16:11 shows a good example of this type of flexibility being entrust-ed to these servants. Concerning this giving of trust, Kevin Bauder notes,

> Antioch. . .was in no position to direct Paul and his companions during their missionary journeys. Communication was slow, and decisions had to be made quickly. Even if communication had been possible, people in Antioch could not be expected to know enough of Paul's circumstances to be able to direct him wisely. The bulk of the decisions had to be made by Paul's team as he traveled. . .the team had considerable latitude to make its own decisions. It determined its own direction in ministry and managed its own personnel. Even Paul was not above submitting to direction, most likely from other team members, but certainly from a source other than his own local church (Acts 17:14–15).[21]

21. Bauder, "The New Testament and Service Organizations" www.centralseminary.edu/publications/20051104Print.pdf.

The implication is that a trusting congregation is willing to trust each other with authority and responsibility. The majority of decision-making authority should rest with the brothers and sisters who are actually performing that ministry.

13) A CORPORATE AND INDIVIDUAL COMMITMENT TO PLEASE GOD AND NOT MAN

Once a decision has been made, and the leaders or ministry believe that its foundation and final form is right both in biblical wisdom and in practical application, there may still be detractors. Paul reminded the Thessalonian believers (1 Thessalonians 2:4–6) that as ministry is accomplished, the ultimate goal is the pleasing of God, not of man. What is our choice? We could forsake our mission and all would be well. But as soon as we give in to the pressure, Jesus is no longer the supreme Lord. He has been replaced by loyalty to family, colleagues or ambition. Even when others leaders disagree with a decision we've made, if Jesus of Nazareth is the compass-north, then the commitment to living the truth in love, focusing on our character and leaving our testimony in the hands of God will result in respect. In Luke 14:25, Jesus said, "If anyone comes to me and does not hate his father and mother, his wife and children, his brothers and sisters, yes, even his own life, he cannot be my disciple."

14) A CORPORATE AND INDIVIDUAL COMMITMENT TO A CONNECTION BETWEEN RESPONSIBILITY AND AUTHORITY

No matter how a church organizes its pastors, elders, deacons, teachers, ministry leaders and other offices or positions in the church, congregations do best when responsibility is wed to authority.[22] There must be a consistent approach to delegation. L.A. Allen defines delegation as *"entrusting responsibility and authority and establishing lines of accountability."*[23]

Responsibility may demand a portion of the budget. While it may be correct to come to the deacons or elders for permission for more than what has been budgeted, a leader who has been entrusted with that ministry

22. MacArthur, *Pastoral Ministry,* 67–80.
23. Hendrix, *Management for Christian Leaders,* 89–102.

should have authority over that portion of the budget. Leaders who agree to take on a task but who must continually seek permission to do this or that in its execution are presented with a serious disconnect to this principle. These kind of approaches to so-called delegation do nothing more than frustrate effectiveness and undermine a spirit of trust with co-leaders who typically are already sacrificing much for sake of the ministry. While there is a legitimacy to accountability, it is frankly demoralizing to work under the leadership of a leader who wants to micro-manage every decision you make. This only results in discouragement amongst the faithful. It is also a formula for ministries to continually lose their sharpest servant-leaders to other ministries who will appreciate their work and who will allow these leaders a responsible level of freedom to accomplish the ministry tasks that they are responsible for.

FINAL THOUGHTS

Local bodies may have acceptable variety in the area of decision-making. This may include variety in mission or vision, and in the makeup of the leadership structure and congregation. If the congregation consists mostly of new converts, or if another congregation doesn't have enough male leaders to serve as elders or deacons, or if the strongest and most faithful congregants are women, there should be wiggle room to accommodate these challenges in congregational decision-making, while still adhering to biblical absolutes. In some cases, the lead pastor may have to be a bit more authoritarian than he normally would be, or he may need to be patient and methodically teach key leaders of the congregation before a set of decisions can be tackled. Sometimes a lead pastor might have to maintain a secular job while trying to shepherd his congregation. It has been common down through the centuries for church leaders to be bi-vocational. Special logistical issues may give more or less checks to his decision-making.

In whatever manner the church makes its decision, it must remember that not all decisions are created equal. Care must be taken not to over-emphasize less important decisions and under-emphasize more important ones. Kennon L. Callahan divides decisions into four different categories and responds to each based on where it falls on his scale. This is his taxonomy:

> *Matters that are both important and urgent are #1 decisions. Matters that are important but not urgent are #2 decisions. Urgent but*

> *not important matters are #3 decisions. Matters that are neither important nor urgent are #4 decisions. Many congregations live out their lives together focusing on #3 and #4 decisions rather than #1 and #2 decisions they should be concerned with. . .Effective congregations invest most of their decision-making time on those matters that qualify as #1 and #2 decisions.*[24]

Applying Callahan's observations is important. No sense of priorities in decision-making is irresponsible. Spending the same amount of time on a high level objective as a trivial matter is irresponsible.

As others have essentially noted, a strong and spiritually vibrant servant leadership coupled with an involved and spiritually adept congregation gives the best balance of harmony and peace between all decision-making bodies of an assembly. If there is a glaring spiritual deficiency with either the pastor/staff/deacons or the congregation, decision-making may erupt into open warfare and tragically wound the body of Christ and mar the testimony of the Gospel.

The larger a particular church grows, the more that church has to share its decision-making with its representatives. The smaller a church is, the more decisions can be made by the group at large. Glen Daman said,

> *"When the (small) church acts, it acts as a whole rather than as individual parts. The whole makes decisions rather than a representative few. People desire to know what is going on in every program and ministry even though they are not directly involved. The small church functions as a participatory democracy. . .This is especially true regarding the vision and direction of the church."*[25]

This does not undermine the decisions the pastor-teacher (or senior pastor) makes. Neither does it change the types of decisions the elder/pastor team makes. It does not affect the nature of the decision the deacons, congregation or church members make. What it means is that a larger church cannot discuss to the same degree the congregational decisions that a new church of twenty members can. There is a subjective element to the application of corporate decision-making, no matter what the congregation's polity is. No matter who leads the congregation—the pastor, elders, deacons or even a congregant—there ought to be a spirit of trust and willingness to give decision-making to others, submit to King Jesus and work together in love.

24. Callahan, *Twelve Keys to an Effective Church*, 56.
25. Daman, *Shepherding the Small Church*, 42–64.

How Christ would be honored; how the Gospel would be furthered; how lost neighbors would be amazed if the church of Jesus were unified on the issue of effective and shared decision-making. Each congregation should work to a consensus on what they believe about decision-making and then live consistently (not perfectly, but consistently) with that understanding. Peace would be generated in our communities of worship. God blesses his church when his mandates are followed and decisions are made to the glory of his Son.

What we need today are congregations that are willing not only to be effective in decision-making, be willing to be Christ-like in decision-making. Making decisions can be hazardous. What God wants from congregations as well as individuals is the willingness to make hard decisions, based on principle, righteousness and truth. This is counter to today's culture. Many congregations look for decision-makers who will always keep everyone happy. This is not only a fantasy, but is spiritually toxic and counter to true leadership. Callahan says, *"The decision-making process is solid whenever there is character to the decisions. That is, the decisions reflect courage and backbone rather than simply a willy-nilly effort to please everyone—which usually ends up pleasing no one!"*[26]

Disagreement and disharmony over decision-making can get out of hand. If the persecuted church could see how much the non-persecuted church argues and wastes time over such trivialities, it would be saddened. This is the reality: we who are privileged to be able to work and worship with brothers and sisters in freedom and relative ease have much for which to be grateful. We ought to leverage all of that for God's glory and kingdom. Dietrich Bonhoeffer wrote:

> *"It is by the grace of God that a congregation is permitted to gather visibly in this world to share God's Word and sacrament. Not all Christians receive this blessing. The imprisoned, the sick, the scattered lonely, the proclaimers of the Gospel in heathen lands stand alone. . .It is true, of course, that what is an unspeakable gift of God for the lonely individual is easily disregarded and trodden under foot by those who have the gift every day. It is easily forgotten that the fellowship of Christian brethren is a gift of grace, a gift of the Kingdom of God that any day may be taken from us, that the time that still separates us from utter loneliness may be brief indeed. Therefore, let him who until now has had the privilege of living a common Christian life with other Christians praise God's grace from the bottom of*

26. Callahan, *Twelve Keys to an Effective Church*, 56.

his heart. Let him thank God on his knees and declare: It is grace, nothing but grace, that we are allowed to live in community with Christian brethren."[27]

---

27. Bonhoeffer, *Life Together*, 18–20, quoted by Merkle, *40 Questions about Elders and Deacons*, 11.

Selected Bibliography

BOOKS

Agar, Frederick A. *The Deacon At Work*. Philadelphia: The Judson Press, 1923.

Alexander, Patrick H., John F. Kutsko, James D. Ernest, Shirley A. Decker-Lucke, and David L. Petersen, ed. *The Handbook of Style: For Ancient Near Eastern, Biblical, and Early Christian Studies*. Peabody: Hendrickson, 1999.

Anderson, James D., and Ezra Earl Jones. *The Management of Ministry*. San Francisco: Harper and Row, 1978.

Anderson, Robert C. *The Effective Pastor*. Chicago: Moody, 1985.

Argyris, Chris. *Integrating the Individual and the Organization*. New York: John Wiley & Sons, Inc., 1964.

———. *Management and Organizational Development*. New York: McGraw-Hill, 1971.

———. *Personality and Organization*. New York: Harper & Row, 1957.

Association of Baptists for World Evangelism. *Manual of Church Polity and Practice*. Philadelphia: Association of Baptists for World Evangelism, 1946.

Ayres, Francis O. *The Ministry of the Laity*. Philadelphia: The Westminster Press, 1962.

Avis, Paul. *Authority, Leadership and Conflict in the Church*. London: Mowbray, 1992.

Baker, Helen, and Robert R. France. *Centralization and Decentralization in Industrial Relations*. Princeton: Princeton University, 1954.

Barker, Glen W. *3 John*. The Expositor's Bible Commentary, ed. Frank E. Gaebelein, vol. 12. Grand Rapids: Zondervan, 1981.

Barna, George. *The Habits of Highly Effective Churches*. Ventura, Calif.: Gospel Light, 1999.

Baron, David. *Moses on Management: 50 Leadership Lessons from the Greatest Manager of All Time*. New York: Pocket Books, 1999.

Baxter, Richard. *The Reformed Pastor*. Edinburgh: The Banner of Truth Trust, reprint edition, 1974.

Beasley, Bob. *The Wisdom of Proverbs*. San Diego: Legacy, 1998.

Beeke, Joel R. and Randall J. Pederson, *Meet the Puritans*. Grand Rapids: Reformation Heritage, 2006.

Berkley, James D. *Leadership Handbook of Management and Administration*. Grand Rapids: Baker, 1994.

Berghoef, Gerard, and Lester De Koster. *The Deacon Handbook*. Grand Rapids: Christian Library, 1980.

Blum, Edwin A. *1 Peter*. The Expositor's Bible Commentary, ed. Frank E. Gaebelein, vol. 12. Grand Rapids: Zondervan, 1981.

Selected Bibliography

Blair, Tony. *A Journey: My Political Life*. New Yoirk: Random House, 2010.

Boice, James Montgomery, *Foundations of the Christian Faith*. Downers Grove: InterVarsity, 1986.

————, *Ephesians*. Grand Rapids: Baker, 1988.

————. *Galatians*. Grand Rapids: Baker, 1971.

Bonhoeffer, Dietrich. *Life Together*. Translated by John W. Doberstein. San Francisco: HarperSanFrancisco, 1954.

Briner, Bob, and Ray Pritchard. *The Leadership Lessons of Jesus*. Nashville: Broadman & Holman, 1997.

Brand, Owen and R. Stanton Norman, ed. *Perspectives on Church Government: Five Views of Church Polity*. Nashville: Broadman& Holman, 2004.

Bruce, Alexander Balmain. *The Training of the Twelve*. Grand Rapids: Kregel, 1971.

Bruce, F. F. *Commentary on the Book of the Acts*. The New International Commentary on the New Testament. Grand Rapids: Eerdmans, 1955.

Bush, George W. *Decision-Points*. New York: Crown, 2010

Carson, D.A. *Exegetical Fallacies*. Grand Rapids: Baker, 1984.

Callahan, Kennon L. *Twleve Keys to an Effective Church*. San Francisco: Harper and Row, 1983.

Calvin, John. *Galatians, Ephesians, Philippians, and Colossians*. Calvin's New Testament Commentaries. Translated by T. H. L. Parker, ed. David W. Torrance and Thomas F. Torrance, vol. 11. Grand Rapids: Eerdmans, 1965.

Campbell, Donald K., ed. *Walvord: A Tribute*. Chicago: Moody, 1982.

Campenhausen, Hans Von. *Ecclesiastical Authority and Spiritual Power in the Church of the First Three Centuries*. Translated by J. A. Baker. Stanford, Calif.: Stanford University Press, 1969.

Carr, Clay. *The New Manager's Survival Manual*. New York: John Wiley & Sons, 1989.

Clinton, J. Robert. *The Making of a Leader*. Colorado Springs: NavPress, 1988.

Covey, Stephen R. *Principle-Centered Leadership*. New York: Simon & Schuster Inc., 1990.

Cowen, Steven, ed. *Who Runs the Church: 4 Views of Church Government*. Grand Rapids: Zondervan, 2004.

Dale, Robert D. *Pastoral Leadership*. Nashville: Abingdon, 1986.

Daman, Glen. *Shepherding the Small Church*. Grand Rapids: Kregel, 2002.

————. *The 7 Habits of Highly Effective People*. New York: Simon & Schuster Inc., 1989.

Dever, Mark. *Nine Marks of a Healthy Church*. Wheaton: Good News, 2000.

————. ed. *Polity: Biblical Arguments on How to Conduct Church Life*. Washington, DC: Center for Church Reform, 2001.

Dewer, Donald L. *The Quality Circle Guide To Participation Management*. Englewood Cliffs, NJ: Prenctice-Hall, 1980.

Doriani, Daniel M. *Reformed Expository Commentary: James*. Phillipsburg: P & R Publishing Company, 2007.

Earl, Ralph. *1, 2 Timothy*. The Expositor's Bible Commentary. Vol 11., ed. Frank E. Gaebelein. Grand Rapids: Zondervan, 1978.

Emis, LeRoy. *Be the Leader You Were Meant to Be*. Wheaton: Victor, 1975.

Engstrom, Ted W., and Edward R. Dayton. *The Art of Management for Christian Leaders*. Waco, Tex.: Word, 1976.

Erickson, Millard J. *Christian Theology*. Grand Rapids: Baker, 1983.

Feinberg, John S. ed. *Continuity and Discontinuity*. Wheaton: Crossway, 1988.

Fee, Gordon. *The First Epistle to the Corinthians*. NICNT. Grand Rapids: Eerdmans, 1987.

Fensham, F. Charles. *The Books of Ezra and Nehemiah*. NICOT. Grand Rapids: Eerdmans, 1982.

Finzel, Hans. *The Top Ten Mistakes Leaders Make*. Wheaton: Scripture, 1994.

———. *Empowered Leaders*. Nashville: Word, 1998.

Fisher, Kimball. *Leading Self-Directed Work Teams*. New York: McGraw-Hill, 2000.

Foshee, Howard B. *Now that You're a Deacon*. Nashville: Broadman, 1975.

Friesen, Garry. *Decision Making & the Will of God*. Portland: Multnomah, 1980.

Gangel, Kenneth O. *Competent to Lead*. Chicago: Moody, 1974.

———. *Feeding & Leading*. Wheaton: Scripture, 1989.

George, Carl F., and Robert E. Logan. *Leading & Managing Your Church*. Old Tappan, N. J.: Fleming H. Revell, 1987.

Getz, Gene. *Elders and Leaders*. Chicago: Moody, 2003.

Gill, John. *A Body of Divinity*. Grand Rapids: Sovereign Grace, 1971.

Greenleaf, Robert. *Servant Leadership*. New York: Paulist, 1977.

Grudem, Wayne. *Systematic Theology: An Introduction to Biblical Doctrine*. Grand Rapids: Eerdmans, 1994.

Guthrie, Donald. *The Pastoral Epistles*. Tyndale New Testament Commentaries. Grand Rapids: Eerdmans, 1984.

———. *New Testament Introduction*. 4th edition. Downers Grove: InterVarsity, 1990.

Harris, Joshua. *Stop Dating The Church*. Sisters, Oregon: Multnomah, 2004.

Harris, Murray J. *Exegetical Guide to the Greek New Testament: Colossians & Philemon*. Grand Rapids: Eerdmans, 1991.

———. *2 Corinthians*. The Expositor's Bible Commentary, ed. Frank E. Gaebelein, vol. 10. Grand Rapids: Zondervan, 1976.

Harrison, Everett F. *Romans*. The Expositor's Bible Commentary, ed. Frank E. Gaebelein, vol. 10. Grand Rapids: Zondervan, 1976.

Hartley, John E. *Leviticus*. Word Biblical Commentary. Dallas: Word, 1992.

Hartog II, John. *Pastors and Deacons*. Victoria, BC, Canada: Trafford, 2008.

Hayford, Jack. *Leadership Handbook of Management and Administration*, ed. James D. Berkley. Grand Rapids: Baker, 1994.

Hayhurst, Ron. *How to Interpret History*. Mustang, Oklahoma: Tate, 2007.

Hendriksen, William. *Philippians, Colossians and Philemon*. New Testament Commentary. Grand Rapids: Baker, 1962.

Hendrix, Olan. *Management for Christian Leaders*. Grand Rapids: Baker, 1976.

Hiebert, D. Edmond. *1 Peter*. Chicago: Moody, 1984.

———. *1 Timothy*. Chicago: Moody, 1957.

Hiscox, Edward T. *The New Directory for Baptist Churches*. Valley Forge: Judson, 1894. Reprint, Grand Rapids: Kregel, 1970.

Hooker, Richard. *Of the Laws of Ecclesiastical Polity*. New York: St. Martin's, 1975.

Hort, F.J.A. *The Christian Ecclesia*. London: MacMillan and Company, 1900.

Howell, R. B. C. *The Deaconship*. Valley Forge: The Judson, n.d.

Hughes, Philip Edgcumble. *A Commentary on the Epistle to the Hebrews*. Grand Rapids: Eerdmans, 1977.

Jones, Bruce W. *Ministerial Leadership in a Managerial World*. Wheaton: Tyndale, 1988.

Josephus, Flavius. *The Life and Works of Flavious Josephus*. Translated by William Whiston. Philadelphia: The John C. Winston Company, n.d.

Kalland, Earl S. *Deuteronomy*. The Expositor's Bible Commentary, ed. Frank E. Gaebelein, vol. 3. Grand Rapids: Zondervan, 1992.

Selected Bibliography

Kent, Homer Sr. *The Pastor and His Work*. Chicago: Moody, 1963.

Kent, Homer Jr. *Philippians*. The Expositor's Bible Commentary, ed. Frank E. Gaebelein, vol. 11. Grand Rapids: Zondervan, 1978.

Kilinski, Kenneth K., and Jerry C. Wofford. *Organization and Leadership in the Local Church*. Grand Rapids: Zondervan, 1973.

Kittelson, James M. *Luther the Reformer*. Minneapolis: Augsburg, 1986.

Larsen, David L. *Caring for the Flock*. Wheaton: Good News, 1991.

Leach, William H. *Handbook of Church Management*. Englewood Cliffs, N. J.: Prentice-Hall, 1958.

Leeman, Jonathan. *The Church and the Surprising Offense of God's Love*. 9 Marks. Wheaton: Crossway, 2010.

Lenski, R. C. H. *The Interpretation of the Acts of the Apostles*. Lutheran Book Concern, 1934. Reprint, Minneapolis: Augsburg, 1961.

———. *The Interpretation of I and II Epistles of Peter, the Three Epistles of John, and the Epistle of Jude*. Minneapolis: Augsburg, 1966.

Lindgren, Alvin J. and Norman Shawchuck, *Management for Your Church*. Nashville: Abingdon, 1977.

———. *Foundations for Purposeful Church Administration*. Nashville: Abingdon, 1965.

Longenecker, Richard, N. *Acts*. The Expositor's Bible Commentary, ed. Frank E. Gaebelein, vol. 9. Grand Rapids: Zondervan, 1981.

Lumpkin, W.L. *Baptist Confessions of Faith*. Valley Forge: Judson, 1959.

Lutzer, Erwin. *Managing Your Emotions*. Wheaton: Victor, 1983.

MacArthur, John Jr. *Answering the Key Questions about Elders*. Panorama City, Calif.: Word of Grace Communications, 1984.

———. *Body Dynamics*. Wheaton: Scripture, 1982.

———. *Leading the Flock*. Sun Valley: Grace Community Church, 1974.

———. *Pastoral Ministry*. Nashville: Thomas Nelson, 2005.

———. *Rediscovering Pastoral Ministry*. Dallas: Word, 1995.

———. *The Master's Plan For The Church*, Chicago: Moody, 1991.

———. *1 Corinthians*. Chicago: Moody, 1984.

———. *Worship*. Chicago: Moody, 2012.

Mare, W. Harold. *1 Corinthians*. The Expositor's Bible Commentary, ed. Frank. E. Gaebelein, vol. 10. Grand Rapids: Zondervan, 1976.

Maring, Norman H., and Winthrop S. Hudson. *A Baptist Manual of Polity and Practice*. Valley Forge: Judson, 1963.

Marshall, I. Howard. *Acts*. Tyndale New Testament Commentaries. Grand Rapids: Eerdmans, 1980.

Martin, Ralph. *Philippians*. Tyndale New Testament Commentaries. Grand Rapids: Eerdmans, 1959.

Maxwell, John C. *The 21 Irrefutable Laws of Leadership*. Nashville: Thomas Nelson, 1998.

———. *Developing the Leader Within You*. Nashville: Thomas Nelson, 1993.

———. *The 21 Indispensable Qualities Of A Leader*. Nashville: Thomas Nelson, 1999.

———. *The 17 Indisputable Laws of Teamwork*. Nashville: Thomas Nelson, 2001.

McConkey, Dale D. *No-Nonsense Delegation*. New York: American Management Associations, 1974.

McGregor, Douglas. *The Human Side of Enterprise*. New York: McGraw-Hill, 1960.

———. *Leadership and Motivation: Essays of Douglas McGregor*. Cambridge, Mass.: The M.I.T. Press, 1966.

McLachlan, Douglas R. *Reclaiming Authentic Fundamentalism*. Independence, Mo: American Association of Christian Schools, 1993.

McQuilkin, Robertson. *Understanding and Applying the Bible*. Chicago: Moody, 1988.

Merkle. Benjamin L. *40 Questions about Elders and Deacons*. Grand Rapids: Kregel, 2008.

Morris, Henry M. *The Genesis Record*. Grand Rapids: Baker, 1976.

Murphy, Thomas. *Pastoral Theology*. Philadelphia: Presbyterian Board of Publication, 1877.

Murray, John. *Romans*. The New International Commentary on the New Testament. Grand Rapids: Eerdmans, 1959.

Naylor, Robert E. *The Baptist Deacon*. Nashville: Broadman, 1955.

Newton, Phil. *Elders in Congregational Life: Rediscovering the Biblical Model for Church Leadership*. Grand Rapids: Kregel, 2005.

Nichols, Harold. *The Work of the Deacon and Deaconess*. Valley Forge: Judson, 1964.

Noll, Mark A. *Turning Points*. 3rd ed. Grand Rapids: Baker, 2012.

Osborne, Grant R. *The Hermeneutical Spiral*. Downers Grove: InterVarsity, 1991.

Parsons, Talcott. *Structure and Process in Modern Societies*. New York: The Free Press of Glencoe, 1960.

Perry, Lloyd M., and Norman Shawchuck. *Revitalizing the 20th Century Church*. Chicago: Moody, 1982.

Peters, Thomas J., and Robert H. Waterman, Jr. *In Search of Excellence*. New York: Harper & Row, 1982.

Pink, Arthur W. *The Sovereignty of God*. I. C. Herendeen, 1930. Reprint, Grand Rapids: Baker, 1984.

Piper, John. *Brothers, We Are Not Professionals*, Nashville: Broadman & Holman, 2002.

Piper, John, and Wayne Gruden, ed. *Recovering Biblical Manhood & Womanhood*. Wheaton: Good News, 1991.

Ray, David. *The Big Small Church Book*. Cleveland: Pilgrim, 1992.

Rees, Fran. *How to Lead Work Teams*. San Francisco: Jossey-Bass/Pfeiffer. 2001.

Richards, Lawrence O., and Clyde Hoeldtke. *A Theology of Church Leadership*. Grand Rapids: Zondervan, 1980.

Robertson, Archibald Thomas. *Word Pictures in the New Testament*. Nashville: Sunday School Board of the Southern Baptist Convention, 1930.

Robbins, Harvey A., and Michael Finley. *Why Teams Don't Work*. San Francisco: Berrett-Koehler, 2000.

Ross, Allen P. *Proverbs*. The Expositor's Bible Commentary, ed. Frank E. Gaebelein, vol. 5. Grand Rapids: Zondervan, 1981.

Rush, Myron. *Management: A Biblical Approach*. Wheaton: Scripture, 1983.

Ryrie, Charles C. *Nailing Down the Board: Serving Effectively on the Not-for-Profit Board*. Grand Rapids: Kregel, 1999.

———. *Dispensationalism Today*. Chicago: Moody, 1965.

Schaller, Lyle E. *The Decision-Makers*. Nashville: Abingdon, 1974.

———. *The Change Agent*. Nashville: Abingdon, 1972.

Schaff, Philip. *History of the Christian Church*. Vol. 2 Charles Scribner's Sons, 1910. Reprint. Grand Rapids: Eerdmans, 1967.

Steinbron, Melvin J. *Can the Pastor Do It Alone?* Ventura, Calif.: Gospel Literature International Foundation, 1987.

———. *The Lay Driven Church*. Ventura: Gospel Literature International Foundation, 1997.

Senter, Mark. *Recruiting Volunteers in the Church*. Wheaton: Scripture, 1990.

Shawchuck, Norman. *How to Manage Conflict in the Church*. Irvin: Organization Resources, Vol. 1, 1983.

Smith, Sir William & Samuel Cheetham. *A Dictionary of Christian Antiquities*. London: J.B. Publishing, 1880.

Smith, Rockwell C. *Rural Church Administration*. New York: Abingdon-Cokesbury, 1953.

Snodgrass, Klyne. *Between Two Truths*. Grand Rapids: Zondervan, 1990.

Sorenson, Roy. *The Art of Board Membership*. New York: Association Press, 1950.

Sproul, RC. *1–2 Peter*. Wheaton: Crossway, 2011.

Strauch, Alexander. *Biblical Eldership*. Littleton, Colo.: Lewis & Roth, 1995.

———. *Minister of Mercy: the New Testament Deacon*. Littleton, Colo.: Lewis & Roth, 1992.

Stott, John R. W. *The Message of Ephesians*. Downers Grove, Ill.: Inter-Varsity, 1979.

———. *The Preacher's Portrait*. Grand Rapids: Eerdmans, 1961.

Stowell, Joseph M. *Shepherding The Church*. Chicago: Moody, 1997.

Sullivan, James L. *Baptist Polity*. Nashville: Broadman, 1983.

Tenny, Merrill C. *John*. The Expositor's Bible Commentary, ed. Frank E. Gaebelein, vol. 9. Grand Rapids: Zondervan, 1981.

Thayer, Joseph Henry. *The New Thayer's Greek-English Lexicon of the New Testament*. Reprint, Peabody, Mass.: Hendrickson, 1979.

Thomas, Donald F. *The Deacon in a Changing Church*. Valley Forge: Jusdson, 1969.

Tillapaugh, Frank R. *Unleashing the Church*. Ventura, Calif.: Gospel Literature International Foundation, 1982.

Trentham, C.A. *Studies in Timothy*. Nashville: Convention, 1959.

Turabian, Kate L. *A Manual for Writers of Term Papers, Theses, and Dissertations*. 6th Edition. Chicago: The University of Chicago Press, 1937.

Van Dam, Cornelis. *The Elder*. Phillipsburg: P & R, 2011.

Wagner, Charles U. *The Pastor*. Schaumburg. Ill.: Regular Baptist, 1976.

Walvoord, John F., and Roy B. Zuck, ed. *The Bible Knowledge Commentary*. 2 Vols. Wheaton: Scripture Press, 1988.

Walton, Mary. *The Deming Management Method*. New York: The Putnam Publishing Group, 1986.

Warren, Rick. *The Purpose Driven Church*. Grand Rapids: Zondervan, 1995.

Westing, Harold J. *Multiple Church Staff Handbook*. Grand Rapids: Kregel, 1985.

Whitehead, James and Evelyn Eaton Whitehead. *Method in Ministry*. Oxford: Sheed & Ward Publishing, 1995.

Wiersbe, Warren. *Be Faithful*. Colorado Springs: Victor, 1981.

Williams, Matt. *How to be a Team Player and Enjoy It*. Independence, Mo.: American Association of Christian Schools, 1992.

Winger, Otho. "Church Polity" in *History and Doctrines of the Church of the Brethren*. Elgin: Brethren, 1919.

Wirasinghe, Errol. *The Art of Making Decisions*. Shanmar: Houston, 2003.

Woodbridge, John D., ed. *Great Leaders of the Christian Church*. Chicago: Moody, 1988.

Woolfe, Lorin. *The Bible on Leadership: From Moses to Matthew-Management Lessons For Contemporary Leaders*. New York: American Management Association, 2002.

Young, Edward J. *An Introduction to the Old Testament*. Grand Rapids: Eerdmans, 1949.

Youngblood, Ronald F. *1 Samuel*. The Expositor's Bible Commentary, ed Frank E. Gaebelein, vol. 3. Grand Rapids: Zondervan, 1992.

Zaspel, Fred and Tom Wells. *New Covenant Theology*. Frederick: New Covenant Media, 2002.

Zuck, Roy B. *Basic Bible Interpretation*. Wheaton: Victor, 1991.

DICTIONARIES, ENCYCLOPEDIAS AND PERIODICALS

Bauer, Walter. *A Greek-English Lexicon of the New Testament and Other Early Christian Literature*. Translated by William F. Arndt and Wilbur Gingrich. Revised and edited by Frederick William Danker. Chicago: University of Chicago Press, 2000.

Brown, Colin, ed. *New International Dictionary of New Testament Theology*. 4 vols. Grand Rapids: Zondervan, 1975–1985.

Cairns, Alan. *Dictionary of Theological Terms*. 3d ed. Greenville: Ambassador Emerald International, 2002.

Decker, Rodney J. "Polity and the Elder Issue" *Grace Theological Journal* 2 (1988): 258–77.

Fee, Gordon. "Reflections on Church Order in the Pastoral Epistles, with Further Reflections on the Hermeneutics of Ad Hoc Documents" *Journal of the Evangelical Society* 28 (1985): 149–50.

Harris, R. Laird, Gleason L. Archer, Jr. and Bruce K. Waltke, *Theological Wordbook of the Old Testament*. Chicago: Moody, 1980.

Hays, J. Daniel, "Applying The Old Testament Law Today" *Bibliotheca Sacra* 158 (2001): 21–35.

Hock, Carl B, "The Role of Women in the Church: A Survey of Current Approaches" *Grace Theological Journal* 8 (1987): 241–51.

Inrig, "Called to Serve: Toward a Philosophy of Ministry" *Bibliotheca Sacra* 140 (1983): 336–50.

Kittel, G., and G. Friedrich, eds. *Theological Dictionary of the New Testament*. Translated by G. W. Bromiley. 10 vols. Grand Rapids: Eerdmans, 1964–1976.

Lewis, Robert M. "The 'Women' of 1 Timothy 3:11" *Bibliothea Sacra* 136 (1979): 168–76.

Liddell, Henry George and Robert Scott. *A Greek-English Lexicon*. Revised by Stuart Jones. Oxford: Oxford University Press, 1996.

McCune, Rolland D. "Doctrinal Non-Issues in Historic Fundamentalism" *Detroit Baptist Theological Journal* 1 (1996): 178–79.

Moritz, Fred. "Congregational Church Government." *Frontline* (March/April 2009): 10–12.

Rushdoony, Rousas John. "Biblical Law and Western Civilization" *The Journal of Christian Reconstruction* (Winter, 1975–76): 5–13.

Stitzinger, James F. "Spiritual Gifts: Definitions and Kinds" *Masters Seminary Journal* 14 (2003): 143–76.

Young, Jerry R. "Shepherds, Lead!" *Grace Theological Journal* (1985): 330–36.

UNPUBLISHED MATERIALS

Bauder, Kevin, "Thinking About the Gospel, Part Seven: Frontloading the Gospel," In the Nick of time - www.centralseminary.edu/publications/Nick/Nick127.html, July 27, 2007

Selected Bibliography

————., "The New Testament and Service Organizations," In the Nick of time – www.centralseminary.edu/publications/20051104Print.pdf., November 4, 2005.

Bixby, Bob, "The Emerging Middle." http://bobbixby.wordpress.com/2007/08/04/the-emerging-middle, August 2007.

Brown, Jeffrey, "Corporate Decision-Making in the Church of the NT," Ph.D. thesis, Central Baptist Theological Seminary, April 2009.

Cianca, James, "The Nature of Biblical Leadership." D.Min. diss., Central Baptist Theological Seminary, 1998.

Doran, David M., "Part One: Foundations of Ministry Management." Lecture to M-532 Ministry Management, Detroit Baptist Theological Seminary, Detroit, Mich. Spring 1994.

————, "The Foundations of the Pastorate." Lecture to M-524 Pastoral Leadership, Detroit Baptist Theological Seminary, Detroit, Mich. Fall 1994.

Doerksen, Vernon. "An Inductive Study of the Development of Church Organization in the New Testament." Th.D. diss., Grace Theological Seminary, 1971.

Hiemela, John., "Especially Those who Labor in the Word: 1 Timothy 5:17 and the Pluarlity of Elders (CTSJ 10:2, Fall 2004) – www.galaxie.com/article/7539

Holmberg, Bengt., "Paul And Power: The Structure of Authority In The Primitive Church As Reflected In The Pauline Epistles." Ph.D. diss., Lund University, 1978.

Leadership Resource Notebook, Southeast Valley Baptist Church, Gilbert, Ariz. Unpublished church leadership manual from, Winter 2000.

Leadership Policy and Procedures File, Southeast Valley Baptist Church, Gilbert, Ariz. Unpublished church policy and procedures, Winter 2001.

McCune, Rolland D. "Dispensationalism." Lecture to M-335 Dispensationalism, Detroit Baptist Theological Seminary, Allan Park, Mich. Summer 1992.

Nehrbass, Daniel, "A Biblical Model of Church Decision-Making." M.R.E. thesis, Indiana Wesleyan University. March 5, 2001

Tetreau, Joel C. "The Deacon's Role in the Decision-Making Process At Southeast Valley Baptist Church." D.Min thesis, Central Baptist Theological Seminary, 2004.

Tetreau, Joel C. "Lines in the Sand Redux: A Plea to Type A Fundamentalists." http://sharperiron.org/article/lines-sand-redux-plea-to-type-fundamentalists, February 29, 2012.

Tuttle, Jeffrey P. "An Analysis of Christian School Compensation Patterns in Pennsylvania." D. Ed. diss., Bob Jones University Press, 1988.